The Bare Essentials Guide for
Martial Arts Injury Prevention and Care

SECOND EDITION

The Bare Essentials Guide for
Martial Arts Injury Prevention and Care

SECOND EDITION

by
Trish Bare Grounds, Ph.D., ATC/L
*USA TAEKWONDO Medical Committee Chairman,
Medical Coordinator
AND
US National Taekwondo Team Head Athletic Trainer*

          Turtle Press   Hartford

THE BARE ESSENTIALS GUIDE FOR MARTIAL ARTS INJURY PREVENTION AND CARE, 2ND EDITION

To contact the author or to order additional copies of this book:
Turtle Press
P.O. Box 290206
Wethersfield, CT 06129-0206
1-880-77-TURTL

ISBN 9781880336892
LCCN 2005030533
Printed in the United States of America

10 9 8 7 6 5 4 3 2 1 0

Library of Congress Cataloguing in Publication Data

Bare Grounds, Trish.
The bare essentials guide for martial arts injury care and prevention / by Trish Bare Grounds.-- 2nd ed.
    p. cm.
ISBN-13: 978-1-880336-89-2
ISBN-10: 1-880336-89-8
1. Martial arts injuries. 2. Martial arts--Health aspects. I. Title.
RC1220.M36.B37 2005
617.1'027--dc22
                            2005030533

Dedication

This book is dedicated to the constant memory of Aimee L. Gunnoe, my best friend, my daughter's Godmother, my partner in crime for the many sports medicine endeavors I decided to undertake, and the one who kept me on track when life wanted me to get lost.

Even though you left us all far too early in life, I thank God to have known you, to have worked with you and to have been the last person to hug you goodbye before you left the event that faithful night never to return home safely.

The world will always be a better place because of the marks you made on our lives and our hearts.

Aimee L. Gunnoe, MS, ATC/L
1972-2002

IMPORTANT NOTE TO READERS:

The treatments and activities suggested in this book have been developed by the author from her experience in the treatment of martial arts athletes and through education as an athletic trainer certified by the National Athletic Trainers Association (NATA) and licensed by the State of Florida Health Professions. However, every sports injury, and the reaction of the injured individual, is unique. The treatment or activity which is appropriate in most cases of a particular injury may not be appropriate in others. Accordingly, the treatments and activities described in this book may be inadvisable in certain circumstances. Athletes, instructors and coaches are advised to seek and follow the advice of their preferred medical professional in the treatment of all injuries. Furthermore, instructors and coaches are recommended to obtain certification in Emergency First Aid and CPR and to seek the aid of medical professionals in the event of a serious injury to an athlete during a practice or competition.

Acknowledgments

I want to personally thank all those people who played a large part in the production and inspiration for this book. Without your generosity and words of encouragement this book would have never been completed.

First, I want to thank Dr. Sang Kim & his wife Cynthia at Turtle Press for believing in me, my knowledge and experience enough to produce not only the first edition of this book, but a video and this second edition. Without them and their support, neither of the books or the video would have been able to be produced. Thank you from the bottom of my heart Cynthia for taking that first step, and Dr. Kim for flying down to Florida to do the video shoot personally.

I want to say thank you from the bottom of my heart to Jean Lopez, 2004 Olympic Taekwondo Coach, & Paris Amani, owners of Elite Taekwondo Center, for allowing me to use their athletes as models for the first book, and their school as the backdrop. Jean and Paris you have been and always will be very special athletes, coaches and friends near and dear to my heart. Thank you for always supporting me and trusting me with your health and the health of your athletes.

Thank you to 2000 & 2004 Olympic Gold Medalist Steven Lopez, Mark Lopez, Diana Lopez, Mandy Meloon & Masumi McLaren for graciously agreeing to be models for the first book. Not only are all of you great athletes but wonderful people and friends who make my job extremely enjoyable. The words "thank you" could never express what I feel for all of you.

I must also congratulate the Lopez's for being the first family in which three siblings took Gold at the same World Championsihps while being coached by their brother. Way to go Steven, Mark and Diana, and of course you too Jean! And congratulations to Mandy, too, for her World Championship medal.

Thank you also must go out to a much smaller athlete, Sam Harton, who was gracious enough to get up bright and early on a Saturday morning to be a model for this book. Sam is the son of Stan Harton who runs the Hurlburt Youth Center Taekwondo program on my husband's Air Force Base. Thank you to both Sam and Stan for their contributions and patience in the production of the first book.

Thank you to Phuong Hoang, my newest model for the second edition of this book who is not only one of the best athletic trainers and strength coach. I have had the privilege to watch coming into her own right, but a really great friend. You will always be my Mighty Pocket Hercules! Thank you for your well-valued suggestions as we completed the marathon photo shoot.

Thank you to Aubrey Yeagle who at the last minute was a replacement for one of my models, as we were all dealing with the aftermath of Hurricane Ivan. Aubrey jumped into the photo shoot like a pro! You are on your way to being a great star Aubrey! Thank you for helping this book to shine!

Thank you also must go to another of my former student athletic trainers who is now an ATC herself, Elizabeth Speed. Best of luck in PA school.

Thank you must go out to my smallest model, Olivia Bare Grounds, my daughter. You have given my life so much more meaning than I could have ever imagined! Thank you for asking to be one of the models in this book.

Thank you to the many members, athletes, parents, officers and staff of the United States Taekwondo Union, and the newly formed USA Taekwondo, Inc, for your support and patience with me through the years. A special thanks goes out to those I have worked personally with over the years who have enabled me to remain with this sport for so long: 2004 Olympic Coach Jean Lopez, 2000 Olympic Coach Han Won Lee (Olympic Bronze Medalist), USOC Director of Sports Partnerships Jay Warwick (Olympic Silver Medalist), the former USTU/present USA Taekwondo Administrative Staff including Jeanna Mendoza and Monica Paul, my many wonderful Sports Medicine Volunteers: ATC's & PT's, Maj. Tony Bare,

Phuong Hoang, Jonathan Lawrence, Jen Louie Pejo, Bill Spivey, and Sheri Walters (among tons of others); and Doctors, Dr. Ken Gordan, Dr. Steve Isono, Dr. Jimmy Kim (Olympic Gold Medalist), Dr. David Kung, Dr. Sherri LaShomb, and Dr. William "Buddy" Ramsey, and many others whom I do not have room here to thank but you know who you are and how much you mean to me. Thank you for always being there, and for believing in me and our mission as a Volunteer Sports Medicine Team.

Thank you to ALL of the athletes, coaches, referees, parents and medical professionals I have met and worked with over the years who have encouraged me to do such a book. Thank you also to all of those parents, athletes, referees, coaches and medical personnel that purchased the first book and encouraged so many others to do the same. Your words of praise have been greatly appreciated and treasured. Also, your suggestions and feedback of what else you needed to see in this second edition have been a tremendous inspiration, thank you all.

I would like to thank my mother, Eileen Bare, the president of my "fan club", my secretary, my personal assistant, my nanny, my counselor, and my friend, no matter what I do. Thanks for always being there, even for this book as a model and critic. Your encouragement and support have always been my lifeline, thank you. I would not be the person and professional I am today without your leadership, direction and love.

Lastly, I wish to thank my husband, Mark A. Grounds, who also graciously posed as a model for the first book, being taped and re-taped, but who was unable to make a repeat performance due to his military obligations. Thank you also for all of your support and undying belief in what I do as a professional. Your love and respect mean the world to me, and I would be nowhere without it.

Contents

Staying
Healthy

Injury Prevention

1

Every athlete knows that the best treatment for injuries is to prevent them from ever occurring in the first place, and the martial arts are no different. Martial arts athletes have to not only learn the correct forms and mechanics of the sport, but also be in tune with their body's needs. The body needs to be strong, yet flexible, highly trained, and yet not over-trained, well nourished but not over nourished, and herein lies the dilemma for most athletes. Most athletes and instructors know how to perfect their abilities as an athlete, simply by practicing how they will perform in competition....and practice, and practice.

Prevention of athletic injuries, also known as sports medicine care, involves exactly the same. It means an athlete must get into a routine prior, during and following any workout of any kind to reduce the chances of becoming injured. If the athlete does become injured the time to recover will most likely be reduced as the mind and body have been fine-tuned as to how to correctly care for an injury before it becomes worse.

Sport is not always about working your way through the pain, although there are times where an athlete must use mind over matter to get through a competition day, or even a strenuous practice. This does not mean, though, if an injury has occurred that it is ignored until it has become so painful that continuing is impossible. This does mean that an athlete and his/her instructor learn to recognize an injury, treat it immediately to better ensure a complete recovery, or prevent an injury before a more serious injury develops.

This book is designed to help prevent the athlete from getting injured and manage an injury if it does occur. These are simply outlines that should become part of an athlete's and instructor's daily workout routine.

Stretching

Ask one hundred different people how to stretch and you will get one hundred different answers, but there are some basic rules that should guide an athlete through a proper and meaningful stretching routine. Here are some starting guidelines:

Stretching should always be part of any workout program, whether it is a sport, exercise or weightlifting program, BOTH BEFORE AND FOLLOWING ANY WORKOUT.

The key here is BOTH BEFORE AND FOLLOWING ANY TYPE of WORKOUT. Stretching is not something that should be done only when you have time, or when you are cold, but should be done EVERY TIME you work out. Whether you are in your dojang, a weight room, running outdoors or at a competition, stretching should be the first thing in your routine and always on your mind. In cases of those who have chronically "tight" muscles, who have reached the middle of their lifespan or later, or who are pregnant, may in fact need to begin stretching before they even get out of bed in the mornings, or during their morning showers.

Think of it this way, your muscles and tendons are much like a sponge. If you take a sponge that has been sitting around all day, which is pretty dry and stiff, and then try to twist it quickly, what happens? It will crack and tear won't it? If you take that same sponge and gently warm it with water, slowly bending it until it is completely loose, then what happens? The sponge will bend and stretch with little or no tearing or cracking. Your muscles are exactly the same as the sponge. If you want them to last without any tears you need to take the time to warm them up and stretch them out properly.

The same goes for after a workout. You should never end a workout, whether in a dojang or a weight room, by simply stopping without allowing your heart and muscles to calm down slowly. If you take five to ten minutes to cool down and stretch out following a workout you are less likely to become sore and stiff later. There are many excellent ways of doing a cool down, from a slow gentle stretching out on the floor to use of a Swiss Ball or yoga. Think about it, you have been asking your heart to rapidly pump a lot of oxygen-filled blood with nutrients to all of your muscles for the past hour or more, and then you want it to simply stop pumping as hard because you no longer need it to?

The body functions much better if you take the time to slow the pumping of your heart down following a workout. By simply slowing your pace down and slowly stretching out you are giving your body a chance to cool down naturally rather than asking it to shut down all together. A gentle jog or ride on a stationary bike, followed by a five to ten minutes of stretching out the muscles you have been using will do wonders. Never go from a strenuous workout or run directly to your car for a ride. This allows lactic acid build-up to stay in your muscles and increase your soreness and stiffness in the following couple of hours and even days.

Another trick to reduce soreness and swelling which accompanies a workout giving you that "dead leg" feeling is to follow a short stretch of your legs by "putting them up a wall" and allowing the blood flow to be slowed. Simply lay on your back and put your legs up on a wall or an object higher than your heart to help reduce the flooding of blood cells into your legs. While you are lying there you can continue stretching your arms and wrists as you begin to cool down, and even work on visualizations to clear your mind and therefore aid in the slowing of your heart. This is especially beneficial during long competition days when your legs may have to last through five, six or seven matches.

> Stretching should follow a brief five to ten minute warm-up in which you get your blood flowing, and a good sweat going, but without any quick or hard movements (such as kicking full speed). This gives the muscles a chance to begin to move more easily.

Always start your workout routine, whether weights, running or kicking, with a minimum of five to ten minutes of bringing your body to a sweat without any fast or hard motions. Warm-ups can come in the form of a light jog, riding a stationary bike, jumping rope, punching bag exercises, or typical dojang warm-up exercises done at half-speed and half-power. In this manner you will get the blood flowing to the muscles before you ask the muscles to do anything strenuous, including stretching. This is normally something you can begin prior to class or a workout or as part of a group warm-up. The main point here is that you should be warm and sweating before stretching or beginning any type of workout.

If the weather is cold, or the room in which you are working out is highly air-conditioned or simply cold, then extra care and time should be committed to having a good warm-up and breaking a sweat before any other activity is begun. If you are late to a practice this does not mean skip the warm-up in order to get into class. It may mean that you don't get your full ten minutes to warm up, but it should never mean you skip it all together. Having the muscles warm and fully stretched out is one of the best preventatives to injury an athlete can do.

Stretching should take eight to fifteen minutes to complete, using slow movements which are not forceful and which do not cause a "knife-stabbing" pain. Stretching should take longer in colder climates or rooms, especially if it is hard to maintain a sweat in the room. Plus, stretching should never be painful. It will be uncomfortable but never deeply painful.

Stretching should feel good once you are done, although it may be "uncomfortable" while you are stretching. If you warmed-up properly, stretching should be a lot easier to do and more meaningful to your muscles. You should NEVER feel any sharp, stabbing pains like someone is stabbing you with a knife. Rather, you should feel a "pulling" sensation that is not deeply painful but not necessarily comfortable. If you can simply lie down into a stretch and don't feel a good pull, the stretch is doing nothing for you and you are wasting your time. Always push the limits to a comfortable stretch and take it a step beyond, but never to the point of sharp pain.

Often it is easier to have someone else stretch you to take you out of that comfort zone of an easy stretch into a meaningful stretch, but they should never take you into a torturous stretch. If you partner up, you can usually guarantee that your partner will not overstretch you because you will be stretching them next. Also, you should never overstretch a joint as you can make it too loose and therefore more prone to injury. For example, if when you stretch, you make a joint look like it is "bent backwards" or in a weird position you have probably overstretched this area and need to back off some.

Stretching should NEVER involve ballistic movements or BOUNCING. This does not mean you can't move from one side to another and then back, but don't sit and bounce down into a stretch to try to get further. Bouncing actually makes your muscles tighten up or tear in reaction to the bouncing.

Athletes and coaches alike believe that you can "bounce down into a stretch" to get a better stretch, but you actually are decreasing your stretching ability. If you bounce into a stretch you activate a stretch reflex that tightens the muscle more, making it more likely you will become injured. NEVER, EVER bounce while stretching. Instead, you can move from one position to another, say stretch on your right for a few seconds and then move to the left and then back to the right. Each time you should aim to stretch a little bit further than the last time, but do not bounce at the end of the stretch to help move into the stretch of the opposite leg. It is not required that you sit in a stretch for long periods of time. Five to seven seconds can be sufficient if you are truly stretching the muscles and not just sitting there talking while in an easy stretch, nor is there reason to torture yourself for thirty seconds. Quick movements that cause you to bounce, though, can weaken the muscle fibers as well as tighten the muscles, setting you up for injury, the very thing you are trying to prevent from happening.

> **Stretches are most successfully completed with a partner and can be done with what are known as PNF Patterns. PNF stands for proprioneuromuscular facilitation.**

PNF is a group of stretching patterns with one of the most common patterns involving you either to partner up with another athlete or a wall, taking the muscle to a full stretch and then pushing against a person or wall for five to ten seconds, then relaxing. During the relaxed phase the muscle is pushed into a deeper stretch before pushing against resistance once again. These stretches should be done three to six times for each muscle.

This form of stretch also helps athletes encourage each other to push it a little bit further, increasing their flexibility without "torturing" them. No quick or hard movements should ever be used. If you feel sharp pain, your partner needs to back off immediately. This form of

PNF Pattern Stretching is known as a "contract-relax" stretch. You will be able to stretch further in less time using these stretches.

PNF stretches can be done on any muscle of the body by simply having someone or a wall apply resistance against you as you try to contract the muscle against them. If using a partner, your partner can encourage you to push harder as you begin to fatigue, therefore increasing the amount of stretch that is achieved.

An athlete can do slow "rolling" motions of a joint, such as neck rolls or ankle rolls if performed slowly in A NORMAL MOTION FOR THE BODY as long as NO FORCE is applied against the joint during the rolling.

Neck rolls become dangerous when done quickly or against resistance or before a person has begun to sweat from a warm-up. If your joint cracks a lot when doing a rolling exercise you should immediately stop. This is an indication that your body is trying to adjust to a movement which may either be too fast for the joint or in a position which the body does not like to be in and therefore must make accommodations to protect itself from damage. **Never force any joint to crack or pop** as this helps to break down the protective cartilage within the joint.

Never put a joint in an unnatural position, such as bending the knee behind you and then laying back on it. This puts too much pressure on the joint and the protective cartilage in between the bones of a joint, leading to damage. It would be much better to lay on your stomach, bend your knee as if to kick your butt and have a partner lift your leg from the floor and help take your foot closer to your butt to stretch the quad muscles. This way you are predominantly stretching the muscle and not damaging the joint and cartilage.

Remember ALL MUSCLES of the body should be stretched prior to a workout, not just the big ones. So, you should be stretching your thighs, calves, ankles, butt, lower back, shoulders, forearms, wrists, and neck in order to be properly ready for any workout.

Athletes are notorious for only stretching the muscles they feel they use or those they simply like to stretch because they are not uncomfortable to stretch. But, in the martial arts every muscle of the body is used and therefore needs to be warmed up and stretched prior to any workout in order to reduce the chance of injury. Athletes and instructors need to devise a routine in which the same muscles are stretched every time, whether this is done using a chart on the wall or a check-off list that everyone must complete prior to a workout. Usually it is easier to start at one end of the body or the other and progress all the way through the body. Here is a typical check off list that can be used:

• **Neck:** forward, backward, bend head towards each shoulder, turn chin towards each shoulder

• **Shoulder:** internal rotators, external rotators, traps, triceps, biceps, pects

• **Forearm/Wrist:** wrist flexors, wrist extensors, supinators

• **Back:** upper back twist both directions, lower back twist both directions, back stretches on the knees

• **Leg:** quads, hamstrings, piriformis, IT band, groin, calves (both bent knee and straight knee),

• **Ankle/Foot:** side to side, up and down

> **If you feel yourself beginning to get tight during a workout or in between rounds/matches at competitions, stop and take a few moments to re-stretch. It is better to take a few extra minutes to stretch than risk an injury that could take you out for weeks!**

Stretching at the beginning of the day or the beginning of a routine does not always guarantee that you are set for the rest of the day! If you stop working out, or rest for a while between matches your muscles will tighten back up, especially if you lose your "sweat". As you cool down it is natural for your muscles to return to their original unstretched state. So, if your instructor stops a workout to talk with athletes for more than a few minutes, you need to stretch again. To avoid wasting time, you can simply stretch while intently listening to your instructor, keeping arms, legs and back lose for the drills to follow.

If, during a workout, you begin to feel a "pull" in a muscle it is better to stop and take five minutes to restretch the muscles before an injury occurs. If you "pull" a hamstring, for instance, it can take anywhere from six weeks to six months, even a year, to fully repair and heal, not exactly what an athlete wants to go through. So, it is better to take five minutes to stretch again properly, reducing your chance of injury, rather than having to sit out for weeks on end because of being too stubborn to listen to your body.

On the other hand an athlete should never use the need to stretch as an excuse to get out of a difficult drill. After completing the stretching the athlete should be expected to complete any drills or workout he/she missed out on while stretching, unless an injury is suspected, and then injury care treatment should be followed rather than return to a workout. Many times simply taking a moment to stretch will allow the athlete to feel better and therefore work harder instead of "babying" a muscle that does not feel quite right.

Stretching is an essential portion of any workout, and even on those days that an athlete does not workout, a stretching program should be followed to help maintain the flexibility of the muscles. Stretching can be done in silence or to music, individually or with partners, alone or in groups, but nonetheless it should be part of every athlete's daily routine. If the athlete has more than one workout each day, then there will be a need for a separate stretching routine for each routine, both prior and following each workout. For this reason athletes must learn to organize their time well, planning adequate time to warm-up, stretch and cool-down for each workout schedule during the day.

Stretching Exercises

Here are some of the basic stretching techniques that should be used prior to and following any workout on a daily basis. All of these stretches are safe to be completed by athletes of any age, pre-adolescent to senior citizen. Stretching should not only become a daily routine but a way of life for the rest of your life, as it will help to reduce injuries and some of the ailments of aging later in life.

Ankle:

Sam is pictured here stretching his ankle by pulling his toes into a pointed position for resistance as he attempts to work against his hand with his foot for a great stretch prior to kicking.

Gastrocnemius Stretch
the runner's stretch for calf muscles

Mark is performing the typical runner's stretch for the calf muscle by putting his toes on an incline from his heel and leaning his entire body into the wall to stretch the muscle of the lower leg. Notice that Mark is standing tall with shoulders back and buttocks tucked under him as opposed to leaning his chest into the wall while sticking his buttocks out behind him. This position allows for a much better stretch of the calf muscle. This stretch can also be accomplished off of the edge of a step or incline board.

Soleus Stretch
the deep calf muscle

Notice how Mark's right knee is bent as he is performing a standard calf stretch. His knee is bent in order to stretch the deep calf muscle, the soleus, beneath the gastrocnemius of the calf. Both muscles need to be stretched to reduce the chance of injury. Also note that Mark is standing tall with his shoulders back and his buttocks under him as opposed to leaning his chest towards the wall and allowing his buttocks to stick out behind him. This is the proper position for this stretch.

Calf & Hamstring Stretch
towel-assisted

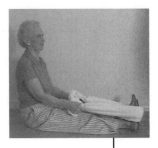

This stretch is another way to stretch both the calf and the hamstrings at the same time, for those who cannot touch their own toes. Put the towel around the bottom of your foot, gripping both ends of the towel with your hands. Keep your back straight (no over arching), and shoulders back. Gently pull on the towel bringing your chest closer to your legs without causing pain, while maintaining a flat back and square shoulders.

Lunging Hip Flexor Stretch:
the front of the pelvis

Phuong is demonstrating the stretch used for the hip flexor, a muscle with a tendon running between the front of your pelvis and the front of your upper thigh. Begin by stepping out in a lunge position with toes pointed forward, knee bending perpendicular to the floor, & shoulders held back over torso, while your hand applies pressure to the hips and pelvic region from the backside of the hip.

Lean your pelvis towards the ground as pictured. You should feel the stretch up the front of the pelvic region but no sharp pain should be felt.

Butterfly Stretch
further stretching the groin

The butterfly stretch is done by bending both knees in and placing the bottom of both feet against each other, then pulling the feet into the groin as much as comfortably possible. Notice Diana is sitting tall with her shoulders back and looking forward (not down).

Mandy assists her in this stretch by gently applying pressure to Diana's low back arch region as Diana leans forward into the stretch, never looking down or "humping" her back.

Butterfly Stretch Supine
lying on the back

The butterfly stretch from the supine position is a greater stretch for some individuals. From the seated butterfly position described previously lay back onto the floor. Use your hands to give added pressure to the insides of your thighs while maintaining your heels as close into the groin area as possible without causing pain. Pre-adolescent children should work on bringing the feet in close to the groin without applying pressure.

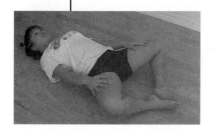

Children should learn at an early age proper stretching techniques to build good habits. A child is never too young to begin to learn to stretch. Olivia has been stretching since she was only a few months old. She sees it as a fun game.

Seated Straddle Stretch
Groin & Hamstring

Sam begins this stretch by sitting tall, shoulders back (not rolled forward), feet spread comfortably apart, toes pointed straight up in the air, eyes looking forward.

Sam then reaches for his calf, leading with his chest as he stretches his groin and hamstring.

Seated Straddle with a Partner

The seated straddle stretch can also be accomplished with a partner stretching either to the side or to the front, or both. Here Masumi begins by sitting tall with her shoulders back.

Mandy applies gentle pressure to the lower arch of her back as Masumi goes forward into her stretch while maintaining a comfortable position.

Notice Mandy does not apply any pressure to Masumi's shoulders or upper back during this stretch.

Even athletes who do not have quite the same flexibility as Masumi can undoubtedly benefit from this partner stretch. Notice how Steven keeps his shoulders back and his chest forward as he moves into the straddle. Mark assists in the stretching by applying gentle pressure to Steven's lower back during the forward stretch.

Inverted Wall Straddle Stretch

This stretch is for those who need a little assistance from gravity to get a good straddle stretch without putting undue stress and strain on the lower back. As pictured to the right, Phuong begins the stretch by lying on the floor near a wall, placing her feet up on the wall, then backing her buttocks as close to the wall as she can tolerate without sharp pain.

Phuong allows gravity to assist her as she opens her legs into a straddle, letting the legs slowly drop into the furthest position of the straddle stretch that she can comfortably tolerate, holding for 7-15 seconds before slowly raising the legs to the start position. Be cautious not to allow the lower back to arch during stretch. The back should remain pressed against the floor throughout stretch.

Position shown above is also excellent to use immediately following a match to reduce the chances of "dead leg" feeling during competitions, or as part of a cool-down program.

Wall-Assisted Hamstring Stretch

Phuong is illustrating a hamstring stretch technique for those who either have extremely tight hamstrings or chronic low back pain to aid in taking the pressure off the lower back. Position yourself in a doorway or facing a doorway with one leg going through the doorway, running the leg to be stretched up the wall. Lie with the back completely flat on the floor pushing the buttocks as close to the wall as is comfortable.

Once you can attain a 90° stretch, sit up into the stretch as Phuong shows, while maintaining the proper arch in the lower back by supporting upper body with arms outstretched. There should be no sharp pain during the stretch. Hold for 7-15 seconds.

If your upper body is too tall to fit in the doorway as Phoung demonstrates, simply turn so the leg not being stretched is going through the doorway while the leg being stretched runs up the side of the doorway.

Towel-Assisted Hamstring Stretch

For those who still need a little bit more assistance to get the hamstrings stretched, try using a towel. Place the towel behind the leg, gripping both ends with your hands and pulling the leg in towards your chest as far as is comfortable, not allowing your low back to arch or knee to bend.

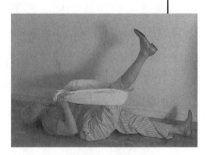

This is an especially good way to stretch the hamstrings which are chronically tight, adding to low back pain, or following a back injury.

PNF Hamstring Stretch

This is one of the "contract-relax" or resistive stretches. Notice Mark begins with both of his buttocks flat on the ground along with a flat back and shoulders. Mark will maintain this position all throughout the stretch. Mark stretches his leg as far as he can comfortably before Diana begins to apply pressure to push it slightly farther.

Mark then attempts to push against Diana's hands as she resists him (but allows some movement) for five to seven seconds. As Mark relaxes Diana pushes his leg into a further stretch before Mark begins to resistively work against Diana once again.

Note the positions of Diana's hands with one on the calf near the ankle, and the other hand just above the knee but not on the knee. Never apply pressure directly to a joint during stretches.

Seated Hamstring Stretch

Sam demonstrates a seated hamstring stretch. Note how Sam sits tall while leaning towards his legs with his chest.

Seated Hamstring Stretch with a Partner

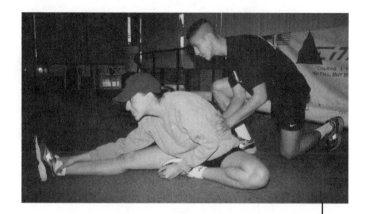

The hamstring can also be stretched in a seated position with or without a partner. Here Diana bends the uninvolved leg in towards her groin while taking her chest towards her straight leg. Mark assists in this stretch by gently applying pressure to the arch of Diana's lower back. Note Diana's eyes are looking forward not down, preventing her from "humping" her back, thereby getting a much better stretch.

Lunging Hamstrings

This is a typical stretch for both the hamstring (foot turned out) and groin (feet face forward). Notice Sam does not hump his back.

Lunging Groin

Basically the same stretch as hamstrings only feet face forward as Sam squats towards the lunging (bent) leg. Stretch should be felt in the groin area of the outstretched leg. Notice Sam keeps his buttocks under him as he stretches.

Quad Stretch
Laying Position with a Partner

This stretch is very beneficial for those athletes with tight quadriceps muscle and/or knee pain. As seen with Steven, the starting position begins by laying on his stomach and bending his knee up behind him at a 90° angle while Mark grabs Steven's thigh & then applies pressure to Steven's buttock with his other hand. No direct pressure is applied to the knee.

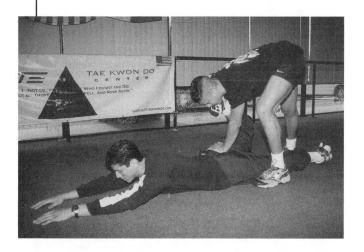

Mandy demonstrates this stretch by gently lifting Diana's thigh while using her shoulder and body to slowly bend Diana's leg towards her. Note Mandy is not applying a lot of force to Diana's leg, just enough for Diana to get a good stretch up the front of her quads.

Standing Quads Stretch
with or without a Partner

Using the opposite hand to grab his foot, both Steven & Sam stretch their quadriceps muscle while standing, pulling the leg directly behind them and not out to the side. Steven uses Mark for balance while Sam uses a wall.

Piriformis Stretch
the "pain in the butt" muscle

The piriformis is a muscle which lies deep within the buttocks but which is needed to perform many martial arts kicks. For this stretch Steven takes Mark's leg, bending it at the knee of the side to be stretched and externally rotating the leg to bring Mark's foot and lower leg across his body.

Steven then applies pressure to Mark's thigh just above the knee pulling back towards him while Steven's other hand is pushing Mark's lower leg toward Mark's chest and bending Mark's hip closer to him (all at the same time). Note though, Steven is not applying pressure directly to the knee but rather just above it. This stretch should burn deep within the buttocks.

Standing Upper Back Twist

This stretch is designed to help loosen the muscles of the upper back. It will help loosen the lower back as well since all of the muscles overlap and work together. You can use a wall (as Sam is showing) or a bar (as Steven is showing below). It is important to take your arm across your body grabbing the bar or wall and then turning away from your arm, keeping your back and shoulders straight without having a "hunchback" or sticking your buttocks out.

Laying Lower Back Twist

Diana and Mandy are demonstrating one of many ways you can stretch your lower back and IT Band. Note Mandy has her hand placed on Diana's thigh, not hip or knee, with the other hand applying gentle pressure to Diana's shoulder. Diana attempts to keep her back and shoulders flat on the ground.

Lower Back Stretches

Diana is performing some of the best low back stretches for a sore and tight back from kicking. The first step (below) Diana sits back on her knees while reaching her upper body out in front of her. Notice Diana is looking forward not down.

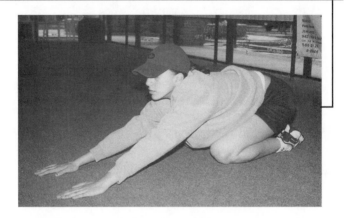

For the second step (above) Diana slowly rocks her pelvis forward creating an arch in her lower back. If your back is sore or if you have a lot of pain you do not have to reach a large arch, simply rock your pelvis forward to a comfortable position.

Cat & Camel Low Back Stretches

Sam is demonstrating stretches often used in therapy programs for low back pain. In the first step Sam drops his head and arches his back towards the ceiling while keeping his knees facing forward, shoulder width apart.

In the second step Sam slowly tilts his pelvis and stomach down to the floor creating an arch in his lower back and lifting his head. If putting an arch in your back inflicts any pain, only take this stretch to a flat back with no pelvic tilt.

Fetal Position Low Back Stretch

Start position for this stretch is to lie on your back, pulling your knees in towards your chest along with your chin.

Final stretch position has your chin tucked into your chest with your hands pulling your knees into your chest as far as is comfortably possible without eliciting pain beyond normal discomfort. To come out of this stretch slowly "unfold" your body, using no quick or sharp movements. You should not feel any sharp pains in the neck or back at any time when performing this stretch properly.

Feet Over Head Back Stretch

Begin this stretch lying on your back, with your arms & hands, as well as the head and neck, flat on the floor. Lift your legs and buttocks up towards the ceiling by tightening the abdomen.

Curl the midsection inwards allowing the feet to go up & over the head. If possible the toes should touch the floor above the head. This motion should be slow and controlled, both going into and out of the stretch.

Upper Back Stretch

This stretch allows you to stretch the upper back even if the lower back is painful. Stand facing a wall. Place your hands on the wall with your arms extended above your head as far as you can comfortably reach. Walk your feet back until the body is at an angle with the wall, dropping your head below your arms, and simply allowing your body to "sink" into the stretch. Walk your feet back in towards wall before trying to take your arms down.

Remember: Do not stick your buttocks out or overly exaggerate the arch in your lower back by maintaining a "flat back" throughout the stretch.

Simple Neck Stretches

The neck should be stretched in all directions as Mark and Sam demonstrate. These stretches should never be forceful or quick, rather only a comfortable pull. As Mark demonstrates here, begin by gently pulling the head towards your shoulder, bringing the ear closer to the shoulder, not the shoulder to the ear.

To continue stretching your neck, take your hand and gently pull your head so your ear goes toward your shoulder (as Mark demonstrated on page 55), your face towards your chest (above), and then turn your face towards the shoulder (below) as Sam demonstrates.

Shoulder Pendulums
loosen the shoulder

For those returning from a shoulder injury or who are suffering from a "frozen shoulder", this is one of the first stretching exercises you need to use. Simply lean forward, bending at the waist allowing your arms to hang in the air.

Begin creating large circles going clockwise, bringing them down to very small circles and then back to large circles. Reverse and go counterclockwise first with large circles then to small and back to large again.

Upper Body Stretches for Shoulder, Upper Arm & Lats

Diana is helping Mark to stretch triceps and lats by pushing Mark's bent arm behind his head. For an added stretch Diana holds the arm resisting Mark's push against her hand. This is another beneficial PNF stretch. Diana can then push Mark's arm farther behind his head when he relaxes after 5-7 seconds of resistive stretching.

This exercise can also be done alone, as Sam demonstrates.

Shoulder Stretch Across Body and Pects Resistive Stretch

The stretch that Sam is doing here can be done with or without a partner, using resistance either against a person or wall. Note Sam stands tall at all times.

In the Pects Stretch, both arm & wrist remain flat on wall as Sam turns away from wall, pressing his arm into wall stretching his pects.

Pects Stretch with Partner

Mandy is stretching Masumi's pects by bringing her arm directly behind her with thumbs pointing up at all times. Mandy then lifts Masumi's arms higher than shoulder level to get a shoulder stretch combined with the pects.

Notice both Masumi and Steven stand tall without hunching their backs and looking forward at all times. Mark and Mandy can apply resistance for an even better stretch. Note how Steven turns his thumbs out to change the stretch on his shoulders.

Pects Stretch & Shoulder Stretch
Gravity Assisted

If you do not have a partner to help you stretch, or simply want additional stretching, this may be the stretch for you. Simply lock your fingers together with your arms behind your lower back and lean forward allowing the arms to "drop" towards the head, stretching the chest and shoulder.

Shoulder Rotator Cuff Stretches with a Partner
External Rotation

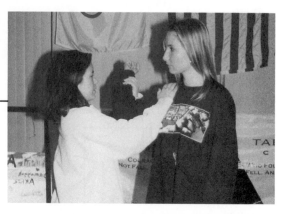

Notice that even though Masumi and Diana stand in different positions, one hand grips arm just below wrist while the other is placed on the shoulder as the forearm is pushed towards Mandy & Mark's backside. The hand on the shoulder is used to stabilize and not allow the shoulder to turn in. Not a lot of pressure is applied to the shoulder.

Shoulder Rotator Cuff Stretches with a Partner
Internal Rotation

For internal rotation stretch of the rotator cuff muscles the arm position of Mandy and Mark is turned so the elbow is at a 90° angle to the ground. Once again Masumi and Diana place one hand just above the wrist with the other hand at the shoulder. They pull Mandy & Mark's arm back behind them, trying to not allow any twisting of the upper body or shoulder by stabilizing the shoulder with the other hand. Note Mark and Mandy remain standing tall and looking forward at all times.

Elbow & Forearm Stretch

This is a combination stretch of the muscles of the elbow and forearm. Begin by crossing your arms one over the other with the palm of the arm to be stretched facing up. Lock your fingers together and try to twist the arm a little bit further.

Wrist Extensor Stretch

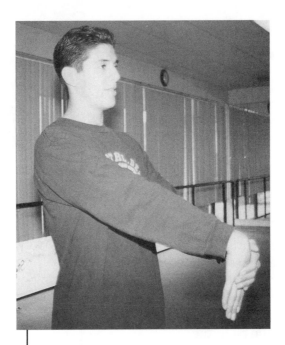

It is important to stretch the wrist and forearm prior to punching or grabbing workouts. Steven is pushing on the top of his right hand while keeping his arm straight in order to stretch his wrist extensor muscles. Steven can also apply resistance to his hand as he tries to extend his wrist for an even greater stretch.

Wrist Flexors Stretch

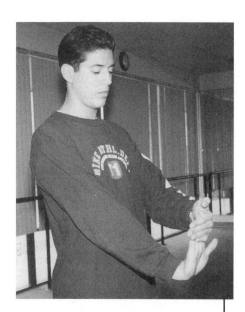

This is a similar stretch, only this time Steven is stretching his wrist flexors by pulling his hand and fingers up while keeping his arm straight. Steven can apply resistance as he tries to straighten his wrist against his hand for an even greater stretch.

Workout Equipment, Workout Surfaces and Proper Footwear

Having good working equipment and workout areas, as well as proper footwear, is essential to any workout program whether in a gym, weight room, dojang, or outdoors. Once again there are a few simple guidelines to follow to help prevent or reduce the chance of an injury occurring:

All equipment should be in good working order.

Equipment should be regularly inspected for safety, function and general wear and tear. If equipment is torn or broken it should be removed from use until repaired. This is simply common sense, but not always followed due to budgetary restraints. Never "rig" equipment to get by, for that makes the equipment unsafe. The safety and well being of the person using the equipment is much more important than having one less piece of equipment to use.

Equipment does not always need to be replaced once damaged, but it does need to be properly repaired before allowing the continuance of its use. Never put yourself or another athlete at risk simply because you feel "you can fix it later". It is wiser to change a workout routine to omit use of a piece of equipment than to use some piece of equipment that may potentially injure either the athlete or instructor.

Choose the proper workout surface to reduce the chance of injury.

Workout surfaces are another cause of injury for varying reasons. If a surface is too hard and non-yielding the athletes will undoubtedly sustain overuse injuries such as shin splints and stress fractures.

Such injuries are very bothersome and take a long time to recover from, often requiring the cessation of weight-bearing activity until the injury has fully healed.

The optimum surface for any workout is a moderately padded floor, which allows for some give without being "too soft". Throwing forms of martial arts tend to prefer softer mats than sports involving spinning. Surfaces which are soft can lead to a greater number of knee injuries but reduce the number of shoulder injuries seen in throwing forms of the sport. If a wooden floor is used there should be a space below the floor which allows the wood to "give" and bend slightly, absorbing some of the shock rather than requiring the athlete's body to absorb all of the energy of a workout. Workouts should never be conducted on a solid concrete floor or asphalt surface as these surfaces are non-yielding and detrimental to the joints.

Carpet has its advantages and disadvantages: it does allow some cushioning for jumping drills or running, but when used barefoot it can also cause skin burns and blisters. Great care must be used to introduce new athletes to a carpeted surface, allowing the use of shoes all or part of the time in order to help protect their feet while trying to "toughen" the feet up.

Workout surfaces should never be slippery, as many more injuries can occur from a slick padded surface. If purchasing new mats, be sure to clean them appropriately several times in order to "roughen" the surface prior to use. Never clean a floor and then immediately begin using the surface before it has completely dried, otherwise you are asking for injuries.

Grass surfaces can be used if the terrain is smooth, without any holes or lumps that may cause an athlete to lose their balance and become injured. Grass surfaces should never be used early in the morning or following a rain as the grass becomes very slippery, increasing the risk of injuries. This is not to say that grass surfaces cannot be used, only that the area needs to be inspected prior to use to ensure its safety.

> **Proper surfaces for running activities should not be too firm or too soft. Appropriate footwear should be worn.**

As for running surfaces, the surface once again needs to be "yielding" and give some when running to prevent overuse injuries such as shin splints and stress fractures. If running in a dojang or a gymnasium for extended periods of time, wear properly fitted and maintained running shoes, not martial arts shoes. The arch and the lower leg need the support provided in running shoes which is not found in martial arts shoes. Running shoes, though, are not appropriate to use when doing a normal martial arts workout with kicks and spinning as they do not slide well and can lead to ankle injuries.

Judge the appropriate needs for each situation. If an athlete is running outdoors, a soft, dry or slightly moist (but not slick) surface is the optimal choice. It is preferable to run in the dirt or grass along a sidewalk or road as opposed to the concrete sidewalk or asphalt road. The earth, as long as it is dry or slightly moist, but not too dry, will "give" more when running on it. This will reduce your chances of shin splints, which are very painful and difficult to treat.

One of the best surfaces to run on is sand that has been moistened by the water, but that which is not wet or partially submerged in water. Beach sand where the tide was coming in previously but which is not presently wetting the sand, is a great surface to run barefoot upon. This type of surface when available, reduces the risk of overuse injuries, and actually makes the joints work more to find their "center" or proprioception (body's knowledge of where it is in space), thereby strengthening the muscles which support the joints of the legs. Running on sand is the one exception to the rule of wearing proper running shoes. If you choose to run on sand it is more appropriate to run barefoot in the sand that is moist but not soaked. Avoid areas of heavy shell or rock deposits, and be aware of jellyfish that may be littering the area, which can pose the risk of another type of potential injury. Sand running can prove to be a quite a workout, so do not expect to be able to run as far or as fast when initially beginning a program. The change of scenery and type of workout though, may actually increase the desire to workout harder.

Running on dirt trails can be safe as long as the dirt does not contain loose rock or pebbles and is not extremely compact and hard. Outdoor running can often be much more enjoyable with a change of scenery than indoor, but precautions still need to be taken to ensure safety. Always inspect a route prior to running. Look for any safety hazards, such as holes or obstacles to avoid. When leading a group, map out the route so athletes who fall behind will know where they are going when they lose the rest of the pack.

When shoes are worn for a workout, properly maintained shoes are essential, especially running shoes. Many athletes have their "favorite" pair of running shoes that they will wear until the shoes fall off of their feet, which can lead to overuse injuries. Once the tread begins to wear, particularly if it wears unevenly on one side as opposed to the other, or the arch support becomes worn, the shoes are no longer properly supporting the foot and ankle and therefore can lead to ankle injuries, shin splints, stress fractures, tendonitis of the knee, etc. They should be replaced by new shoes before the wear becomes excessive. Generally speaking, if you are running on a daily basis, or even every other day, you should be replacing your running shoes every 3-4 months.

Protective Equipment

Besides the normal protective gear that most martial artists are accustomed to wearing: chest protector, head gear, forearm pads, shin guards, foot pads, gloves, wrist/hand protection, and genital protectors, there is one other piece of equipment that all athletes should wear, the mouthpiece. Many athletes skip the use of the mouthpiece because they feel they cannot breathe with it or that the mouthpiece is uncomfortable to wear. If you go to your dentist to have a form-fitted mouthpiece made from a mold of your mouth it should be very comfortable. Most dentists will gladly produce a form-fitted mouthpiece, often at no additional charge. There are also many companies nowadays that will send you a kit to make an impression of your teeth, which you then send back to them to produce a very thin mouthpiece. As for breathing, wear your mouthpiece during all practices to become accustomed to it, and therefore accustomed to breathing properly with one in your mouth.

Mouthpieces are not only designed to protect your teeth and jaw, but also the head and brain as follows:

• Having a mouthpiece properly fitted can help reduce the chances of a serious concussion and even a potential loss of consciousness in a knock out.

• Mouthpieces will not prevent head injuries or concussions, but may reduce the overall severity of the injury, often meaning the difference between continuing a fight or ending a fight due to injury and/or knockout.

• Mouthpieces reduce the chance of a dislocated jaw by not allowing abnormal movement to occur to the joints of the jaw when struck during a fight.

• Mouthpieces help to reduce the chance of fracture by holding the mouth in a less vulnerable position.

• Mouthpieces protect teeth from damage or loss. They can prevent teeth from being chipped and broken, or knocked out of the mouth altogether.

• Mouthpieces protect not only the teeth but the lips and inside of the mouth of those wearing braces affixed to the teeth, which may become cut or torn by the wires when hit

Unless you like that "hockey player" look or that "punch-drunk" feeling it is a very wise investment to have a mouthpiece made by your family dentist or commercially produced from a mold taken of your own mouth and teeth.

A properly fitted mouthpiece should completely cover all teeth of the maxilla, that is all of the teeth in the upper portion of your mouth, from the right temporal-mandibular joint (TMJ) of the jaw to the left, not just the very front teeth. The mouthpiece needs only to be a thin layer of shear protective material. It does not need to cover the roof of the mouth in any manner. Many boxers, as well as martial arts athletes, today actually use mouthpieces that fold over and cover both the upper and lower teeth for maximum protection of the teeth, jaw, head and brain.

Although adding color to the mouthpiece helps to increase the use of mouthpieces by adding a "fun factor" or even comic relief, always have a second clear mouthpiece available as a back-up for competitions requiring mouthpieces to be clear or white. This way you avoid having to buy a non-fitted mouthpiece at the last minute.

In recent years many head injuries, including serious concussions, dislocated jaws, broken jaws, knockouts and even deaths of prominent martial artists and national team members have been attributed in part to not wearing a mouthpiece during competition. These injuries kept athletes out of practice and competition from thirty days up to three months following the injury. If these athletes had been wearing a mouthpiece at the time they received a blow to the head the injury could have been substantially reduced, therefore shortening the recovery period and allowing athletes to return to competition more quickly.

All protective equipment should be inspected on a regularly basis for tears or damage to the soft padding and/or straps used to keep them in place. If the equipment at any time shows signs of wear and tear, or damage, the equipment needs to either be sent back to the manufacturer for repair or a new piece of equipment needs to be purchased to replace it. Recently, the ASTM (American Society for Testing and Materials) was asked to set safety standards for martial arts equipment and mats, as it has done for many other sports such as soccer and gymnastics. The ASTM takes equipment and puts it through various testing procedures to see whether or not it is going to properly protect the user. In 2004, the ASTM set the first of many safety standards for martial arts equipment, beginning with the headgear or helmet. Soon, headgear will be required to have a label showing that it has passed ASTM safety standards testing and is therefore a protective piece of equipment. Many martial art competitions, as well as insurance companies that insure martial art schools, will soon be requiring athletes to use only equipment which has passed the ASTM Safety Standards Testing. Presently, only the headgear has a set safety standard, ASTM: F 2397-04a.

Jewelry

Jewelry causes many injuries every year that could be prevented simply by not having it on. Many athletes practice and compete with jewelry on their body without ever giving it a second thought. But think about it, jewelry is metal, a hard substance which is not allowed in competition for safety reasons. Injury prevention means looking at all possible causes of injuries and reducing the chances of those injuries occurring, and this includes the removal of all jewelry. If you wear jewelry often enough during workouts or competitions, you will eventually experience an injury, either to yourself or to your opponent, and it is simply not worth the risk.

Jewelry worn on the head is the most dangerous, including all piercings and chains. Earrings, either lower lobe or upper cartilage earrings can either be torn from the ear or smashed into the athlete's head upon contact from an opponent's foot or hand. Piercings of the face (eyebrow, nose, lip, etc) are even more vulnerable as the athlete usually has no protective gear covering the jewelry. Opponent's can also be injured from facial jewelry.

Piercings of the tongue are especially dangerous as there is no protection from injury, allowing the ball of the piercing to be driven directly into the palate, or roof of the mouth. An injury of this nature can cause serious damage if the jewelry enters or becomes lodged between the palate (roof of the mouth) and the nasal cavity or becomes infected following such an incident. This piercing can also come loose during activity with the person swallowing part or all of the jewelry, causing internal damage to the body. Injuries from tongue rings and barbells can occur even with those pieces of jewelry that are imbedded down into the tongue.

Necklaces can also cause serious injury to the neck and throat, often getting caught and either pinching or strangling the athlete. The same goes for bracelets and ankles bracelets that often become easily tangled, damaging the area or an opponent, even those bracelets/ankle bracelets that are tied on like a string or rope. Rings on fingers, thumbs and toes cannot only be dangerous for the person wearing them, but also to the person being struck by them. Fingers and toes can swell to a point at which the ring cannot be removed and eventually prevents adequate blood supply to reach the digit, as well as becoming a weapon to both the wearer and the person struck by the ring. Lastly, belly button rings, nipple rings, and genital rings, although this jewelry is not readily seen during competition, can also cause serious injury if ripped from the skin. These areas are also very vulnerable to infection should an injury from the piercing occur, as well as the risk of heavy scarring of the damaged tissue. Obviously the best policy is for athletes not to wear any jewelry during practice or competition. Jewelry can always be put back on later, a torn ear or damaged mouth cannot.

Chapter One Key Points

✦ Injury prevention through correct form, mechanics and staying in tune with your body's needs is preferable to caring for an injury after the fact.

✦ Stretching should be done before and after every workout, even on days you do not other type of workout.

✦ Stretching should always be preceded by a five to ten minute warm-up to raise your body temperature.

✦ Stretching should be done slowly and should not be unbearably painful.

✦ Never bounce during a stretch.

✦ Joint rolling exercises are okay as long as no force is applied to the joint and the rolling motion is natural for the joint.

✦ It's a good idea to stretch if you tighten up during a workout or between rounds of a match.

✦ Workouts should never be conducted on solid concrete or asphalt surfaces.

✦ Martial arts shoes may be worn to protect the feet when training on carpeting, but running shoes should always be worn when doing any type of sprinting or distance running.

✦ A properly fitted mouthpiece can reduce the risk of head injuries.

✦ All jewelry should be removed before any practice, workout, or competition to reduce the chance of injury to yourself or your opponent/partner.

Strength & Conditioning 2

Although strength programs have played a large part of many other athletic programs for decades, the martial arts is an area where strength and conditioning is just beginning to be used by many athletes . Martial art athletes have always been afraid to use weights for fear of "bulking up" and losing speed or flexibility. But this does not have to be true if a proper program is designed. Athletes who participate in martial arts should be on a routine strength and conditioning program in addition to a plyometrics program, and a core strengthening & stability program. These types of programs help to reduce the risk of injury by strengthening the muscles necessary for participation in the sport, while maintaining power, speed, agility, coordination, quickness, and flexibility. Strength and conditioning programs which involve weightlifting and plyometrics, as well as Pilates, Yoga and Swiss Ball workouts, are the best source for burning fat of any type of workout, another incentive for weight-restricted sports such as martial arts. As mentioned earlier, these strengthening programs must include an appropriate warm up and stretching routine prior to and proper cool down immediately following every workout in order to maintain flexibility and reduce the chance of injury.

As with any new workout program, ensure that you are in good health and capable of handling the requirements of such a program **by always first visiting your physician** for an annual physical and release for participation in a strength and conditioning program, as well as for any other form of workout (running, martial arts participation, etc.). Many unknown conditions, such as heart and lung conditions, could become evident from participation in such programs and it is better to know that your body is capable of handling the demands of such a program rather than collapsing during a workout. An annual physical should be part of any athlete's life anyway to ensure the body is maintaining its highest level of performance. It is also wise to seek the knowledge and direction of a licensed professional in the field of strength and conditioning, such as a Certified Strength & Conditioning Specialist (CSCS) from the National Strength & Conditioning Association (NSCA), and/or a Certified Athletic Trainer (ATC) from the National Athletic Trainers Association (NATA), before designing a strength and conditioning program. Both of these fields require a college degree in one of the following: athletic training, biomechanics, exercise science, kinesiology, or sports medicine, plus successful completion of a national board exam in the related field of health science or allied health field. Unlike a personal fitness trainer, who is also certified, the CSCS & ATC require a college degree plus successful completion of a national board exam, and in many cases state licensure, so you can be guaranteed their knowledge base is going to be higher when dealing with athletes, particularly those who have special sports specific needs. An NATA Certified Athletic Trainer (ATC) can additionally evaluate injuries, providing the initial treatment and recommendations for further evaluation or treatment by a physician, as well as give insight into preventative measures which can be used to greater reduce the risk of injury from participation.

A strength and conditioning program can take many different shapes but the basics should all be relatively the same. For athletes under the age of 8, no weights or resistance should be used (except the athlete's own body weight) during exercises, where the focus should be on basic proper technique. Programs which involve proper flexibility training and balance/coordination training are paramount at this age, such as various yoga programs, exercise ball or roller training.

Ages 9-11 should begin on progressive weightlifting with low weights, adding new styles of exercise with little to no resistance, with continued emphasis on basic proper technique. It is at this age that sports specific components of strength and conditioning with weights should be begun, as well as non-traditional programs such as Pilates. For ages twelve and up, a weightlifting program should involve a higher number of repetitions per exercise (12, 15 or 18), a moderate to high number of sets (3 or 4), and a low to moderate amount of weight (moderate: 50-60% of your maximum ability to lift in one lift) with continued emphasis on flexibility and balance training.

By age 16, regular adult components of a weightlifting program can be incorporated. Athletes age 40 and older need to remember that there are physiological changes taking place in their body, so weightlifting overhead will become more difficult to complete, and some modifications to their program may be necessary to reduce the risk of injury. Flexibility at this age also begins to make changes, requiring more time and effort to maintain, with some joints losing previous flexibility levels. But this does not mean that individuals over the age of 40 should cease weight-training or flexibility workouts. Rather this is when these individuals need to focus more on strength and conditioning as well as flexibility, and there is no reason a program cannot be begun after the age of 40 (or 60 or 80) once your physician has given the okay for physical fitness. And yes, I have a 77 year old mother who still lifts weights and stretches, and even kicks and punches.

As for pregnant individuals, we will discuss your workout in Chapter 9, as there are many precautions to take, but not as many as one might think!

If you are returning to workouts following an injury, first get your release for activity from both your physician and either your licensed physical therapist or certified athletic trainer (not personal fitness trainer).

Many of the exercises described in this chapter begin from a reduced difficulty, moving into more progressively difficult techniques. These lower difficulty exercises are where BOTH a person starting their first strength program (or starting a new program after years of not doing one) or someone who is returning from an injury, following release from their physician and/or physical therapist and/or certified athletic trainer, should begin their program. You should NEVER return to the strength and conditioning program you were participating in at the same levels as before your injury. Rather you should use progressive steps to return to your baseline program. It is very wise after you have sprained ligaments/cartilage, strained muscles/tendons, dislocated/subluxed a joint, or fractured a bone, to request from your physician a prescription for physical therapy or wellness program rehab prior to return to participation in activities. Even if you can only get a prescription for two weeks, you can gain knowledge and guidance in how to create a program of strength and conditioning necessary to return to your original level of play.

Once you have been cleared by your physician for participation in a strength and conditioning program (and/or your Licensed Physical Therapist or Certified Athletic Trainer if you have been injured) it is wise to do some functional movement tests for mobility and stability. One such program is known as the Functional Movement Screen[SM] (FMS) which was developed to determine baseline assessment of mobility and stability. The FMS has 7 test components and can be utilized with athletes from any sport at any age, including all forms of martial art. The tests are as follows:

1. Deep Squat

2. Hurdle Step

3. In-line Lunge

4. Shoulder Mobility

5. Active Straight Leg Raise

6. Trunk Stability

7. Rotary Stability

Deep Squat

A normal deep squat is performed while holding a bar (can even be a broomstick or mop handle) held overhead. A perfect score of III is attained if the torso remains parallel with the lower leg when in the deep squat (both vertical), knees are aligned over the feet and the bar aligned over the feet. Any inability reduces the score and shows reduced functional ability of either the hips, knees, ankles, shoulders or low back.

Hurdle Step

While standing erect hold bar on your shoulders behind your head while stepping over a raised obstacle, such as a hurdle. A perfect score of III is attained if the hips, knees and ankles remain in alignment, the low back remains extended (not hunched), and both the bar and the obstacle remain parallel to each other. The score is reduced if there is any movement of the lower spine, the alignment of the hips, knees and ankles is not maintained, toes touch obstacle or the bar and obstacle do not remain parallel. Start with the toes just under the obstacle, which in this picture is a cord.

In-Line Lunge

While standing on a 2 x 6-inch board place the bar vertically behind your head and back. Grasp with one hand from over the shoulder/behind the head and one reaching up behind from the lower back. Take a lunge step forward on the board until the trailing leg's (back leg) knee gently touches the board, then stand and take a lunging step with other leg. A perfect score is attained for proper position of the knee in line with the toes of the lead lunging leg. The trailing leg knee should remain in line on the 2 x 6 board and touch behind the heel of the lead leg. There should be no movement (wobbling) of the torso, which would reduce the score.

Shoulder Mobility

Place the bar behind the head and back in a vertical position, grabbing the bar with one hand from over the shoulder and back behind the head, while the other hand grasps the bar from lower, coming up behind the back, trying to get the two fists as close together as possible on the bar. A perfect score is attained if the 2 fists are within one hand-length of each other while maintaining an erect posture.

Active Straight Leg Raise

While lying on the floor place 2 x 6 board crossways behind knees. Press the lower back to the floor. Lie with your hands at your side. Lift one leg up in a straight leg raise without bending the knee or allowing the lower back to raise up from the floor. At this point drop the bar vertical to the floor next to leg not being tested directly next to the ankle on the inside of the leg being raised. A perfect score of III is attained if the bar is dropped at a point which is mid-thigh to groin region of the untested leg. If the bar is dropped lower than the mid-thigh region (towards the knee region) a reduction of score is assessed.

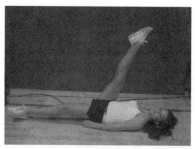

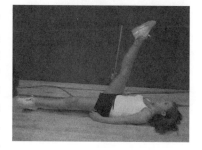

 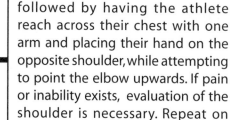

The shoulder mobility test is then followed by having the athlete reach across their chest with one arm and placing their hand on the opposite shoulder, while attempting to point the elbow upwards. If pain or inability exists, evaluation of the shoulder is necessary. Repeat on both shoulders.

Trunk Stability Push Up

Performance of one push-up is done with hands in two different placements for male vs. female. For men, place hands together forming a diamond so when the push-up is at the floor level the forehead/hairline touches the diamond; for females the diamond is placed so the face and chin touch the diamond.

Diamond formation with hands	Hand placement for males

Hand placement for females

Notice that Phuong's back, hips, shoulders & neck are like a plank, flat, with no differences in level between the shoulders to the buttocks, knees are extended, and face looking down at the floor.

Rotary Stability

Place the 2 x 6 board longways on the floor; get on the hands and knees over the board with one knee resting on the board. While maintaining a flat back with no arch (plank), lift the hand and knee of the same side. Bend the elbow and knee in towards each other while remaining parallel with the board below and maintaining a stable balanced position. Next extend the arm out in front of you and the leg back behind you, maintaining balance and plank torso, before returning to the bent position. If you can complete this exercise with good balance and proper mechanics you receive a perfect score of III. If you can complete this using the opposite arm and leg you receive a II, if unable to perform in either fashion receive a I. You receive a zero if any pain is associated with this exercise.

One point would be deducted in this case as Aubrey loses her balance momentarily as she brings the elbow and knee together.

Lastly, get on the hands and knees, sitting the buttocks back on the heels while the arms are outstretched in front of you. If pain occurs, even if you received a III prior you will receive a 0.

Other functional performance tests can include the vertical jump, standing medicine ball chest pass, 40-yard sprint, anaerobic power tests (such as a 300 yard shuttle run or line drills), agility and body control tests, and aerobic power tests (such as 2-mile run or 3-minute step test). Functional tests can also be sports specific, incorporating maneuvers which are typically used by an athlete in the sport, or mechanisms to record and analyze the movement of the athlete, such as telemetry mechanisms that graph mechanical movement to be analyzed for proper technique.

Core Strengthening

A Core Strengthening Program is essential to any strength and conditioning program, but especially for martial artists, as your power from kicks, punches and throws originates in your core muscles, enabling your legs and arms to perform proper technique. So, what is core strengthening? Your core encompasses your abdomen, back and chest, the largest part of your body, to which your arms and legs are attached. If your core is not strong and flexible then you have to compensate for the weakness when kicking or throwing by "hunching" the body instead of standing tall allowing for the most power and force to be delivered to your opponent. The greatest part about core strengthening is that any age can do some form of core strengthening, from toddlers to teenagers to adults to the elderly, even pregnant women can do some core strengthening exercises (more on pregnant martial artists in Chapter 9). Not only do you gain strength and power from core strengthening, but also a great looking stomach, back and chest! Even for those of us with an extra layer of fat on our midsection, the core can still be strengthened and help to burn fat. A core strengthening program should be done on a regular basis in addition to weightlifting, cardiovascular training, balance training and sports specific training.

In addition to core strengthening components that will be described in the use of free weights, resistance and weight machines, Swiss Ball and such, here are a few key core strengthening exercises you might want to consider adding to your strength and conditioning program:

The Traditional Push-Up

Back, buttocks, hips, shoulders and legs remain in a flat "plank" position, with little to no bend in any joint. Eyes are looking at floor. Control your body movement to floor and then "push up" to original position in a slow controlled motion.

Children can be taught proper technique too. Since only their own body weight is being used it is safe at even the early age of 3, before bad habits have been formed.

Diamond-Hand Push-Ups
Positions at Chest & Face

Use diamond hand position described previously in this chapter for all three of these push-ups, and use the technique previously described for push-ups with diamond hands at the forehead/face/chin also previously mentioned.

Position hands in diamond formation directly under your chest, keeping your body in a plank position.

Diamond at chest

Diamond at forehead position

Lower your body to the ground in a slow and controlled motion without letting the entire body drop to or touch the floor. Then push back up in a slow controlled motion, maintaining the flat "plank" position of the body, eyes looking at the floor at all times. NEVER drop into or bounce up out of a push-up, as severe injury can occur.

Wide-Stance Push-Up

Place your hands directly out from the shoulders in as wide of a position as is comfortable. Your hand position should be one in which you can complete the push-up with proper technique and control of your body at all times.

Fingertip Push-Ups

This is a traditional push-up completed up on the fingertips instead of flat-handed. Place your hands in a comfortable position near your shoulders, using proper technique to maintain "plank" body in a slow and controlled motion.

Push-ups from the knuckles are not recommended as this can cause permanent damage to joints and protective cartilage of the hands leading to arthritis, or damage to the growth plates in young, developing athletes.

The Traditional Crunch

Begin by lying on your back with your knees bent in a comfortable position, fingertips behind the ears, eyes looking at the ceiling. Press your low back to the floor by tightening your abdominal muscles, and continue pressing until you have completed ALL crunches.

To begin the crunch, lift your shoulders and upper back straight up off of the floor by tightening your abdominal muscles, while keeping the low back pressed to the floor. Return to the start position in a slow and controlled fashion. Never allow your hands or fingers to pull at your neck or head. Your eyes should always look towards the ceiling. NOTE: Stop when at any time you cannot keep your back pressed against the floor while crunching or any sharp pain occurs in the neck or back.

CAUTION: abdominal cramping lasting hours or even days may occur from performing excessive number of crunches; progressively add sets/reps to your core strengthening program to reduce the chance of severe cramps.

Pike Sit-Up

This is the traditional sit-up with an added leg component to work both the upper and lower abdominal muscles. CAUTION: if you have a back injury or weakness, DO NOT attempt this exercise unless under the direct supervision of a licensed physical therapist (PT) or certified athletic trainer (ATC).

Begin by lying on the floor with your legs straight and arms extended overhead, low back pressed to the floor. Perform a sit-up by reaching with your arms as you lift your legs into the air, with the ending position of the fingers reaching the legs in the air, eyes following the fingers. WARNING: DO NOT excessively arch the back prior to the sit up as this can cause severe back injury. Your back should be flat on the floor. Return to the start position in a slow & controlled fashion. CAUTION: if you have a low back injury or weakness you should not attempt this exercise without direct supervision of a PT or ATC.

The advanced version is to raise the arms straight above the head bringing the legs up further and creating a "V", hold, then let them open into a wide "V" & hold for 5-7 seconds.

Froggy Crunch

Same technique as the traditional crunch except you put your feet and legs in a butterfly stretch, bringing the heels of your feet as close to your groin area as possible.

Straddle Pike Sit-Up

This is an advanced version of the pike sit-up previously described, and should not be attempted until the pike sit-up has been mastered, as it requires more balance and body control to complete properly. CAUTION: do not attempt this exercise if you have a back injury or weakness unless under the direct supervision of a PT or ATC. Do not attempt until you have mastered the pike sit-up even if you have no back injury/weakness.

Begin by lying on the floor with your arms extended above the head, your legs extended in straddle position and your low back pressed against the floor.

Begin the sit-up by bringing arms from over head lifting your body and straddled legs up off of the floor until the arms reach between the legs. DO NOT excessively arch the low back prior to sit-up as this may cause severe injury.

Advanced position for this exercise has only the very low back and buttocks touching the floor when at the peak.

Lower Abdominal Leg Lift

Begin by lying on the floor, arms at your side, low back pressed to the floor, eyes looking at the ceiling. Tighten and then lift legs off of floor. If you have any sharp pain STOP.

Lift the legs until perpendicular with the floor while your low back is still pressed to the floor (no arching). Arms remain on the floor at your side.

Slowly lift your legs up as high above your chest as possible in a controlled motion, with your shoulders remaining on the floor. Slowly "roll" your body back to the start position.

Reduce difficulty: place hands under the buttocks while pressing the low back towards the floor. Lift as high as comfortable. Hold.

Advanced Version – Jacknife: continue to raise the legs until only the shoulders are touching & the legs are bent toward the face at about a 45° angle from the floor. Hold.

Superman

This is an abdominal exercise in which you lay on the floor on your stomach and attempt to bring both arms and both legs up, looking like superman. Hold for 10-15 seconds.

Obliques

These are the muscles of your side that aid in twisting the torso (also where we find "lovehandles" when gaining weight/fat). They assist martial artists by providing power and strength during spinning kicks and twisting throws. Since the obliques are often untrained and weak in many individuals these exercises may be extremely difficult at first, but continue to attempt them, as any movement towards performing the exercise is strengthening upon which you can build.

Obliques Exercise #1

Begin by lying on your side, with your arm closest to the floor bent 90°, legs extended out straight and your other arm at your hip as Phuong illustrates. Your entire body from shoulders to ankles should be in line to start.

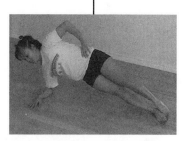

Using the muscles of your sides (obliques), raise the hips upwards towards the ceiling, causing a "sidebend". Do not push with your feet or arms. Use only the oblique muscles. The stronger they are the more of a side pike you will attain.

CAUTION: if you have balance problems or an elbow injury, this exercise may not be advisable, check with your MD, PT or ATC before attempting.

Obliques Exercise #2

This is the more difficult of the 2 sidebending exercises for the obliques.

Begin by lying on your side, arm extended above your head, head held in the air, eyes looking forward, legs extended straight, one on top of the other.

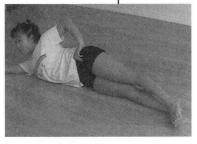

You may only get minimal movement when first attempting this exercise, but keep trying.

Using the muscles of your sides (obliques) bend the body upwards towards the ceiling, taking your shoulders towards your hip, top arm on hip (or laying on your side), other arm extended out above head but not supporting the body. No arching of the back. Return to start position in a slow controlled motion.

Obliques Exercise #3

Lying on your back, put your hands up behind your head or ears, then bend your knees and "twist" them to one side. From this position attempt a crunch keeping your mid-back pressed against the floor, raising the shoulders from the floor like Aubrey does below.

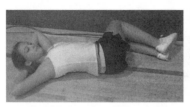 

Weightlifting

Athletes in the martial arts are not like bodybuilders or power lifters in that they do not need to see how much weight they can lift at one time. Rather, martial art athletes need to be able to lift a reasonable amount of weight numerous times in order to build stamina as well as power. Even heavy weight fighters do not have to lift heavy weights, as they are usually at the greatest risk of losing flexibility. Both male and female athletes should be lifting weights three to four times per week in a regularly scheduled routine.

The weightlifting portion of a strength and conditioning program can be followed in several different manners, either by doing the entire body every workout (three times per week) or all upper body one day then all lower body another day (lifting upper two times/week, lower two times/week). Some athletes like to do a program in which opposing muscles of both the upper and lower body are completed in one day and the rest of the muscles worked the next day (four times/week). For example, some athletes will do all large opposing muscles one day (like hamstrings/quads, pects/lats, rotator cuff/deltoids/traps, biceps/triceps) then the next day do all small opposing muscles (like lateral leg/groin, calves/shins, ankles, forearm/wrist) while completing back and abdominal strengthening every day. I personally prefer to lift the entire body for each workout 3 times per week, have a plyometrics workout 1-2 times per week, a Swiss Ball or roller training, Pilates or Yoga workout 1-2 times per week, cardio only workout one day, and complete my back and abdominal exercises along with stretching 7 days per week.

Whichever method you choose to follow ensure that you have a twenty-four to forty-eight hour recovery period for your muscles before lifting with the same muscles again. Stretch all muscles even on days off from lifting. Also, make sure that all opposing muscles (muscles that work against each other) are given equal workouts so as not to create an imbalance in your muscle structure. Do not simply complete those lifts that you enjoy and skip the more difficult lifts as you will set yourself up for injury.

This book is not intended to design a strength and conditioning program but to give you some basic guidelines as to what is needed to develop a good program. There are many great books and videos already on the market which are designed for this exact purpose, some even directly designed for martial arts athletes. But here are a few basic guidelines which athletes in the martial arts should include to ensure that the all of the muscles are exercised during a good strength and conditioning program:

• Wrist flexors and extensors of the forearm — dumbbell wrist curls and hyperextensions work the best along with wringing exercises plus gripping exercises for the hand which strengthen the forearm for punching

• Biceps & Triceps — dumbbell and/or machine work, dips from a bar or chair

• Deltoids, Traps & Rotator Cuff — resistance tubing or dumbbells and barbells usually have the best results (these take your shoulder in all directions, do not skip any direction); can be completed standing, sitting, or lying on the edge of a bench or table

• Pects — dumbbells, barbell and/or machine can be completed in several different positions to isolate pects only or also include the shoulders

• Lats — dumbbells, resistance tubing and/or machines

• Abdominals — various crunch exercises and sit-ups along with machines work wonders; also medicine ball drills work great

• Obliques — twisting workout either with barbell or machine

• Back — back extensions from a bench and/or machine (do not overdo as these can make your back extremely sore and/or tight when kicking or throwing)

• Hamstrings & Glutes — leg curls using resistance tubing and/or machine in addition to walking lunges. Should be performed with NO KNEE PAIN. If completed properly with good mechanics you should only feel the exercise in your butt and hamstrings.

• Quads — leg extensions and leg press with resistance tubing and/or machines; can add free-standing squats if you do not go below 90° of knee flexion in reference to the ground (do not overload weights as this can cause severe knee pain when kicking)

• Lateral leg/IT band — resistance tubing or multi-hip machine

• Groin — resistance tubing or machine

• Calves — barbell while standing on floor or step or seated or supine machine (be careful not to overload the weight here as this one may appear too easy and you will be sore later!)

• Ankle — resistance tubing in all four directions of ankle movement is the best

All exercises should be performed using proper mechanics and without any pain. You want your weightlifting program to be a good workout but it does not need to be exhausting or make you extremely sore each time. Caution needs to be given to athletes ages twelve to sixteen as heavy weight lifting can affect the growth plates of their growing bones. Growth plates are located near the ends of each bone, and when damaged can close prematurely stopping the normal growth of the bone. Children under the age of nine should not be lifting weights over one to five pounds in addition to their own body weight, and should not do more than one set of ten reps in a set. It is better to use resistance tubing exercises with young athletes as opposed to using weights, and work on proper mechanics of movement and lifting. The following pages will also give you some direction on the exercises that can be incorporated into a strength and conditioning program for injury recovery and/or for a basic workout. This series of photos includes workouts using free weights, a Total Gym® machine, resistance tubing, and a Swiss Ball. Many other workout systems can be easily incorporated, but these selections were chosen to show proper mechanics and give some insight into the many possibilities that are on the market and in gyms.

TOTAL GYM® is a free standing resistance training machine which uses your own body weight as well as gravity to create a workout. Olympic plate weights can be added to increase the workload, or the incline of the glideboard can be changed to increase/decrease the difficulty of the exercise as well. This machine was designed to incorporate all aspects of resistance and weightlifting techniques needed for a strength and conditioning program, while creating a piece of equipment versatile enough to fold up under your bed. It has both private and industrial level machines, for home, clinic and gym strengthening programs. The Total Gym® will be utilized to demonstrate several techniques that can be used by athletes of many ages.

Total Gym Upper Body

Upper body strength is not only of key importance in throwing sports such as judo, but essential for punching and blocking kicks in martial art forms which utilize the foot and fist, such as karate and taekwondo.

Lats: "swimmer's muscles"
muscles of the upper back and sides of the torso

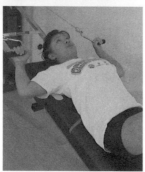

Start Position: Lay on the glideboard with your feet supported by the foot platform (easier) or on the glideboard (harder), depending on the difficulty desired. Grasp the handles, first by extending your arms up above your head to reach handles, then bending to initiate the first movement.

Continue moving your arms from the overhead position, straight over your face and body until they rest next to your sides. For those who have yet to gain enough upper body strength to complete this exercise, you can push off of the platform plate to initiate the movement, but as you progress in strength, place your feet on the glideboard using bent knees. Changing the level of the incline of the glideboard also greatly increases or decreases the difficulty of the exercise.

This same exercise can be completed on a traditional Lat Pulldown Machine found in most health club and workout facilities.

Rowing

Lats, Shoulder, Biceps, Triceps, & Upper Back

This exercise is an overall good exercise if close attention is paid to proper technique, otherwise you can be injured and the exercise is rendered useless. Phuong demonstrates the proper position to begin the rowing exercise, seated at the front end of the glideboard, legs comfortably straddling over edge, back stiff with proper lower back arch, shoulders back, hands grasping the handles with the palms facing inward towards each other. Note that the incline is low for this exercise until you can complete it comfortably with proper techniques.

To perform the rowing exercise, Phuong lifts her feet off of the floor and steadily bends and pulls her elbows back keeping the handles in a straight line from the start point and pulling them towards her chest, then slowly and in a controlled manner returns to the start position.

To **increase the difficulty** of this exercise you can increase the incline level of the glideboard or you can do this exercise from a kneeling position rather than a seated position. To **decrease the difficulty** eliminate the incline, positioning the glideboard parallel to the floor, and sit with legs outstretched in front of you on the glideboard. To isolate the triceps, kneel on the glideboard with your face between your knees, pulling the handles until the arms are fully extended behind you.

**Can also be done on a traditional rowing machine

Inverted Jack Knife

Workout for the shoulders, arms, abdominals & hip flexors

This is a twist on the traditional jack knife exercise. Beginning position: place your hands on the rear crossbar, and then kneel on the glideboard with feet higher than your head.

Initiate the exercise by extending your legs upward, causing the glideboard to slide up the incline until your legs are fully extended. Your face should always be looking downward as to not put any pressure on the neck.

In the final position, your body is flat on the glideboard: back is flat, buttocks in line with the shoulders and no bend in the hip or knees. Return to start position by slowly bending hips and knees, controlling the movement of the glideboard.

To **increase/decrease the difficulty** of this exercise adjust the incline or add plate weights to the weight bar on the glideboard. Difficulty can also be increased by doing this exercise on one leg, alternating from one side to the other.

Chin up/Pull up

Upper arm, shoulder, and lats workout

To perform the chin up grasp the bar with palms up. For pull up grasp the bar palms down.

Phuong pulls up with her arms on the bar causing the glideboard to slide up the incline with her on it. She continues to look down to avoid straining her neck.

Finish with your chin over the bar. NOTE: do not just release your hold, instead slowly allow your body on the glideboard to reach the initial start position in a slow and controlled motion, otherwise injury could occur.

To **increase/decrease difficulty** of this exercise raise/lower the incline of the glideboard to allow for the athlete to struggle on the last couple of reps without compromising proper technique. Plate weights can also be added to increase the difficulty of the exercise.

Inverted Push Up
shoulders, chest, and abdominals

Attach the pull up bar to the rear crossbar, then lay on the glideboard on your stomach with your feet higher than your head & bent up towards your buttocks. Grasp the bar palms down.

Push with your arms through your hands causing the glideboard to slide up the incline as shown below. NOTE: always look down. Do not lift your head to avoid neck strain. Return to the initial start position in a slow and controlled motion.

Difficulty can be increased/decreased by simply adjusting the incline of the glideboard and/or by adding plate weights to the weight bar on the glideboard.

Total Gym ® Lower Body Workout

Calf Raises

Phuong begins by standing on the platform while resting her back and body against the glideboard. Her heels are hanging off of the back of the platform beginning in a calf stretch position.

She then raises her body to stand on her toes, causing a small upward slide of the glideboard, tightening the muscles of her calves. To return to the initial start position she slowly lowers her heels back to the starting position in a controlled fashion, not simply dropping back into position.

Difficulty can be increased/decreased by increasing/decreasing the incline of the glideboard. Difficulty can also be increased by adding plate weights to the glideboard on the weight pole. To isolate the Soleus (deep calf) muscle do this exercise with bent knees.

Single Leg Squats

Same technique as basic squat on page 107, only using one leg, holding unused leg away from the platform.

Basic Squat
upper thighs, buttocks and calves

Unlike the freestanding squat or one completed in a Smith Machine®, when doing the squat on the glideboard of the Total Gym®, the back is always supported, reducing the chance of lower back injuries so common with this exercise due to using poor technique with an unsupported back. The exercise also begins in the squat position rather than standing erect.

The start position begins with Phuong lying on the glideboard with her back pressed flat against it (by tightening the abdominal muscles). Her feet are planted shoulder-width apart on the platform, knees bent to 90°, shoulders back against the glideboard and hands at her hip.

The exercise is executed by pressing upwards with the legs causing the glideboard to ride up the incline until the legs are fully extended, but not locked out. Return to the initial start position is done by slowly bending the knees back to 90° in a slow and controlled motion, don't just drop.

Difficulty can be increased/decreased by increasing/decreasing the incline of the slide board. Plate weights can also be added to the glideboard to increase the level of difficulty of the exercise.

You can also **increase the difficulty** of the squat exercise and isolate the workout to one leg by performing Single Leg Squats (see page 106).

Sprinter's Starting Block
upper thigh, buttocks and calf muscles

Start with one knee on the glideboard at the edge closest to the leg performing the exercise. The body is leaning towards the glideboard and resting on the elbows. The other foot is supported by the rear crossbar with the knee bent like a sprinter in a starting block.

To perform the exercise, push up on the leg from the rear crossbar causing the glideboard to slide up the incline. To return to the initial start position, slowly bend the leg allowing a controlled slide back to the start position. NOTE: be careful, DO NOT let fingers get caught on glideboard runners as it may cause serious injury.

The difficulty of this exercise can be **increased/decreased** by increasing/decreasing the incline of the glideboard. Difficulty may also be increased by adding plate weights to the weight bar on the glideboard. Difficulty can also be increased by alternating legs for each repetition, but be careful not to get your feet caught between the glideboard and the rear crossbar as serious injury could occur.

This exercise can also be done for cardio fitness, by 1.) doing it for timed speed, and 2.) by alternating legs for each rep for a timed speed.

Hip Abductors/Adductors

muscles of the groin and outside of the upper thigh

Begin by standing to the side of the machine, facing the glideboard, placing one foot just past the rear crossbar and the second foot on the upper portion of the glideboard with the knee bent at a 90° angle (or close to it), in a semi-straddle position. Shoulders are back, with a normal arch in the low back. Maintain this position throughout the exercise.

This exercise is done by pushing the foot and leg on the glideboard up the incline causing the glideboard to slide upwards. This places you in a standing straddle position, with the foot remaining flat on the glideboard, then reversing this action in a slow and controlled motion to work opposing muscles.

Difficulty is **increased/decreased** by increasing/decreasing the incline of the glideboard, or by adding plate weights to the weight bar on the glideboard. **Caution: ensure that you are fully stretched out before performing this exercise, as serious injury could occur.**

Front Lunge

upper thigh and buttocks

Start position: Stand tall with your shoulders back and tail tucked under. Place the support foot just in front of the rear crossbar and the second foot on the upper portion of the glideboard with the knee bent at a 90° angle & the foot flat on the surface. Hands can either be at the side or on the hips, eyes looking forward.

Initiate the motion by sliding your foot on the glideboard forward as far as you can and still maintain balance. Keep the shoulders back, body vertical and support leg straight, with both feet flat on the surface. Using control, slowly return to the start position NOTE: you should NEVER feel pain or pressure on your knee. If you do you are leaning too far forward. Your chest should never lean in or over the knee as serious injury could occur.

You can **increase/decrease** the difficulty of this exercise by adjusting the incline or by adding plate weights to the weight bar on the glideboard.

Exercise should be completed on each leg.

Backward Lunge

upper thigh and buttocks

Phuong starts by turning her back to the glideboard and placing her standing foot just inside of the rear crossbar on the floor with the other foot on the glideboard directly beside her leg. She stands erect with her shoulders back and eyes forward.

Phuong remains standing erect, leaning slightly forward as she pushes the glideboard up the incline with her toes and leg, and then slowly controls the downward movement of the glideboard to the original position.

To **increase/decrease the difficulty** of this exercise adjust the level of incline of the glideboard and/or add plate weights to the weight bar on the glideboard. Difficulty can also be increased by performing a squat on the support leg while the rear leg pushes the glideboard up the incline, with the arms being held straight out in front of you. Ensure you can perform this exercise with proper technique (no wobbling or overarching of the back) before increasing the incline or adding weight.

Inverted Leg Pull

upper thigh, buttocks, hips, & abdominals as an option

Begin by lying inverted on the glideboard with the feet higher than the head. Place the toes under the pull-up bar, positioning the buttocks at the upper end of the glideboard, with the hands resting on the abdomen or on the hips.

Begin the exercise by hooking your toes under pull-up bar and using legs to pull the glideboard up the incline as far as comfortably can go without arching the lower back. ALWAYS keep low back pressed down on the glideboard by tightening the abdominals. Keep the knees up and apart. Return by slowly allowing the knees to extend to the start position. Never just let go as serious injury could occur.

The difficulty of this exercise can be **increased/decreased** by simply adjusting the incline of the glideboard or by adding plate weights to the weight bar on the glideboard.

Difficulty can also be increased by performing the exercise using one leg at a time, but always begin this variation at the lowest incline level to ensure proper technique before raising the incline level, as serious injury may occur.

Swiss Ball or Exercise Ball

The Swiss Ball is a large exercise ball (much like a heavy duty kick ball) used to increase strength, flexibility, balance and coordination. It is especially great to use with beginners or those returning from injury. In the following pages we will demonstrate the various uses of the Swiss Ball, as well as discuss the endless other ways you might want to consider to enhance your strength and conditioning program. This is a tool that can be varied for each individual, dependent on their  needs, their age, and their overall strength. It can be used with the very young as well as the very old, and everyone in between, males and females alike. The ball can be inflated to make very firm and therefore increase the difficulty of balancing on it, or it can have some of the air removed making it rather "soft" and easier to balance upon, depending on the needs of the individual. Swiss Balls come in all age-appropriate sizes to fit any body type from petite to obese. For those injured, it allows you the opportunity to continue in a strength and conditioning program to aid in maintenance of fitness level while allowing the injuries to heal properly. Dumbbells and medicine balls can be utilized with the Swiss Ball to aid in core stability strengthening as well as balance. Many of the stretches previously discussed can be performed on or using the Swiss Ball.

Basic Sit

When selecting a ball you need to have one with which you can perform the basic sit comfortably and easily. In order to do this you must be able to sit on the ball as Phuong is doing, with buttocks centered in the middle of the ball, feet comfortably touching the floor, shoulder width apart, torso sitting up tall, shoulders back and square with your hips. You should not have a lot of weight in your feet, just enough to balance yourself with your weight centered over the ball in your midsection or abdominal region, with legs slightly straddled. Do not hold your breath as this does not help your balance.

You can increase/decrease the difficulty of exercises on the exercise ball by adding/releasing air from the ball. The more firm, the more balance you must have, but be careful not to let too much air out, as this also increases difficulty as the ball no longer supports your body weight appropriately. Choose balls for age, weight and height appropriateness, and fun colors and designs for children.

Even toddlers Olivia's age and size can workout on an exercise ball. Olivia's ball is actually a hop-a-long ball with a handle to give her an added sense of stability. If she feels like she is losing her balance she can grab the handle to regain her center before letting go again.

> Advanced position: bend your knees, pulling the feet up onto the front of the ball while holding your arms spread above your head, in a high "V" position.

Basic Kneel

This is a step up in difficulty from the basic sit requiring you to straddle the ball, while squeezing the ball with your knees to maintain your balance. Your torso should be held erect, shoulders back, and hands at your hips as Phuong demonstrates. There should be no "sag" in your abdomen or your back, no hunching or over-arching. You should feel like there is a string coming out of the top of your head pulling your body upward and looking tall. There should not be excessive squeezing by the knees once you gain your balance.

This exercise is not only excellent for working on balance and coordination, but also as part of your core strengthening program. In order to maintain your balance you must engage the muscles of the abdomen, back, chest, groin and hips to keep from falling over.

To increase the difficulty of this exercise for advanced core strengthening and balance training, throw a ball (small or medium size) or a weighted medicine ball at the athlete while they are balancing on the ball, then have them throw it back, throwing from the chest, overhead, twisting from the side or from a low position while maintaining their balance and their tall stance on the ball. Throws can range from a soft toss to a hard pass to continue to increase the difficulty of this exercise.

NOTE: DO NOT attempt balancing exercises such as this before being cleared by a physician if you have inner ear or balance problems, or are taking medications which can lead to light-headedness, nausea or dizziness, or have not gained the core strength necessary to maintain your balance on the ball, as it may lead to serious injury or illness.

Finding Center on Your Ball: it is extremely important for you to find your "center" on the ball in several positions, including the just mentioned basic sit and basic kneel. Your center is where your body weight is centered while on the ball. You should never have a lot of weight distributed in your hands or feet, but rather feel like you are light on the ball, balanced and in control. For females your center should be somewhere between your navel (belly button) and the center of your hips. For males this center is generally higher, finding it somewhere between your navel and the center of your chest. There are times when these do not apply, and actually the opposite is true, but generally females tend to carry the majority of their weight from the stomach down, while males carry their weight from their belly up. Being able to find your center and maintain it allows you to increase your balance control and coordination, while strengthening the core muscles and aiding in better proprioception (the ability to know where your body is in space without having visual or audio hints, allowing the body to have a better sense of balance).

Centering in a Supine or Bridge Position:

Notice that the weight is in the area of Phuong's and Olivia's stomach, not in her hands or feet. This is also a very good way to stretch out the entire back, by simply rocking the ball back and forth. Also, a great way to do crunches, especially for children or someone new to the exercise ball as they have to learn balance and control.

Centering in Prone Position

Note: no pressure in the hands or feet, and actually seen in the region just above the hips.

Steps to Obtaining "Superman"

One of the best exercises to build balance and coordination on the Swiss Ball, while being a great core strengthening exercise, is known as the "Superman" pose. Several steps must first be mastered before an individual can attain this position with balance and coordination.

Step 1:

Centering achieved with little to no weight in hands or feet, as previously described.

Step 2:

Raise arms from the floor while remaining light on the feet, focusing on centering your body weight over the ball not your feet.

Step 3:

Raise feet from floor while keeping the weight light in the hands, once again focusing on centering the weight on the ball.

Step 4:

This can also be performed on your hands and knees without the ball, or over a smaller ball to strengthen your lower back.

Raise opposite hand & foot at the same time while maintaining center of balance over the ball. This is an excellent strength exercise for the low back, but should not be attempted without the direct supervision of a PT or ATC if you have low back problems. NOTE: back is a plank, not arched.

Step 5:

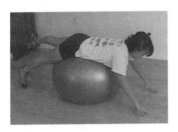

Begin lifting fingers and toes an inch or so off of the floor while maintaining your center of balance over the ball, hold for 5-10 seconds. NOTE: eyes are looking at the floor, not ahead.

Step 6: Superman Achieved

Superman is achieved with body, arms and legs fully extended while maintaining center of balance over the ball. Hold 5-10 seconds while maintaining a plank body, eyes looking at the floor.

Butt Bridging

This exercise helps to isolate the gluteal muscles of your buttocks, which are necessary for productive kicking or holding your ground. This exercise also is a great core strengthening exercise by having to maintain balance and control of the ball.

Begin by lying on the floor with the back pressed against the floor so it is flat and your feet are up on the ball, not allowing the ball to roll around. Squeeze your buttocks to lift the buttocks off of the floor while also keeping the stomach tight in order to keep the ball from rolling around. Hands can be on the floor next to you to help to support your hips for beginners.

For beginners someone may need to hold the ball initially until you gain control of your balance, or use a wall to stabilize the ball.

Advance this exercise by doing single leg bridging while controlling the ball with your foot, especially if one leg is not as strong as the other leg.

Butt Bridge with Ball Roll

This exercise goes one step beyond the butt bridging just mentioned, not only strengthening the buttocks and abdominals, but incorporating balance and coordination.

From the butt bridging position previously described, roll the ball out with the feet, and then roll ball back into the bridging position with bent legs, while maintaining a plank body (body is as straight as a board or plank). To maintain plank, both abdominal and back muscles must be engaged (tightly contracted).

NOTE: do not attempt if you have a low back weakness or injury as it may cause serious injury to your back.

Remember, this is an ADVANCED core strengthening exercise & should not be attempted before mastering the butt bridging exercise previously described, with full control of balance & coordination as well as proper technique. To increase the difficulty of this exercise, perform the above described exercise with only one leg at a time, with uninvolved leg held extended in the air.

Crunch

Traditional mid-abdominal strengthening exercise. Doing crunches on the ball increases the level of difficulty but also increases the chances of using proper technique, therefore reducing the chance of creating a lower back injury or soreness.

Lay your back across the ball with your feet flat on the floor, shoulder-width apart, fingertips behind the ears with no pressure or pull applied to the head or neck, eyes looking at ceiling. IMPORTANT: press your back into the ball until you achieve a flat back & a tight abdomen, maintain tightness throughout the exercise.

With back pressed against the ball, "crunch" the body up raising ONLY your shoulders and upper back up off of the ball. Your lower back remains flat on the ball throughout the exercise. Motion should be slow and controlled both going up and returning with as little weight in the feet as possible. Eyes look at ceiling with no pulling by the hands on the neck.

I like to do crunches in 3-4 sets of large numbers of reps, such as set 1-50 reps, 2-60 reps, 3-60 reps, & 4-50 reps, but you can choose a set-up that is appropriate, increasing in number and adding new styles as the workout appears to become easy. ALWAYS focus on proper technique, with the low back pressed against the ball to reduce the chance of injury.

Modifications of Crunch

For those that the crunch proves to be too difficult, I propose the following modifications until you can attain the strength to perform the exercise on the ball.

Position yourself in a supine position on the floor as you would on the ball, with the back pressed to the floor. Place your feet and/or legs upon the ball to keep your knees in a bent position. While keeping your back pressed against the floor "crunch" the body upwards, raising the shoulders and upper back from the floor. Maintain a slow and controlled motion with proper technique to return to start position. If it still proves too difficult to control the ball while doing the crunch, position the ball against a wall or in a corner until you increase your strength. If you are unsure if your low back is touching the floor, roll up a small hand towel and place in the small of your back. If you do not feel pressure of the rolled towel pushing back against you, you have an arch in your back and need to press the back down further and maintain this position.

To increase the difficulty of the crunch exercise, try incorporating the start position at right, but always ensure the use of proper technique of keeping the back pressed flat onto the ball at all times.

NOTE: if you are prone to light-headedness or dizziness, or are on medications that may cause dizziness or are pregnant, this position may not be suitable for your use as it may increase the likelihood of dizziness occurring. Speak with your physician, physical therapist or certified athletic trainer before attempting.

Obliques

Your oblique muscles are the abdominal muscles that wrap around from your sides allowing for twisting action. These are usually some of the weakest muscles, but in martial arts they are of key importance for both throwing and kicking.

Obliques Exercise #1:

Start by lying on your side on the ball, with your feet supported by a partner, wall or other heavy object. Place your fingertips behind your ears with no pressure or pull on the head or neck. Make sure that your shoulders are back creating a flat back from the rear view. Your weight should be centered on the ball, not in the feet or the object the feet are propped against.

From here do a sidebend upwards in the air, feeling a tightening of the muscles on the side of your abdomen. This motion should be slow and controlled from start to finish to return to the start position. This exercise may only produce a few reps initially, or very little movement at all, but you should build up to several sets of high numbers of reps, paying close attention to proper technique and controlled motion.

Advanced technique does not have any assistance at the feet by a wall or partner, but rather is freely moveable and unsupported.

Obliques Exercise #2

Begin by lying on your back with your back pressed against the ball, feet flat on the floor and fingertips behind the ears with no pressure or pull on the head or neck. Maintain your center of balance over the ball.

Tighten the abdominal muscles then twist your body to each side while maintaining your balance and keeping the back pressed against the ball. Only shoulders & upper back should move off of the ball, while abdominals and low back remain tight throughout the exercise..

Modifications of Crunch using the Ball
(See pages 121 and 122 for Crunch instructions)

Other modifications: instead of legs up on the ball, squeeze the ball between your legs while performing the crunch technique, with the ball resting on the floor or with your legs holding the ball in the air. Once again, a great exercise for small children as you can make a game out of it.

Back Extensions

As part of your core strengthening program it is essential to not only tighten abs, but also the back. This is one of the traditional methods, only we are using the ball instead of a bench. You will need either a partner, wall, or something weighted to keep your feet from sliding until you gain strength and control of your body on the ball.

Begin by lying with your stomach across the ball, feet on the floor (may have someone hold you at your ankles). Do not apply ANY pressure from the hands to the head or neck. Your weight should be centered over the ball and not heavy in your feet.

Arch up from the ball to first attain movement off the ball, progressing to a flat back (plank) and eventually progress into a hyperextension of the back with a dramatic arch. During the entire exercise keep the abdominal muscles tight to reduce the chance of injury. Use a slow and controlled motion.

To **decrease the difficulty** of this exercise, kneel on the floor with the ball in front of you at your abdomen, then lean forward laying your abdomen and chest onto the ball. From this position perform the hyperextensions as described above. Eventually progress to completing on the ball, progressing to no support at feet/ankles. To **increase the difficulty,** place the ball at your thighs and bend body over the ball with your face beginning near the floor surface.

Push-Ups

There are a couple of variations of push-ups that can be done using the Swiss Ball, with you hands or feet on the ball.

Hands on the Ball Push-Ups

Position your hands on the ball with the body in a plank position, and then find your center before continuing.

As with a traditional push-up, slowly lower your body towards the ball while maintaining a plank. There is little to no bend at the hips or knees, but you must maintain balance and proper technique.

To **increase the difficulty** of this exercise, position the ball so the hands are holding ball at the forehead level or at nipple level. Moving the position of the hands to a more narrow hold will also increase the difficulty of this exercise. Lastly, hold the ball by the fingertips rather than the hand to also increase the difficulty level.

Feet on Ball Push-Up

From prone position, walk your hands out on the floor until the ball is at your toes (or to mid-calf or mid-thigh if needed to reduce the difficulty), with your body in a plank position, eyes looking at the floor. You should have little to no bend at the hips or knees, NO BUTT IN THE AIR.

In a slow and controlled motion, lower your upper body to the floor without allowing your body to touch the floor, or allowing the ball to roll underneath your feet (or legs). Then slowly press your body back up to the start position, maintaining a plank position at all times while maintaining control of the ball beneath your feet or legs.

Beginners can support the ball and their feet against a wall. Children may need to be reminded to keep a flat plank back by gently placing your hand on their stomach to remind them to tighten their tummy.

These two styles of push-ups can be used alternating from one style to the other, producing several sets of high number of reps, as long as close attention is paid to proper technique. Stop at any time that you feel a sharp pain or pull, or you cannot complete the exercise with the proper mechanics. Never allow your butt to raise higher than your back or your low back arch creating a "sway back" while performing this exercise.

Ab Contraction to Pike Position
Advanced Abdominal Exercise

Begin with your feet on the ball in a push-up position, with body in a plank position, eyes looking at the floor as Elizabeth demonstrates.

Slowly contract the abdominal muscles to roll the ball towards your mid-section, causing the hips to bend while maintaining extended knees & a flat back, eyes looking at the floor. Slowly roll the ball back to push-up position to finish. DO NOT USE THE HANDS TO WALK BACK TO THE BALL.

To **decrease the difficulty** of this exercise position the ball at mid-thigh to knee area instead of at your toes to start (decreased difficulty push-up position). Then when rolling ball in towards your mid-section, rock back onto your knees on the ball rather than going to the pike position, pulling the ball in close to the buttocks.

The Plank

This is another stability exercise to improve body control and coordination. With your feet on the floor, lean on the ball. Your forearms are flat on the ball, with the body completely flat, no arching of the back or "pooching" of the stomach.

Ball Squeezes

Also known as pillow squeezes, used to strengthen the adductor muscles located in the inner thigh & groin area. Perform exactly like it sounds: put the ball between your legs and squeeze with the inner thigh muscles, hold 10 seconds.

You can **advance this skill** by squeezing the ball between the legs, and then lift legs into the air, while maintaining a flat back pressed to the floor as Aubrey and Elizabeth are doing above.

Examples of how you can use the exercise ball to stretch:

Quad stretch with Ball

Both exercises require you to engage core muscles and to maintain balance and control of the ball while completing the stretch.

Upper Back Stretch with Ball

Standing Exercises with Ball

Beginners as well as those recovering from an injury often cannot begin a strength and conditioning program using free weights or a resistance training machine, so the Swiss Ball offers some viable alternatives for a few exercises. Also it is not wise to use weights or resistance for the very young, and with some of our elderly populations; here the Swiss Ball works quite well. The following are several recommended exercises that can often be incorporated into a new program. **NOTE: if you have been injured in the past, or are recovering from an injury, speak with your physician, physical therapist or certified athletic trainer before attempting these exercises as they could lead to serious injury if performed incorrectly or before the body is prepared for such exercises.**

Wall Squat

Begin by placing the ball between a wall and your back, step your feet out slightly to be able to press your back flat against the ball. Keeping shoulders back and square, place feet shoulder-width apart, with hands at your hips.

Slowly begin to sit, rolling the ball down the wall until your knees reach a position of 90° from the floor, keeping your back pressed flat against the ball. Try not to drop below this position as it puts added pressure on the knees. Then slowly rise back up causing the ball to roll back up the wall.

Modification to Wall Squat with Swiss Ball: there are several methods to increase the difficulty of the wall squat.

First this same exercise can be performed using only one leg with the uninvolved leg either extended out in front of the body or bent up behind the body. Your arms are either extended out to the side or out in front, or the hands can be placed at the hips for added difficulty.

Second, is what are often referred to as "negatives" in which once you get to the position of 90°, you then begin to roll the ball back up the wall but instead of completing the motion you stop only a few inches after starting, then hold the position for 15-20 seconds, or until your legs begin to feel a little bit weak.

Free Standing Squat, Holding Ball

Once you have conquered the wall squat you can move away from the wall and put the ball in your hands to perform another squat.

Begin by placing the ball in your hands, extending the arms out directly in front of your body, standing with feet shoulder-width apart, toes forward, shoulders back and square, eyes looking forward, with the proper arch in the lower back without overarching.

Slowly sit into the squat position until the knees reach 90°. Try not to squat any lower as it may put undue pressure on the knees leading to pain and injury. Slowly return to the start position without allowing yourself to wobble, create a greater arch in your low back or dropping your arms and shoulders. It should feel like you are trying to sit into a chair that you know is not there.

This exercise can also be performed with the toes turned out at a 30-45° angle to work the inner and outer thigh muscles in addition to the buttocks.

To decrease the difficulty of this exercise, instead of the ball get the back of a chair to use for balance as you perform the squat motion to increase stability during the maneuver, or perform as a wall squat with back flat against the wall while holding the ball in front of you.

Advanced version can be completed on one leg while holding ball during a free standing squat.

Squat and Twist with the Ball

To extend the free-standing squat one more step, incorporate a twist to the side, then stand, repeating on each side.

This creates a workout not only for the thighs and buttocks, but also the abdominal and oblique muscles, adding to the core strengthening program. For children, you can have them squat and twist to hand off the ball to the next person in a circle, to build up stamina as well as strength.

Young children should not be working with weights or resistance but they can work with a ball. Lifting the ball and then slowly controlling into a squat, either freestanding or as a wall slide. Also works well with those athletes of any age returning from injury of the shoulders, back, knee or hip – ensure proper technique is used.

Stand, Twist & Reach

This is one step further from the squat and twist, incorporating all of the major muscles of both the upper and lower body, as well as the core muscles.

Begin by standing tall with feet shoulder-width apart, toes pointing forward, ball in extended arms directly in front of chest. Your shoulders are back and square, low back arched properly (no over-extending), eyes forward.

Reach with ball first over one shoulder as high as possible, following the ball with the eyes, keeping the arms fully extended, twisting at the waist. From here, twist in the opposite direction while taking the ball down and across the body, ending next to the opposite leg with arms fully extended and knees bent slightly. Repeat.

Free Weights Workout on Ball

Many of the traditional upper body lifts that are normally done while standing or seated on a bench can be performed while sitting on the Swiss Ball. Workouts include those that strengthen the biceps, triceps, forearm/wrist/hand, lats, deltoids, pects, rotator cuff, traps, and chest (including chest press, military press & incline/decline press) using either dumbbells or weight bars with/without weights. The advantage to doing these traditional lifts while seated on the ball is that you must engage your core muscles to maintain balance and not fall from the ball, making the benefits of the workout two-fold. You can increase/decrease the air pressure in the ball to adjust the difficulty of the exercise and lift.

On the following page Phuong demonstrates a traditional biceps curl with supination, as an example of how to conduct such a workout. This exercise has a start position normally with the hands at the side of the body, palms facing the leg or facing to the rear, with the lift causing the arm to twist as the arm bends, ending with the palms up and the forearm flexed up towards the upper arm. The reason for adding the twist is that the bicep muscle is not only a strong flexor muscle of the arm but also a supinator. Supination is the motion of turning your hand from palms down to palms up, like you do when turning a door knob or with the reversal of some punches used in forms.

Biceps Curl with Supination on the Swiss Ball

Begin in a basic sit position, obtaining your center with your weights held at your side before beginning any lift. Shoulders are back, and there is a proper arch in your lower back. Feet are slightly straddled and flat on the floor. This is the basic start position for most lifts conducted on the ball. Remember: body weight is centered over the ball , not in the feet.

Flex your forearm up towards the upper arm while rotating the palm to an upwards position, maintaining a "stiff" wrist. No movement should occur in the wrist, only the arm.

Finish by ending the motion with the palm up and the arm flexed as close to the upper arm and shoulder as possible. Your motion should be slow & controlled at all times. Return to start position in a slow, controlled motion.

Even the bench press can be performed on the exercise ball, either with the entire back supported by the ball for more support, or in the advanced forms, only supporting the shoulders as Aubrey demonstrates. Watch for arching of the back leading to pain.

COOL DOWN

After stretching, cool down your mind & body, allowing your heart rate to return to normal. This is a great time to do visualizations or meditation. Always spend at least 5-10 minutes in a cool down following any form of exercise or workout.

Notice no weight in hands or feet

Other Exercise Products

Another great training tool is what is known as a slide board with angled box ends, which you can buy commercially with other plyometric and agility equipment (for example from Perform Better®, M-F Athletic Company® or Power Systems®) or produce yourself (Refer to drawing on page 148). With a slide board you can work on lateral movements and speed, which are necessary for participation in some forms of martial art. You can begin with simply the slide board, allowing you to work on sliding laterally at a quick rate of speed. The surface must be slick enough to slide on, like a newly waxed vinyl floor. To increase the sliding ability of a surface, put a sock over your shoe to reduce friction. You can then add in the angled box ends (as pictured), remove the socks covering the shoes and work on quick feet pushing off of the lateral angled end boxes in a quick feet program, or leave the socks on and work on advanced lateral movement development.

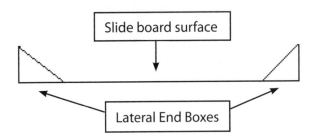

Other items that can be incorporated into your conditioning program beyond the traditional free weights, lifting & resistance machines, punching bags and dummies, speed bags and paddles, include the of the following:

• Parachutes – used for resistance training while running

• Hurdles – for jumping and agility drills

• Plyometric boxes – for jumping and plyometric drills

• Cones with and without hurdle bars for plyometric and agility drills

• Ladders – designed for agility drills, lay out on the floor

• Jump ropes – of various weights at height appropriate lengths

• Medicine balls – of various weights and shapes

• Agility rings – used for fast feet plyometric and agility drills

• Z-ball – a dimpled bouncing ball, increases reaction time and ability

• Mini-trampolines – used for rehab, as well as for reaction drills

• Swiss Ball – used for core strength training and coordination/ balance programs

• Wobble boards – used for balance, and proprioception training

• Balance boards – used for coordination, balance & proprioception training

• Foam rollers – used for balance and motor skill development; can use the styrofoam "noodles" children use in swimming pools

• Resistance Tubing and Bands – for resistance training when weights are not appropriate or in addition to using weights

Free Weights/Dumbbells

Some athletes prefer the use of the traditional free weights either instead of or in combination with alternative methods of strength and conditioning mentioned previously. The problem is, many athletes are never taught proper technique and form, and then become injured from using poor mechanics, not from the actual weights themselves. As discussed earlier, athletes under the age of 16 should not be lifting heavy weights. Under the age of 8, no weights or resistance outside of their own body weight should be incorporated into a strength and conditioning program. Those individuals over the age of 40, and women past menopause also need to remember that precautions should be taken when lifting, specifically lifting heavy weights over their heads, because physiological changes begin to occur at this time in their lives. But once cleared by your physician, and under the direction of a Strength & Conditioning Specialist or Certified Athletic Trainer, lifting weights can be a great way to get into shape, increase power and strength. So, the first thing you must learn about lifting weights is how to do it properly. The following pages are not designed to set up a weightlifting program for you, but to teach proper technique of the most traditional lifts, in hopes of reducing your chances of injury. There are many books, videos and trained professionals out there who design programs for a living that you should seek out when you are ready to create your own program.

Types of Grips:

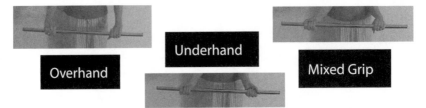

Overhand

Underhand

Mixed Grip

Lower Body
Squats without weight

Begin by standing erect, feet shoulder-width apart, toes pointing forward, shoulders back & square, fingertips behind the ears with no excessive arching of the lower back, eyes looking forward.

Sit straight down as if sitting on a chair, keeping your tail tucked under without excessive arching of the lower back. Keep the shoulders in line with the knees & toes. The knees should not go past the end of the toes when squatting, with the safest range being up to 90° of knee flexion. Below this range may result in knee pain and injury or loss of balance.

Squats with Barbell

Mechanics are the same as squat without weight. The only difference is that the hand placement moves to a comfortable position to grip the bar. Proper technique is key to injury prevention.

Skater's Squat

Same technique as traditional squat, only on one leg, with your other leg lifted to the side and held parallel with the floor while maintaining an upright posture.

Great for balance training while strengthening the legs. To decrease difficulty, perform with back flat against a wall.

Temple Squat

Same technique as previously described squats, except the foot position has changed, turning both feet out as far as possible while maintaining an upright and erect posture.

Walking Lunge, with & without dumbbells

Begin with your feet shoulder-width apart, arms at your side (dumbbells in hand if desired) or at waist, shoulders back and square, eyes looking forward. Take an exaggerated step forward, but not a giant step. Both legs are slightly bent, keeping the weight back in the hind leg, shoulders back and square, eyes looking forward not down.

From the step out position allow your body to "sink" straight down with your body weight remaining on the hind leg and buttocks. Little to no weight should be allowed or felt in the forward leg and knee. The forward knee should NEVER go past of the position of the toes (you should be able to look down and see your toes past your bent knee), or serious knee pain & injury can occur. The shoulders should be back and square, eyes looking forward, not down, at all times. If you wobble at all when dropping into the lunge you have taken too large of a step. Do not take rear bent knee down to floor. You should only reach several inches above the floor to reduce the chance of injury from the knee hitting the floor. To finish, push forward with your hind leg and buttocks into next step position, should feel tightening of the buttocks. NO PAIN OR "PULL" SHOULD BE FELT IN THE KNEES EVER.

Stork Stands

This exercise is used for balance and proprioception training for both healthy individuals, as well as those returning from ankle, knee, hip or back injury. Since so many techniques in martial arts require an athlete to be able to stand and balance on one foot, stork stands can help in balance training for such techniques.

Stork stands are an exercise which ask you to stand on one foot and balance yourself without leaning or wobbling, keeping the body in perfect alignment from head to toe, standing tall while only on one foot. Stork stands can be done for short or long durations, with or without dumbbell weights. You can even incorporate medicine ball throws from overhead, down low, passed from chest level, or twisting from one side to the other. You can punch a speed bag or a large punching bag while performing stork stands. You can do one leg squats from a stork stand. Stork stands can also be done on wobble boards, balance boards, mini-trampolines, foam rollers or even on a 2 x 6 board to increase difficulty. Even further advancement of difficulty for throwing forms of martial arts is to have a partner try to push you over while doing a stork stand, especially while standing on a foam roller or 2 x 6 board.

Note how tall Phuong looks as she stands balanced on one leg, as if a string runs from her heel up through the top of her head pulling her up into proper posture as she balances on one leg.

Advanced Position: raise leg to the side and balance. Notice Aubrey shows no signs of leaning, instead maintaining an upright body alignment.

Buttocks & Abductors

The following two exercises strengthen the muscles of the buttocks and the outer side of the leg, known as the abductors. Both exercises begin with the athlete on their hands and knees, with back in plank position.

First exercise has Aubrey raising her leg directly out to the side to hip level while maintaining a flat back.

Second exercise has Aubrey lifting her leg up behind her with a straight leg. Exercises can be performed with either a straight leg or bent knee for an advanced workout.

Negatives can also be performed to increase the difficulty further by having the athlete take their leg to the highest level and then back off slightly, holding for 5-10 seconds.

One Leg Shoulder Bridge

Strengthens buttocks, abdominals, hamstrings & quads.

Begin with your back flat, arms at your side, one leg bent & one leg extended.

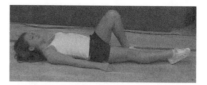

Squeeze your buttocks and tighten your abs as you press your body towards the ceiling, keeping only the shoulders and arms on the floor. Maintain a flat back and fully extended leg. Slowly return to the floor in a controlled motion. Do not use arms to assist unless you need to decrease the difficulty.

Hip Abductors & Adductors, Sidelying

Begin by lying on your side. For abductors raise the leg on top into the air; for adductors raise the bottom leg into the air, both while maintaining your balance with no overarching of the back.

Hip Adductors

Hip Abductors

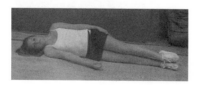

Upper Body

Triceps Extensions

Strengthens the muscles used in upper arm for extending the elbow, such as with punching or blocking. Always keep your elbows close to your ears.

Sit on a bench or in a chair with your shoulders back, sitting tall, feet flat on the floor. With a dumbbell in your hands, your arms are bent behind your head, eyes are looking forward.

Lift the dumbbell straight up behind your head fully extending your arms, being cautious not to hit the back of your head. Sit tall with no excessive arching of low back, eyes looking forward.

Dips (Triceps)

For those who cannot do dips on dip or parallel bars against your full body weight, here are some alternative methods to build up the strength in your triceps (the muscles on the back of your upper arm responsible for extending your elbow). With either legs straight or bent, begin with elbows bent, shoulders back, pressing your body straight up, fully extending the elbows.

Once your arms are fully extended supporting your body in the air, slowly return to the start position in a controlled motion, do not simply drop. Push to extension should come from your pressing hands into chair as extending the arms, no help from the legs!

Legs straight is more difficult than legs bent as part of your body weight is supported by your legs when bent. Once you have mastered bent leg move to straight leg, then move onto a dip bar.

If exercise is still too difficult even with knees bent, consider working out on a triceps press machine before moving onto these modified dip exercises.

Biceps Curl

Begin standing or seated on a bench or chair, shoulders back and square, normal low back arch, dumbbell in hand with your palm facing towards the rear, arms fully extended at your sides.

As you bend your arm, begin "twisting" the arm to rotate the palms up. As you continue to flex the forearm up to the upper arm with the weight ending up at shoulder level, keep the elbow at your side at all times and avoid excessive arching or hunching of the back. Return to the start position in a slow and controlled motion, never simply dropping the arm as serious injury could occur.

Wrist Flexion Exercise

Begin with your wrists fully extended, (hyperextended as shown, if capable), palms up (with or without weights), with the forearm bent at the elbow (foreares may be supported by a table if needed). Shoulders back and square, normal arch in the back.

Flex your wrists up towards forearms without "twisting". Keep the movement straight and fluid at the wrists, with a light grip in the weights. Return slowly to the start position in a controlled motion.

Wrist Extension/Hyperextension Exercises

Exercises for the wrist and forearm are crucial for strengthening punching and gripping, as well as for blocking.

Begin with your elbow bent, forearm either held in the air or supported on a table/bench, palms facing down, shoulders back and square.

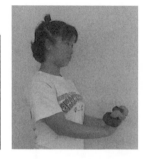

"Bend"your wrist upwards as far as comfortably possible, then slowly return to the flat wrist position in a controlled motion, without dropping the weight and hands.

Wrist Wringing

exercise for forearm, wrist and grip strength.

This exercise is the same as if you were wringing out a towel, starting with your hands on a bar (or mop handle), palms down. First turn with one hand then the other, turning the bar in a clounter-clockwise direction, shoulders back and square. To increase difficulty, add a piece of twine/string with a plate weight hanging off the end of the twine. Wrist wring until the twine is wound up onto the bar, with the weight at the bar, then reverse.

Hitchhikers Thumb

wrist strengthening exercise

Put your wrist in a position that would be used by a hitchhiker, with the thumb-side of the wrist up, palm facing towards your side (with or without weights), elbow bent, forearm either held in the air or supported by a table/bench, shoulders back and square.

First "bend" the wrist and thumb up as high is comfortably possible, followed by "bending" it downwards away from your face as far as is comfortably possible. You should never feel any sharp pain in the wrist, hand or elbow. If you do, stop and look at your mechanics and the amount of weight you are trying to use. You should be using 0 – 10 pounds for this exercise. A small soup can works well as a weight for beginners.

Empty Cans (with or without dumbbells)

This is an exercise for the shoulder, traps & deltoids. Your hand position is thumbs down as if emptying a can. Small weights can be placed in the hands to increase the difficulty of the workout.

Angled: Begin with your arms at your side, raising straight arms at a 45° angle from chest, shoulders back & square, thumbs down.

Raise your arms only to shoulder level, not above, before returning slowly to the start position. Do not simply drop arms, but use a slow, controlled motion.

Straight: Same as above, only raise your arms from the side of your body straight out to shoulder level with thumbs down.

Full Cans

deltoid and rotator cuff muscles of the shoulder, along with traps

Full Cans is exactly the same as Empty Cans, except for the hand position, with the thumbs pointing up like a hitchhiker instead of down. Done both with the arms at a 45° angle from the body as well as straight out to the side of the body, raising shoulder level only, with or without weights, or you can use resistance tubing.

Bench Press

While lying with a flat back on a bench take a pole, weighted bar or dumbbells and press up directly over your face in a slow and controlled motion being cautious not to drop the bar once you hit full extension. Your motion should be slow and controlled coming back down. The bench press is used to strengthen the muscles of the chest. If your feet do not reach floor either bend your legs and place your feet on the bench or fully extend the legs as Aubrey demonstrates (pay attention to keeping the back flat at all times, not recommended when using heavy weights). Works well when using low weight (15 pounds or less) and makes you work your core muscles to maintain balance.

Military Press & Incline Press

Both the military press and the incline press are completed from a seated position, with the incline press being in a reclined position (not pictured) while the military press has you seated upright as pictured. Take the bar from the chest level and press straight up (both military and incline press) until your arms are fully

extended. The back should maintain a normal arch. Sit tall, controlling the motion both as pressing up and returning to the start position. To increase difficulty, use a decline bench to perform press.

Forward Lifts/Shoulder Flexions

Grasp the bar with an overhand grip in front of your body and raise to shoulder height, ensuring that you ARE NOT shrugging the shoulders during the lift. This exercise can also be completed without the weight bar, with plates on the bar or with two dumbbells.

Resistive Tubing and Bands

Resistive tubing and bands are often equated with physical therapy and rehab programs to aid in recovery from an injury and regain strength, but that is not the only use. Resistive tubing and bands can also be used by healthy individuals who do not like to work with free weights and weight machines for particular parts of the body, or for parts of the body that are difficult to strengthen, such as the ankle. Resistive tubing and bands can be purchased through pretty much any sports medicine or rehab product catalog, such as Sports Health® and Econoline Sports Medicine Products®, or many other fine companies. It comes in various strengths from very little resistance (such as red) to very strong resistance (such as silver), with varying degrees of difficulty in between. If you do not have the means to purchase such products, you can either obtain surgical tubing or bands (the same stuff that is used on your arm when you give blood to restrict the blood flow), or use an old bicycle inner tube (varying the strength by the amount of air, the more air the more resistance). Many of the exercises shown using free weights or weight machines can be performed using resistive tubing and bands. You simply have to anchor one end of the tubing/band in a position similar to the angle of pull you would otherwise get. The next few pages will give you a few ideas of the more popular exercises using tubing and bands, although there are endless exercises that can be done.

Lower Body

Groin Exercise

For those of you who do not have access to an ab/ad machine or a multi-hip machine, or even a Total Gym®, this tubing exercise works great to help strengthen weak muscles in the groin region. This is a muscle that needs to be strengthened as a counter balance for the strong IT Band used to pull the leg out to the side (located down the outer edge of the thigh). This is also a great balance training exercise as well. Simply tie a loop in each end of the tubing, place one end under a desk or bed leg, and the other end around your ankle.

Stand tall, shoulders back, with your leg held in the air by the tubing as Phuong illustrates.

While standing tall, bring the leg with tubing around the ankle across the body with a straight leg, maintaining balance and good posture. Bring your leg as far across the body as possible before slowly allowing it to return to the start position. Do not hunch or over-arch the back. The farther you stand from the anchor the more resistance you create, increasing the difficulty.

IT Band Exercise for Abduction of the Hip & Leg

Start the opposite of the groin exercise: attach one loop of the tubing to a bed or desk and the other to your ankle. Shoulders are back with good posture and balance.

Pull your straight leg across your body as far as possible while maintaining your balance and proper erect posture. Slowly control the return to the start position. You should not do any sidebending, over-arching of the back or hunching of the back to complete this exercise. If this occurs, step closer to the anchor to reduce the resistance on the tubing.

Ankle

The ankle must be strengthened in all four directions of mobility to have a balanced stable joint. The following will aid in ankle strengthening.

Loop the tubing around the end of your shoe near the toes, and ensure that it is tight enough on the foot that it will not slip off during the exercise. Begin with the ankle "rolled" so the toes are pointing at the other leg. While keeping the leg straight and not allowing movement anywhere but in the ankle, pull the toes across the foot/ankle until they point away from the body and the opposite foot. Repeat as many times as possible until exhaustion of those muscles. This is strengthening the motion of eversion of the ankle. Rest 1 minute before working on a new direction.

To strengthen the opposite motion, inversion (the motion most likely to cause an ankle sprain), position the tubing so that it is approaching the foot from the outer edge, with the starting position of the foot turned outwards away from other foot, then pulling inward towards the other foot into inversion. To increase resistance move the foot farther away from tubing anchor, to decrease move closer to anchor. Repeat this exercise as many times as possible until muscles reach exhaustion. Rest 1 minute before working on a new direction.

To strengthen the muscles at the front of the ankle, or the anterior aspect, loop the tubing around the foot with the anchor approaching the foot from the underneath side (plantar surface) as pictured above. With a straight leg, pull up on the tubing with the ankle as far as possible towards your nose, then slowly return to the start, repeating as many times as possible in one set to exhaustion. Rest 1 minute before working on a new direction..

For the last ankle exercise, put your foot in one loop of the tubing and the other loop in your hands. Begin with your toes pulled towards your nose, then push down against the tubing like you are trying to point your toes, return to the start position in a slow and controlled motion. Repeat as many times as possible to exhaustion in one set.

These exercises can be done as part of a regular strengthening exercise, or while watching television, etc. Every athlete should have their own tubing to complete exercises at various times throughout the day as they find the time.

Towel Scrunching
for injured or weak arches and toes

Instead of using tubing or bands to strengthen the muscles of the arch on the bottom of the foot, and the toes, use a towel. First place the towel spread out on the floor in front of your foot.

Curl the toes under causing the towel to gather or "scrunch" up under the foot, then straighten the toes again.

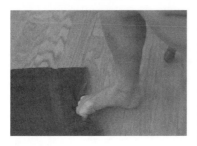

Repeat, curling/straightening until the entire towel has been gathered up under the foot. Stop and relax for a moment if the toes or foot begin to cramp. This means you are doing the exercise too fast or intensely. Slow down.

A similar exercise is to spread a bunch of marbles on the floor, then while seated in a chair pick the marbles up with your toes and put them into a bowl, one by one. This mimics the same action as scrunching the towel; great for weak, fallen or flat arches, which are very common in barefoot sports, such as martial arts.

Shoulder/Rotator Cuff Muscles

These are the muscles required to throw a football or baseball, or to throw an opponent in martial arts. The muscles are located on the back side of the shoulder and shoulder blade area, coming up and over the shoulder attaching on the upper arm.

Internal Rotators can be strengthened from two different positions: from the side or overhead. Phuong demonstrates using the tubing from the side position with the tubing anchored on a door knob at mid-upper arm to elbow level. Begin standing tall with shoulders square and back, no over-arching or hunching of the back, feet shoulder-width apart, with the arm being exercised held at the side (if this position is uncomfortable due to shoulder inflexibility, injury or weakness, roll a small hand towel up and place in between your upper arm and your side, squeezing with arm). The elbow is bent at 90° and rotated out so that the palm of the hand is facing forward when gripping the tubing. Step away from the anchor to create resistance in the tubing at a comfortable level, rotating the arm outwards to the side.

Keep your upper arm in as close to the body as possible (using a rolled towel if necessary) while "swinging" the forearm into the torso, maintaining a stiff wrist (no "flipping" with the wrist from hyperextension to flexion), and keeping the shoulders back and square. DO NOT JUST LET GO OF THE FINAL POSITION as serious injury could occur. Return to the start position slowly, allowing your arm to "swing" back out, while maintaining a resistive pull against the tubing and upper arm squeezed into your torso, until you reach the start position. This exercise can also be used to stretch the shoulder by simply getting in the start position and stepping away from the anchor until you feel a good stretch in your shoulder and arm.

CAUTION: if you feel a sharp pain in the shoulder or elbow at any time, stop immediately as you are applying too much resistance against the joints.

To **decrease the difficulty** of this exercise, perform while lying on your back on a bench or table.

Above, Phuong shows how to use the tubing from the overhead position, anchoring the tubing to a hook at shoulder level on the wall. Proper start position requires you to grasp the loop tied in the tubing with your palm facing forward. Extend your arm out to your side to shoulder level, with the elbow bent at 90° of flexion at the same level as the shoulders, causing the hand grip to be above the shoulder. The shoulders are held back and square, with no over-arching of the back. Your feet should be shoulder-width apart in a comfortable stance. Stepping away from the anchor increases the resistance and pulls the bent arm behind the head. Only step out as far is comfortable and which allows you to perform the exercise with proper technique. This position can also be used as a shoulder stretch by itself.

Pull your forearm forward past your ears to the front of the body against the resistance of the tubing, keeping the shoulders back and square, upper arm & elbow at shoulder level, and elbow bent to 90°. End position should have the palm facing the floor while the elbow still is bent to 90° & at shoulder level. The wrist should

Once you have mastered the highest level of resistance tubing or bands they can be replaced with low weight dumbbells using the same technique. The use of dumbbells for these exercises can be done standing, sitting in a chair, or lying on a table with the involved shoulder just off of the edge of a table or bench (be sure to hang onto the table with the other arm to prevent falling off of the table/bench).

Shoulder External Rotation

Exactly the same as internal rotation, but you start where the internal rotation exercise ends, pulling the tubing across the body.

Shoulder Adduction

Begin by standing with the arm outstretched at shoulder height to your side. Band should be taut, back not over-arching, shoulders back. Pull the tubing down towards the side of the leg.

Empty Cans

Put the center of the band/tube under your foot, and grasp each end with the palms and thumbs down. Lift your arms out from the sides as far as is comfortable. Return to the start position in a slow and controlled motion.

Hyperextensions

Helps to stabilize the shoulder, reducing chances of dislocation/ subluxation.

Anchor tubing on a doorknob or hook at mid-torso level. Start position: face the tubing anchor, grasping the tubing with the palm facing the floor, shoulders back and square, feet shoulder-width apart in a comfortable stance, your wrist and elbow are fully extended, with no over-arching or hunching of the back as Phuong demonstrates.

Pull the hand gripping the tubing straight back behind you with a straight arm and wrist, no bending or "flipping" of the elbow or wrist, shoulders back and square. Pull the tubing as far behind you as possible in a slow and controlled motion. Slowly allow the tubing to pull your arm back to in front of you to the start position. DO NOT JUST DROP YOUR ARM as injury may occur. If you feel a sharp pain in your shoulder, elbow or wrist at any time stop as the resistance maybe too much on the joints.

Plyometrics

Plyometrics is a form of strengthening program that should be added to an athlete's repertoire at least once every week. Plyometrics are various series of exercises and drills designed to enable an athlete to gain strength and power while increasing speed and agility. Plyometrics often include box jumping drills (both with and without weights), medicine ball exercises, quick feet pattern exercises, speed drills, quick feet off of a step drills, and speed bag punching and kicking drills, among many other great drills. An athlete should feel a good workout from plyometric drills but not be so terribly exhausted that further exercise is difficult or impossible. Every athlete, male & female, young and adult should be doing some form of plyometrics at least once per week.

A few safety guidelines are needed before beginning any plyometrics program:

• Remember to fully warm-up and stretch prior to beginning any workout, including plyometrics, for at least 10-15 minutes.

• As with any workout program, the floor needs to be a surface that has some flexibility to it. Such floors include a wooden gym floor that has a space directly beneath it, a floor covered by a padded mat, or a rubberized floor or track surface.

• Proper footwear is also mandatory, which includes wearing supportive tennis shoes, running shoes, or basketball high tops with good arch support (and ankle support if possible). **Never wear martial arts shoes or wrestling shoes for a plyometrics workout, or perform barefoot.**

• When using boxes for box jumping drills, ensure the boxes have been properly constructed and are securely built, with no nails sticking out from any surface. You can cover the top of the boxes with a thin carpet, but not rubber padding or any other slick or sticky surface as this will increase your chance of injury. Ensure that any carpet which is used for boxes is permanently attached to the box by gluing it to the surface.

• **As with all weightlifting programs, children under the age of 12 should limit the dumbbells used for exercise to 10 lbs or less and children age 8 and under should not use any weight at all.** This is simply to protect the health and well-being of pre-adolescent growth plates which can be damaged by use of heavy weights.

• Always begin any plyometrics program with a low intensity, simple workout. Do not try to do all of the advanced drills from the very beginning, or even more than a few drills at one time. The key is to start out slow and smart and build up the program as you progress and need more of a challenge. Once again, **children under the age of 12 should not perform high impact exercises or high intensity workouts to prevent possible damage to their growth plates.** Quick feet , bag work, and agility drills are better plyometric workouts for young athletes than using a lot of box jumping and heavy weights.

Before purchasing a book or entering a plyometrics program do some research. A good program will include agility drills, such as quick feet patterns either on the floor or off of a step (or both); quick hand/arm drills involving either bag or peg stand work; various jumping drills both from the ground and onto boxes of various heights (2", 4", 6", 12", 18" and various multiples of each); as well as various running and jumping/kicking drills for speed and accuracy. Jumping drills can incorporate simple tuck jumps, deep squat jumps, standing long jump, hurdle jumping, standing triple jump, use of horizontal ladders for jumping skills, single-leg bounding, alternating leg bounding, or a combination of all of the above at different rates of speed and from different surface heights, even many of the jumps performed by cheerleaders, such as the traditional toe-touch. One basic drill usually included in most plyometric programs includes placing numbers on the floor, on steps, or a combination of both and having to do a series of quick feet movements in a predetermined sequence for speed and accuracy during 10, 20, 30-second or even one-minute drills, with a specified foot having to touch the designated number in the pre-determined sequence or as yelled out by the coach. Check out the literature which is abundantly available from Certified Strength and Conditioning Specialists (have C.S.C.S. after their name) or from the National Strength & Conditioning Association. Many Strength and Conditioning Specialists have books already on the market, but ensure that they are certified professionals before following their word verbatim, even if they do work with professional athletes. As always, be smart with any workout program, listen to your body when it hurts, feels tired or drained, and care for it accordingly before the problem becomes worse. A good strength and conditioning program which includes a plyometrics workout can strengthen your agility, as well as your speed, coordination and quickness as a martial artist, reducing the chances of sustaining an injury.

Some of the quick feet programs look like this:

#1 One or Two Leg Hop/Step

1	2
3	4

Either call out a number to step on or hop on, or have a pre-set set sequence, such as 3-2-4-1. Can put two of the numbers up on a step or have all four flat on the ground.

#2 Three-Cone Movement

Can use various types of steps (shuffle, sprint, backpedal, grapevine, etc.) moving from cone #1 to #2, back to #1 to cone #3.

Can also be done in a T formation: requires abrupt change in direction.

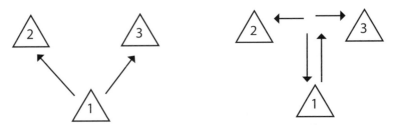

There are unlimited possibilities for designing programs. Take a shot at it!

Yoga & Pilates

Other non-traditional (in other words do not use weights, weight machines or resistance machines) strength and conditioning program modes could include the use of yoga, particularly if there is a need for greater flexibility, balance training, or a need to help control your mind (use of visualizations and breathing skills). Yoga has proven to be very useful in many traditional and non-traditional sports as it combines a lot of the attributes so necessary for a complete athlete, including control of not only the body but the mind. Yoga is a skill that can be learned by any age, any body type, any gender, and especially for those athletes who become pregnant and want to remain in shape. Yoga can take many different directions with various programs designed for each individuals needs. I do believe, though, that if you are to begin a yoga program it should be done initially with a very good and experienced instructor in a classroom, before deciding to use video tapes or books. Much of what is learned begins with the voice of the instructor, so try it and learn to not only listen but focus.

Besides Yoga, a more dynamic alternative is Pilates, which are "spring-based" exercises (created by Joseph Pilates at the beginning of the 20th century) that strengthen muscles without the use of weights, increase flexibility and strengthen the mind. The philosophy is that muscles are strengthened not by isolating them and strengthening them individually, but they are strengthened in combination with each other during motion. As with martial arts, Joseph Pilates believed that you must have a balance between the physical, mental and spiritual parts of your body. Visualizations (or visual imageries) are a large part of the program. Pilates does not use heavy weights, but rather only the amount of weight necessary in coordination with flexibility and balance training. Once again, if you decide to start a Pilates program, I suggest you first enroll in a class with an experienced instructor, before creating your own individualized program using books and/or video supplements. There is a lot to be learned from simply the presence in a class that you cannot possibly absorb from a book alone. Ensure that the instructor is a Certified Instructor in the Pilates Method to have the best results and learning experience.

No matter what type(s) or modes of strength and conditioning programs you decide to include, do your research, and enlist the assistance of a professional in the field before trying to create your own program, and only after you have received your "ok" from a physician, physical therapist, and/or certified athletic trainer. This way you ensure the best possible results to benefit your training in the martial arts with a strength and conditioning program.

Chapter Two Key Points

✦ Always stretch before and after your strength training workout.

✦ Have a complete physical and consult with your physician before beginning a new strength training routine.

✦ Focus on moderate to high sets (3-4) of high reps (12-18) using a moderate amount of weight (50% - 60% of your maximum).

✦ Children under the age of 12 should limit weight training to low sets (only 1), low reps (less than 10) of light weights (1-5 pounds). They should also avoid high impact or high intensity plyometrics.

✦ Students ages 12-16 should avoid heavy weight lifting and high impact plyometrics to prevent damage to the growth plates.

✦ Give your muscles a 24 - 48 hour recover period between strength training workouts.

✦ Plyometrics should be done at least once a week by all competitors.

✦ Never wear martial arts shoes or wrestling shoes for plyometric exercises, or go barefoot.

✦ Always begin plyometric exercises from low intensity, simple exercises and build up as your strength and coordination improves.

Eating to Compete 3

Okay, everyone thinks they know the best way to drop weight for competition, but do you really know how to eat for life as an athlete? Instead of always "going on a diet" you should think more about developing an eating program which helps you stay near your fighting weight, and yet keeps you healthy enough to train hard. To do this you need to do several things.

First, you will have to be serious about reading the numbers on labels for everything until you get used to it. It is advantageous to purchase a nutrition book, such as *Nutrition & Diet Therapy* by Lutz & Przytulski (1994, F.A. Davis Company), in order to be able to determine the numbers for foods which do not contain labels, such as fruits, foods from popular restaurants, beverages, etc. The most important thing to remember is to watch for fat and sodium content and kcal/calorie levels. Your diet should only have fifteen to twenty percent of the total calories from fat each day. Fat is found in meats, nuts, dairy products, salad dressings, sauces, fried foods, oils, creams, dressings, etc. **Read your labels and your charts!**

Sodium, better known as salt and/or preservatives, is also a big culprit — the RDA (recommended daily allowance) of sodium/salt is 1000 mg/day (that much is found in two slices of pizza!). As you look at the charts and labels, you will see some foods have more than this in only one serving. Sodium is found in boxed, canned and frozen foods, dairy products, sauces, cereals, etc, anything that has to be processed or preserved and is not fresh. Once again, read your labels and your charts. When in doubt, buy fresh fruits, vegetables, and meats!

Calories or kcals are your last and least concern. If you are working out hard and sweating each day for at least 60 minutes, are at least sixteen years of age, and are within ten pounds of your ideal weight, you should be consuming up to 2500 calories/day for males, and up to 2000 for females. When not working out, athletes should reduce their intake to under 2000 calories/day for males, and under 1500 for females.

Beverages — drink at least two liters of water each day **in addition to** whatever else you like. This actually helps your body flush itself of unwanted by-products. You can add lemon juice for flavor, but nothing else. Back away from caffienated products such as soda, tea, coffee, chocolate, etc. Caffeine dries your muscles out, reduces your ability to have bowel movements and increases your chance for injury when too much is consumed.

I know, I'm telling you to back off of all the good stuff. Well, now you get to find new and inventive ways of eating and cooking. Explore new spices such as basil, oregano, and garlic—great for weight loss and taste buds. Replace butter with butter substitutes, fresh fruit/vegetable salsa, low-fat cream cheese or low-sugar jellies and jams. Replace your high fat cooking oils with olive oil or oils low in trans-fat or saturated fat.

As for proteins vs. carbohydrates, your intake of protein should be up to forty percent of your diet, with carbohydrates finishing up the other forty percent of your daily diet. Protein is found in meats, dairy products, nuts, beans, soy products (tofu), fish and egg whites. Carbohydrates are divided into starches and simple sugars. Starches include pasta, rice, potato, bread, cereal, oatmeal, yellow vegetables (such as carrots & corn), etc. Carbohydrates comprised of simple sugars include fruits and vegetables, as well as sugar containing sweets. For carbohydrate consumption you should concentrate more on fruits and vegetables, especially green vegetables and less on starches or sweets. If you eat starches they should be from brown grains rather than white (for example, brown rice rather than white) or vegetable base (like spinach or tomato), and not consumed late in the evening, but are great to be consumed 30 minutes prior to a workout or to increase energy on competition day.

When you work out your eating habits should be scheduled around it. First, before working out you need to eat a small amount of carbohydrates: wheat bagel, whole-grain cereal, carbohydrates bar, wheat crackers, brown rice, fruit, etc. This will help increase your available energy and allow body fat to be burned for fuel more readily. Secondly, within two hours following a workout (weightlifting, running or martial arts) you should consume some protein with a small amount of carbohydrate to aid in the repair of any breakdown of muscle during a workout. Something as simple as a fruit and protein smoothie or low-fat peanut butter on whole wheat bread does the trick. It is very important to consume this protein in a low fat form within two hours following the workout. But notice, some of the best sources of protein are also high in fat—your best bet are red and black beans, lentils, low-fat/low-sodium dairy products, chicken/turkey (white meat), and fish, along with berries, pineapple, melon or citrus fruit. Bananas are a great source of potassium, a necessary mineral in your diet, but too many bananas in the same day can constipate you, plus they are high in sugar, so add to your diet sparingly.

If you eat food late at night, it must be something you will either burn off before you go to bed, or in your sleep. Do not have a big heavy meal or snack and then go to bed. It is best to have four to six small meals/snacks throughout the day, with the most fattening foods being consumed at mid-day, and your last snack 1-2 hours prior to going to bed. Also, don't deprive yourself of all your favorite fattening foods. Plan for being bad, allowing yourself one bad food in small quantities a few times a week, but that does not mean have an entire bad eating meal or day. So, don't run off to your favorite fast food restaurant and pig out, even for one meal! Your weeks of eating smart can be ruined by one meal at these places, this includes pizza restaurants.

If your digestive metabolism is slow, invest in some Chinese herbal green tea without ginseng (ginseng can possibly lead to a positive on a drug test for a banned substance). It will help boost metabolism as well as being an anti-oxidant, but you must drink lots of water throughout the day and consume the tea following your meals. An anti-oxidant helps rid the body of unwanted substances, reducing the chances of heart-related problems, and is also a great natural laxative to reduce problems of constipation or regularity. There are many purported anti-oxidants out there, discuss the benefits over using various ones in your diet with your nutritionist/dietician or your physician before adding to your daily routine. What works for one individual may not for another due to differences in body types and metabolisms.

It is wise to also add a vitamin supplement to your daily diet. Your supplement does not need to be the relatively expensive "mega" vitamin supplements found in most health food and fitness stores. It does need to be a basic vitamin and mineral supplement with one hundred percent of the RDA (recommended daily allowance) of all essential vitamins and minerals for your age. This supplement can be as simple as a children's daily chewable tablet (one for children, two for adults). Supplements claiming to have two hundred to five hundred percent RDA are not what you need, because the body simply secretes the excess nutrients not immediately used, taxing your organ system or appearing as annoying acne on the skin. If you are a female in your child-bearing years, especially if you are considering getting pregnant or you are pregnant, you also need to take a folic acid supplement. Folic acid taken prior to pregnancy has been shown to reduce the chances of developing birth defects in a fetus and aids in a healthy heart for females. Speak to your OB/GYN physician about the amount you should be taking.

Your supplements need to be taken every day at approximately the same time of day, ensuring you eat first to aid in the absorption process. Vitamins are especially important when dropping weight and cutting back on your food intake. You should note that vitamin supplements are not meant to replace eating properly, but to supplement those vitamins that you may not get enough of. In some cases, your physician may recommend additional supplementation of particular vitamins and/or minerals due to a problem with your metabolism, presence of a disease/disorder, or lack of appropriate levels in your diet. It is an excellent idea to set an appointment with a registered dietician recommended by your physician or certified athletic trainer, to ensure that all your nutritional needs are met by your diet and supplementation habits. Be cautious of various "all natural" products as the FDA (Food & Drug Administration) does not regulate these products, therefore they are not required to list all ingredients on the label, and there is a high possibility that a banned substance might be present in the supplement. If you have any questions about whether or not a supplement is on the banned substance list, contact the US Anti-doping Agency (USADA). USADA is the agency responsible for drug testing national and Olympic-level athletes throughout the United States, under the guidance and direction of the World Ant-Doping Agency (WADA).

Since everyone needs some basic guidelines in order to get started on the right track here is a sample eating program that you can change according to your needs:

Breakfast:

Small portion of carbohydrates such as 1 cup of oatmeal, whole grain cereal, grits or 1 average size bagel -- no added sugar, butter or salt -- can add small amount of fruit or skim milk

1 egg/egg substitute or 2 egg whites or small portion (4 oz) of other protein

1 small fruit (preferably melons or berries)

4 oz skim/low fat milk or 4 oz lowfat yogurt/cottage cheese can serve as protein

Vitamin supplement (such as children's chewable or basic multivitamin)

Snack:

for any time when you have hunger pains in between scheduled meals

Choose only 1 carb in addition to 1 protein

Small box of raisins or other dried fruit

1 Piece of fruit or 1 cup of cut up fruit -- oranges, apples, grapes, melon, berries, pineapple (bananas only occasionally)

½ cup raw vegetables -- broccoli, celery, cucumbers, green beans (avoid carrots, yellow squash and corn)

½ bag of microwave popcorn, unbuttered (or low fat) & unsalted

8 oz fruit juice or lemonade (avoid caffeine and carbonated sodas)

Plus 4 oz of protein (tuna, yogurt or other low-fat dairy product, chicken)

Lunch:

Small salad (1 cup lettuce) with lemon juice, no salad dressing or small piece of fruit (1 cup of fruit)

½ sandwich -- grilled chicken, turkey, tuna, baked fish, lean beef on whole grain bread or 4 oz of soup, low fat, low salt

½ cup of vegetables -- broccoli, peas, green beans, etc.

8 oz lemonade and a glass of water

Snack:

for any time when you have hunger pains in between scheduled meals

Choose only 1 carb plus 1 protein:

Small box of raisins or other dried fruit

1 Piece of fruit or 1 cup of cut up fruit -- oranges, apples, grapes, melon, berries, pineapple (bananas only occasionally)

½ cup raw vegetables -- broccoli, celery, cucumbers, green beans

½ bag of microwave popcorn, unbuttered (or low fat) & unsalted

8 oz fruit juice or lemonade (avoid caffeine and carbonated sodas)

Plus 4 oz of protein (tuna, yogurt or other low-fat dairy product)

Dinner:

1 cup of pasta, rice, beans or small baked potato, with 2-3 tablespoons of low fat tomato sauce, low-fat yogurt or garlic **(do not need starches every day at this meal)**

½ cup of vegetables -- broccoli, squash, spinach, etc.

3-6 oz of meat, chicken, fish, or 1 cup of beans or lentils

8 oz beverage **plus** a glass of water

Snack:

4 oz low fat fruit yogurt (including frozen yogurt), dried or fresh fruit, or Popsicle (preferably low/no sugar added)

**Snack following a workout: Fruit and Protein Smoothie Shake

This eating program will help you to maintain your weight allowing you to safely drop the extra 5-10 pounds in the weeks prior to competition. In the 3-4 weeks prior to competition you should focus on losing no more than 2 pounds per week in order to safely drop weight without losing strength or speed due to lack of nutrition. Waiting until the last week or even until the last days just prior to competition to lose more than 1-2 pounds is very foolish and can have devastating effects on your body, including your organs, your growth (your bones), and even your muscles.

Every year we have athletes that have to be taken to the hospital following weigh-ins because their body cannot handle the dramatic amounts of weight lost for competition. Many more athletes never fully reach the height they were projected to grow to due to many years of harsh dieting in order to make weight. On rare occasions, improper weight loss has lead to organ failure while an athlete has been at weigh-in. Maintaining your weight throughout the year near a more comfortable weight, and burning fat through a good strength and conditioning program is a much wiser choice, allowing you to have optimal strength for competition.

To adjust the above eating program for preparation for competition simply involves dropping a lot of the complex carbohydrates from your daily menu. These include breads, pasta, rices, potatoes, cereals, yellow vegetables (such as carrots and corn), etc. You should still have protein (meats, fish, beans, dairy products) each meal every day, and maintain your fruit and vegetable consumption. Protein choices should tend more towards tuna and other low-fat high Omega-3 fatty acid fish and seafood (tuna being the very best choice, packed in spring water not oil), or white meat poultry, fruit choices should narrow around citrus fruits (especially grapefruit and pineapple), berries and melon.

You should also cut your beverage intake back to only water at this point. If you are having difficulty having a bowel movement during this period you can follow your meals with a cup of hot Chinese Green Tea or supplement with green tea extract, **but ensure that it does not have ginseng or other additives as these may show up during drug testing as a banned stimulant.** Constipation often becomes a problem when removing a lot of the grains and "roughage" from the diet, as well as when water intake is reduced below the body's perceived need.

You should increase your cardio workout during this same period of time to help burn off some of the last few pounds of fat and water weight. Continue with your strength and conditioning programs as these will help to maintain your body's lower fat content levels and help you to have the most successful outcome at your tournaments.

Eating on Competition Day

Okay, now it is competition day, you have made weight, now how do you make sure you stay at your optimum level of performance throughout the day? Simple, by following a few easy to remember rules. Since you have been trying to drop pounds to make weight all week (and if you are smart, for the past month or so), your stomach has now shrunk. DO NOT STUFF YOUR FACE AFTER WEIGH IN! A more suitable method would be to eat a small meal with mainly carbohydrates such as pasta or rice, plus fruits and vegetables, and a small portion of protein, once you have weighed in and drank at least 1 ½ liters of water. For the following morning (competition day), 1-2 hours prior to your first fight: a small portion of carbohydrates (½ cup of oatmeal, grits, rice, cereal, or a bagel); small portion of fruit or fruit juice; lots of water, at least

1 liter; a small amount of protein (but nothing fried!) and a vitamin supplement (such as a children's chewable vitamin). Eating a heavy meal will only make you feel sick to your stomach, and make you feel slow. You can eat small snacks throughout the day to help keep your energy up without making you feel slow or nauseous. Some great snacks to keep around would be: raisins and other dried fruit, fresh fruit (apples, oranges, grapes), pretzels, crackers, bagels and other breads, energy or carbo bars (try not to eat too many protein bars though), raw vegetables (carrots, broccoli, pickles, etc.), rice or a peanut butter and jelly sandwich. Drink a lot of water throughout your matches and throughout the day. Remember to drink enough water that your urine is almost clear. The better your body is hydrated, the better you and your muscles feel and the less likely you are to get injured.

Hydration

Keeping your body hydrated is just as important as doing a warm-up stretch prior to working out or competing. Your body is mainly composed of water and water-containing tissue. So, it makes sense that water is necessary for life, let alone to maintaining your optimum performance level at all times. Unfortunately, it seems to be the first thing athletes cut from their daily routine when trying to make weight. Actually maintaining your water intake and eliminating other forms of beverages will help to reduce the fat content of your body by flushing out unused materials which would normally be converted to fat.

An athlete should average two to three liters (over one gallon) of water every twenty-four hour period, especially on competition day. In general, you should drink so much water that your urine is pale yellow to clear **every day!** Beverages such as carbonated soda, especially those containing caffeine, should be avoided except for occasional consumption and never consumed on competition day. Dairy products, fruit juices, fruit drinks, and sports drinks can be consumed **in addition** to the daily requirement of water, but remember they often are full of "empty" calories, and contribute very little to your nutritional needs. Water need not be ice cold at all times either, unless you will only drink water when it is ice cold. Often simply adding a squeezed lemon or lime slice into the water will add enough flavor to make it palatable for those who do not like the taste of water.

Sport drinks contain necessary electrolytes (sugars & salts) if you are sweating for more than one hour of constant sweating during a workout. This may be true of everyday workouts, but usually does not apply to competition day (unless the you have lost too much weight for competition and therefore much of your electrolyte stores have also been lost). So, ensure that your muscles, organs and body are at their optimum performance level by drinking plenty of water during practices, while dropping weight, during competitions and always following any competition.

Do not wait until you are thirsty to begin drinking—by this point, you are already dehydrated. It takes at least 20-30 minutes for the message to drink fluids to get from your muscles to your brain. Be prepared. Never allow yourself to get that "cotton mouth" dry, thirsty feeling by keeping a bottle of water with you at all times and continuously drinking.

Chapter Three Key Points

✦ Eating properly every day is healthier and safer than dieting to make weight.

✦ Focus on limiting fat and sodium intake first then worry about calories.

✦ Drink at least two liters of water a day to assist in weight loss and hydration.

✦ For competitors, protein should make up forty percent of the diet, carbohydrates forty percent and fats fifteen to twenty percent.

✦ Schedule your meals around your workout plan.

✦ Green tea can help boost metabolism, aid in weight loss and act as an antioxidant if consumed following meals.

✦ A daily multi-vitamin supplement is recommended.

✦ When cutting weight for a competition, lose no more than two pounds per week.

✦ On competition day, drink plenty of water throughout the day to stay hydrated. Don't wait until you are thirsty to begin drinking water.

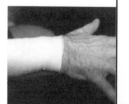

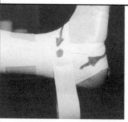

Injury
Care

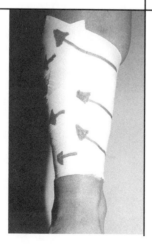

Taping Techniques 4

The use of athletic tape in martial arts, as well as many other sports, is highly controversial. Many instructors and referees do not believe it should be used at all. Others wish to restrict the amount used and the situations in which it can be used, while some feel tape should be used to its greatest advantage without limitations. Taping is beneficial for both prevention as well as protection of injuries, but should never be the sole treatment used to protect a joint or muscle or used to make a body part into a weapon.

When taping is used to protect a joint from injury it needs to be done in conjunction with a strengthening program for that joint. For example, if an athlete has both ankles taped for practice and competition, that athlete also needs to be completing a daily ankle strengthening routine to increase the protection of the joint from injury (as previously described).

Many people falsely believe that taping weakens a joint, such as the ankle, when the exact opposite is true. The tape cannot prevent any and all injuries, it simply is not that strong, nor does it weaken the ankle. What happens, though, is the athlete often becomes relaxed or lazy from knowing they are wearing tape and does not keep the ankle strong to prevent injury. Taping should never replace a solid strengthening program. Tape loses approximately fifty percent of its strength after only thirty minutes of sweating during a workout, thereby losing a lot of its ability to protect the joint. The tape is actually more of a warning signal used by athletes that as they begin to roll their ankle they feel it against the tape and correct the position of their foot.

What tape can do is provide compression of an area of swelling as part of the treatment process of an injury. It can also lend support to weak and stretched out muscles, tendons and ligaments as they heal when used in conjunction with a rehabilitative and strengthening program. Taping does not prevent an athlete from properly kicking or extending their foot as many people believe, because tape is a woven material that gives and stretches with use, particularly with sweating.

The decision to tape depends on the beliefs of the athlete and instructor, the rules of the competition, and the recommendations of a sports medicine professional such as a certified athletic trainer, physical therapist or physician. One point to make though, you should not wait until the day of competition to "try out" using tape. You should initially practice with the joint taped, to determine if you like the feeling. If you become injured and need to be taped it will take some adjusting to get accustomed to working out with tape. But, if you are injured, taping should be continued for three to six weeks during the healing process and not discontinued until the joint has regained its original pre-injury strength. Even if the joint feels "fine" it takes at least three to six weeks to totally heal, and you are at greater risk of re-injury during this period than when healthy.

Here are a few taping techniques which may be beneficial to martial art athletes. Since every form of martial arts has different rules pertaining to taping, be sure to get approval on the use of tape prior to any competition. The techniques shown here will be those approved for use in USA Taekwondo sanctioned events. Variations and changes may be required for other forms of martial arts, and even other sanctioning bodies in the sport of taekwondo.

USA Taekwondo and WTF (World Taekwondo Federation) require that only two layers of tape, or the minimum necessary to contain and protect any injury, be used. Heavy taping is prohibited, as is taping which would give an athlete an unfair advantage over his or her opponent. Bleached (white) tape which is not abrasive, does not contain any hard substance, and does not in any way endanger the safety of an athlete or opponent can be used. The standard tape to use is white 1½ inch or 2 inch athletic tape found in most sporting goods or sports medicine supply stores. The tape often has zinc oxide added to increase the healing abilities of the tape, but also adds to the expense.

A pre-wrap or underwrap is used in conjunction with most tape to reduce the chances of skin irritation. Where pre-wrap is not available it is advisable to shave the area for better adherence of the athletic tape to the skin. Once again, since some competitions limit the number of layers allowed to be used on particular body parts, you need to know if the pre-wrap counts towards these layer limits, and act accordingly.

Certified Athletic Trainers (ATC) will also often use a tape adherent spray to enhance the tape job, allowing the tape and pre-wrap to better adhere to the skin. This spray comes in many forms and is produced by many companies, with the most common being either a tape adherent spray or a quick-drying tape adherent spray. Use of tape adherent spray should only be a light spray of the area to be taped without giving it a thick "super glue" layer. NOTE: if using the adherent spray on or around someone with asthma, take precautions to reduce the chance of them inhaling the spray as it may trigger an asthmatic attack. Also, be aware of any allergies to adhesives or latex as adherent spray may cause an allergic reaction in these individuals.

It is strongly advised not to tape tightly as this may cause blistering of the skin under the edges of the tape or where the tape pinches the skin near a joint. Tighter is not always better! The tape job should be adequately firm (by using gentle tension on the tape) without causing the skin to buckle or fold. Never pull the tape as tight as you can get it, simply tight enough to prevent "buckling" or folding of the tape.

Extra protection is often used in the areas most vulnerable to blistering, for example, the front of the foot where one ties the laces of a shoe, and across the achilles tendon. Commercially produced barrier pads used for this purpose are called heel and lace pads. Heel and lace pads can be made from two gauze pads (make sure they are not abrasive ones!) with either some petroleum jelly or skin lubricant applied to each piece and placed over the tendons in the front of the foot as well as the Achilles tendon near the heal. Commercially produced heel and lace pads are commonly made from Styrofoam or soft foam padding. For the best results, proper tape, pre-wrap, tape adherent and heel and lace pads (for ankle tape jobs) should be utilized to reduce the chances of blistering and increase the durability and longevity of the tape job.

It should be noted that some athletes are allergic to athletic tape, in particular the dry rubber used in most athletic tape, and/or allergic to the tape adherent spray. If you develop a rash following use of tape or spray, discontinue use until a physician can determine the reason for the rash occurrence. It may simply involve discontinuing use of the spray or adding more layers of pre-wrap in order to prevent further rash outbreaks from the tape.

It should also be noted that if you are injured, you should be seen by medical personnel, whether that is a certified athletic trainer, licensed physical therapist or physician, especially if pain or weakness continues without any change beyond a two week period or if swelling and/or discolorization has occurred and not been diminished within the first 5-7 days. The injury may actually be more substantial than you and/or your instructor realizes, requiring more intense medical treatment. If in doubt about an injury of any type at any time seek a medical evaluation by a sports medicine professional immediately.

Tearing the Tape

There are many ways in which tape can be torn, including using both hands or one hand and the body part being taped, but the following is a basic suggestion how to tear tape easily and decrease the chances of damaging your fingernails or developing blisters. You will develop your own methods with time and practice.

Holding the roll of tape in one hand, pinch a short piece of tape between the thumb and first finger on both hands, not allowing your fingernails to touch the tape at any time. Pull the tape taut between the two hands (this is enough to cause some tapes to tear).

Keep your wrists tight and straight. Pull with one hand while pushing down on the tape with the other in a snapping motion until the tape tears. Do not twist the tape.

Ankle

The ankle is the most commonly taped portion of the body in martial arts as well as the majority of sports activities overall. Many martial art athletes tape both of their ankles so they do not feel "lopsided" or off-balance, particularly if they have already sustained an injury to one ankle.

Ninety to ninety-five percent of all ankle injuries are inversion sprains. This injury occurs when the foot "rolls under" often causing the athlete to fall in pain. Inversion injuries can also occur from stepping on an opponent's foot or any object lying on the floor. The other five to ten percent of injuries are referred to as eversion sprains, where the foot "rolls out", very uncommon in martial art athletes. The taping technique that is shown is for inversion sprains.

Step 1

Begin with the ankle.

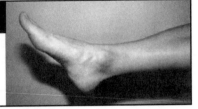

Step 2

Position foot in plantar flexion (pull toes up). Spray with tape adherent. Apply heel & lace pads as shown.

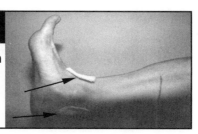

Step 3

Apply pre-wrap beginning at bottom of the belly of the calf (where line is drawn at right).

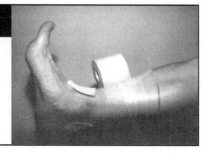

Step 4

Apply pre-wrap to entire ankle area down to instep.

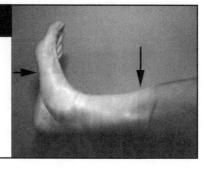

Step 5

Apply 2 base strips just below belly of calf.

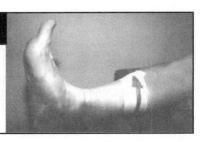

Step 6

Apply two stirrup strips beginning inside of leg to outside, gently pulling. Do not run directly over the bottom of the heel.

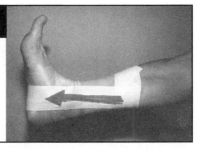

Step 7

Apply another base strip near belly of calf to secure top of stirrups.

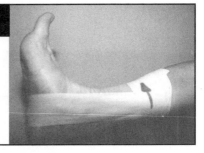

Step 8

Apply horseshoe strips to secure stirrups at ankle.

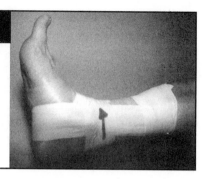

NOTE: FOR COMPETITIONS limiting the number of layers of tape you should SKIP THE STEPS INVOLVING STIRRUPS and horseshoes to keep number of layers to a minimum.

Now you will begin the figure 8 - heel lock combination. You can do this 1-2 times dependent on how stiff the athlete wants the tape. Remember to use only steady tension, do not pull hard or simply lay it on with gaps. Gaps, wrinkles or folds in the tape can lead to blisters and/or weaken the tape job.

Step 9

Begin by placing the end of tape on the lateral (outside) ankle bone.

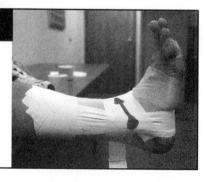

Step 10

Go directly across the front of the leg passing directly across the top of the medial (inside) ankle bone.

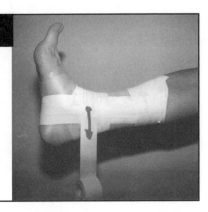

Step 11

As you have crossed over the medial ankle you are going to bring the tape behind the heel and under the lateral ankle as pictured here, known as a "heel lock".

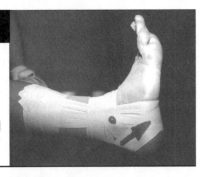

Step 12

Bringing tape under lateral ankle continue under the foot without putting tape on the heel or ball of the foot as pictured.

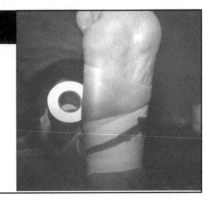

Step 13

Now continue taking tape across the top of the ankle & foot heading directly for the lateral ankle.

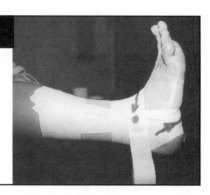

Step 14

Continue taping across lateral ankle to behind the heel.

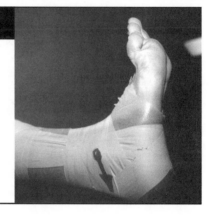

Step 15

As you bring tape from behind heel pass under medial ankle towards the bottom of the foot; no tape on bottom of heel or ball of foot.

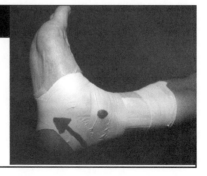

These are known as the heel locks. You can add additional heel locks by simply starting the tape at step 15 (behind heel) and taking through step 17 from both sides of the foot/ankle. Heel locks give additional support.

Step 16

Continue to bring tape across bottom of foot around to top of instep.

Step 17

Cross across the top of the instep and tear tape.

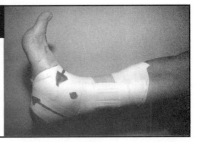

You are now ready to close up the tape job, lending the last bit of supportive tape

Step 18

Use single strips to apply 2 base strips around the foot and instep.

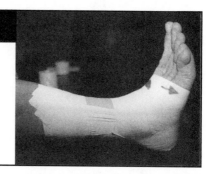

Some athletes prefer not to apply these strips, while others will apply them to just under the ball of the foot to protect their instep. Be sure to press your thumb into the bottom of the athlete's foot, causing the toes to spread and reducing the chances of getting the tape too tight around the instep.

Step 19

Apply single strips around the leg until you reach the bottom of the belly of the calf. You may need to angle the strips to suit the curvature of the leg.

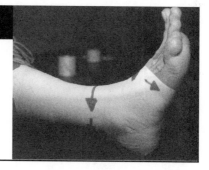

Feet: With & Without Protective Pads

Some martial art athletes use tape and/or protective padding to protect the feet, particularly the instep, from bruising and other injuries. At USA Taekwondo National Events, instep pads are required to be used by all junior and senior competitors. These pads can either be commercially produced with elastic to hold pads on, or applied with tape directly to the insteps of the foot. The padding cannot contain any hard substance, including buckles, shoestrings, metal, casting material or plastic. The pad must extend from the base of the toes up the foot to the joint (but not covering the joint) of the ankle, and from the side to side of the foot, covering all exposed areas of the instep of the foot. Unfortunately, at the present time, WTF International events as well as many other martial art governing bodies, only allow two layers of tape on the instep without any protective padding.

No pre-wrap is used under the tape or over a pad for this tape job. This is to help the tape adhere longer and not slide off the end of the foot when kicking. The use of tape adherent spray when applying pads and/or tape is also highly recommended. Some athletes may want 102 layers of tape underneath the pad to reduce chafing.

Instep Pad Coverage Area: **Taping Instep Pad in Place:**

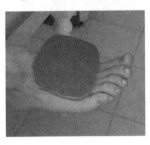   

Single strips of tape, which only circle the foot once before being torn from the roll should be used, layering the strips from the toes up toward the ankle joint, one strip at a time. Pressure should be applied using your thumb into the arch of the foot to spread the foot and toes. This keeps the tape from getting too tight and curling the foot, making it painful or impossible to walk.

Instep Taping without a Pad:

As with taping a pad onto the instep, single strips of tape which only encircle the foot once before being torn from the roll, should be utilized when taping the instep. Press your thumb into the bottom of the foot in the arch region to spread the toes as you apply the tape. No pre-wrap should be used in either case (unless requested by the athlete due to hairy or sensitive skin) as it increases the chance of the tape sliding off once the athlete begins sweating. Tape adherent spray is highly recommended. NEVER apply tape to the ball of the foot or the bottom of the heal, as this may cause the athlete to slip when the dirt collects on the tape creating a slippery surface.

Great Toe (Big Toe)

Believe it or not martial art athletes suffer turf toe as much or more so than athletes who play on the artificial turf surfaces from which the injury gets its name. Turf toe is simply pain and swelling of the joint of the big toe where it attaches to the foot. This injury occurs from being forcibly bent under, up or out to the side, and/or "jamming" of the toe directly into the joint, either from contact with another athlete or workout surface. This injury can be very painful and debilitating, causing athletes to lose time from regular workout routines when not properly cared for. In addition to the injury treatment that will be discussed later in the book, taping the joint at the base of the big toe can add some support and comfort, allowing an athlete to continue working out.

This taping technique by no means takes away all of the pain, but often makes it possible for an athlete to endure while working out or competing. This taping technique is extremely easy to get too tight, so added care must be taken when taping the big toe, as well as removing the tape following a workout or competition. Since martial art athletes should not have tape on the ball of their foot, this taping technique has been modified from the normal protocol used in other sports such as American football or soccer. Taping across the bottom of the ball of the foot creates a slippery surface for athletes which only gets worse as the tape collects dust from walking and competing barefoot.

Step 1

Apply a single strip of tape around the foot and instep below the ball of the foot.*

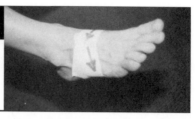

This is the same strip used to tape the instep by itself.

Step 2

Use 1" tape or split your 1 ½" roll of tape — Apply one strip of tape in a "J" formation by beginning on outside of big toe, wrapping across the top of the big toe, between big toe and 2nd toe, under big toe, coming across the joint of the big toe and foot, running tape diagonally across the instep to the base strip of tape previously applied to the instep. Repeat with a second strip overlapping the 1st strip by 1/2 to 2/3.

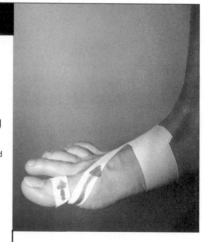

Step 3

Using split tape or 1″ tape run 2 strips of tape from the big toe down the inside of the foot to the base strip of tape on the instep.

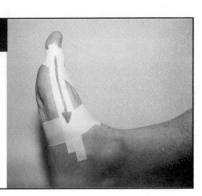

Step 4

Apply one last strip on 1″ tape around toe to secure strips, and then tape instep to close up tape (as noted in step 1).

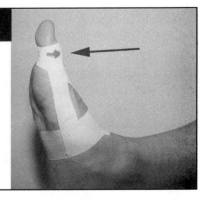

Arch Support

Arch pain is very common among martial art athletes since no supportive footwear is used during competition or practice. Pain can be attributed to bruised or fallen arches, flat feet, high arches, fasciitis (swelling of the tissue that runs through the arch), bone spurs or stress fractures, and can lead to other injuries such as shin splints and stress fractures of the shin region. Since martial art athletes should not have tape on the balls of their feet this taping technique has been modified from the standard taping technique used in other sports. If arch pain is persistent, evaluation by a podiatrist (medical doctor, MD, who specializes in the treatment of foot and ankle problems), especially a sports medicine podiatrist, is highly recommended.

Step 1

Tri-fold (3-way fold) a 3"x3" gauze pad. Place between the 2nd & 3rd toe, below the ball of the foot. Secure with a strip of tape around the instep. As you wrap the tape, press your thumb into the bottom of the foot to spread the toes, reducing the chance of the tape being too tight. If gauze extends downward onto the heel, trim to fit in the arch area only.

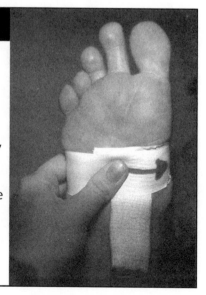

Step 2

Use a single strip of tape to run from the base of the 5th toe down the side of the foot.

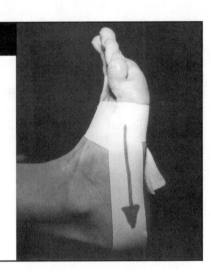

Step 3

Continue under the heel, & then back up the inside of the foot to the base of the big toe. DO NOT PULL TAPE TIGHT.

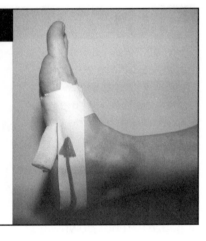

Either use 1" tape or split your 1 ½" tape into 2 strips for steps 4-6.

Step 4

Take one single strip running from tape located under big toe diagonally across foot to other side.

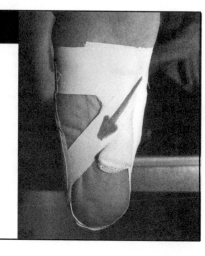

Step 5

Follow with a 2nd strip beginning at the base of the 5th toe running diagonally across the foot.

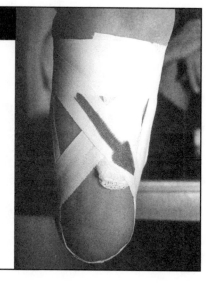

Step 6

Repeat steps four and five 2-4 more times, creating 3-5 "X's" across the arch of the foot, overlapping the strips by 1/2 to 2/3.

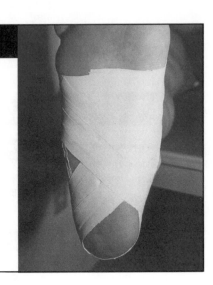

Step 7

Finish by closing up with single strips wrapping around the foot from the arch around the inside of the foot, across the instep & back around to the bottom of the foot as you would when closing an ankle tape job or instep taping.

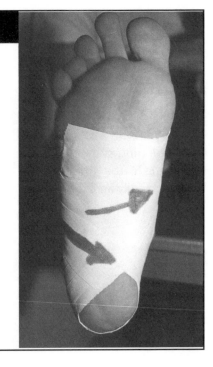

Achilles' Tendon

The Achilles' tendon is the tendon which runs up the back of your heel and allows martial artists (as well as everyone else!) to stand and bounce on their toes when contracted. Due to the fact that many forms of martial art encourage athletes to "stay on their toes", the Achilles' tendon often becomes irritated and inflamed, leading to pain and swelling.

In some cases, when not properly treated, the Achilles' tendon will rupture and/or partially tear, causing a lot of pain and loss of mobility. It is important to compare the size of the Achilles' tendon which is irritated with the one on the other leg, comparing thickness of the tendon, as well as any notable swelling or discolorization. If the tendon is noticeably larger than the other leg, or any discolorization of the skin is occurring, the following taping techniques should not be used as it will only further irritate the tendon, possibly leading to greater damage. Instead, a visit to your Sports Medicine Orthopedist is needed. But for those recovering from an injury, those who simply need a little bit of support, or for those having problems "staying on their toes" the following taping technique can be quite beneficial. Once again, since we do not want to apply tape to the ball of the foot or over the bottom of the heel, this taping technique has been modified to accommodate the needs of martial arts and other barefoot sports. You may see a much different version of taping for the Achilles' tendon in other books on taping techniques.

Step 1

Begin by sitting on a table with the foot in a relaxed position. Do not forcibly point the toes, just relax.

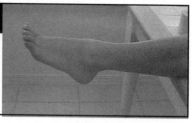

Step 2

Apply pre-wrap in a continuous circular motion beginning at the instep just below the ball of the foot, covering the entire foot (but not the heel) and leg up to the point where the calf muscle begins to bulge.

Step 3

Anchor the pre-wrap with 2 strips of tape around the instep & two around the leg just under the belly of the calf muscle.

Step 4

Attach the end of the tape to the base strip on the arch surface near the ball of the foot, pulling the tape diagonally across the arch with the foot still in a relaxed position.

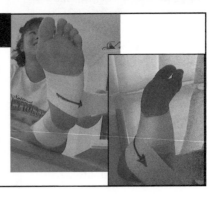

Step 5

The tape comes across the arch and over to the heel side, going behind the heel and ankle, but not covering the ankle. (A reverse of the heel lock used for ankle taping.)

Step 6

The tape will "spiral" in an "S" shape going behind the leg ending at the base tape just under the calf muscle belly (Refer to the arrow direction in photo).

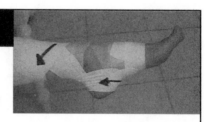

Step 7

Repeat above technique coming from opposite side of the foot and leg, creating a spiral going up the opposite direction (see arrow). Repeat in both directions a second time for more support.

Step 8

Apply single strips to anchor the tape on the instep. Do not create more than 2 layers on the instep. Apply single strips to the leg. Do not pull tightly as the muscles are relaxed and it is easy to tape too tightly.

Step 9

Take a single strip of tape. Start from the inside of the foot and pull up across the front of the ankle, taking it behind the calf, spiraling around and up the shin. Tear tape. Repeat coming from the opposite side of the foot, creating an "X" on the front of the ankle joint, spiraling the tape behind the calf and then up the front of the shin, ending where you already put closing strips. Tear tape.

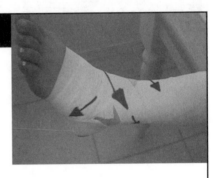

Step 10

Finished product resembles an ankle tape job, leaving no openings or "gaps" in the tape where the skin can get pinched by the tape and cause a cut or blister. Remember, no tape on the ball of the foot or the bottom of the heel.

Shin Splints

Shin splints is a generic term for pain radiating up and down the shin, either on the right or left, or simply the entire region. It can arise from a host of injuries, which are all generally treated in much the same manner. If the pain persists for several weeks, the athlete should be seen by a sports medicine orthopedist to ensure that there is no fracture or stress fracture, or other injury which would require further intervention. Taping for shin splints can be used alone or in conjunction with arch and/or ankle taping techniques. Shin splints are often associated with running in worn out shoes with little arch support, arch injuries/pain, overuse, or poor mechanics. An athlete should examine running shoes and re-evaluate the surfaces on which they run or workout to determine if the surface may be too rigid and therefore contributing to the injury, or that their running shoes are aging and need to be replaced.

Step 1

Begin by placing the heel on a roll of tape and asking athlete to keep their weight forward over the leg by lunging forward while you are taping, to reduce chances of taping too tightly. For best results, do not have any tape go above the bottom of the belly of the calf muscle as indicated by the red line at right.

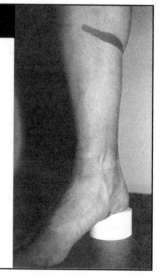

Step 2

Apply pre-wrap to area to be taped. Use as thin of a layer of pre-wrap possible to increase the ability of the tape to adhere to the leg for a longer period of time.

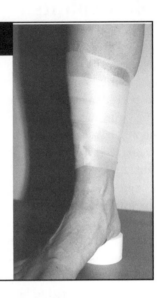

Step 3

Apply single strips beginning straight across leg, going behind leg & circling up and diagonally across front of the shin. This will give an appearance of a "V-shape". Direction of tape depends on where the pain is. If pain runs up the outside of leg, begin on inside, wrapping around leg so it comes diagonally across shin pulling muscle back towards area of pain.

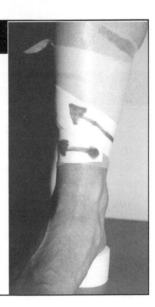

Step 4

When all strips have been applied from the ankle to bottom of belly of the calf muscle, it should look like this.

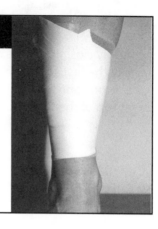

Step 5

Apply 2 strips of tape up the inside of the leg, and 2 strips up the outside of the leg to give added support.

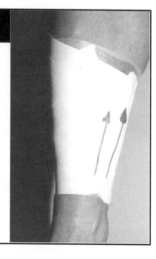

Step 6

Apply closing strips exactly like the first strip, one at the bottom, one in middle, and one at top of the tape job.

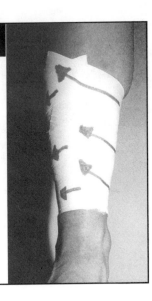

Knee

The knee can suffer countless different injuries as it is a complex joint bearing the weight of the majority of the body. It is not a simple task to evaluate an injury and determine the proper taping technique to best support an injury. When an athlete comes into Sports Med at competitions and wants their "knee" taped, I have to ask several important questions before I can determine which taping technique is best suited. I have to ask:

1. What type of injury is it, ligament, muscle or bone? Do you know?
2. When did it happen, how long ago? What happened? Did you hear or feel anything weird or painful at that time or since then?
3. Have you seen a physician, physical therapist or certified athletic trainer about this injury yet? If so, what were their recommendations?
4. Where does it hurt? Exact point of pain and tenderness.
5. When does it hurt? When you kick, squat, bend, walking up/down stairs?
6. What have you been doing for it? Has it helped at all?
7. Are you still growing?
8. Are you involved in any other sports which may have contributed to or aggravated this problem?

Answers to these questions help to give me direction as to what needs to be done to get the athlete through the competition, but also what I need to tell the athlete to do for the best recovery from the injury once they return home. In many cases, they have no idea what the injury is, have not seen a medical professional, and do not know how it happened, leaving me to start from ground zero. I will first follow the procedures of evaluation explained later in this book to try to determine if there is a possible fracture, or if the damage is to tendon, muscle, ligament, or cartilage. There are five major ligaments supporting the knee, as well as the meniscus (cartilage in between the bones), and numerous muscle tendons and bursas which could have been damaged or irritated.

Since most of you are not medical professionals I am not going to try to instruct you on determining the exact structure damage, but you do need some guidance. Generally speaking, if the pain is on the outside or inner side of the knee joint, at the joint, it most likely involves a ligament or meniscus. If the pain feels like it is in between the bones of the upper leg and lower leg, it is most likely the meniscus as well. If there is an instability problem, that is the knee bends or slides in directions it should not normally, it is most likely a ligament injury. You have a ligament on the outside of your knee to prevent outward bending (lateral collateral ligament, LCL), and an opposing one on the inner side of the knee (medial collateral ligament, MCL), which prevents your knee from bending toward the other knee in an inward direction. You then also have two ligaments running from the bone of the upper leg to the lower leg directly through the knee joint which prevent forward sliding (anterior cruciate ligament, ACL) or backward sliding (posterior cruciate ligament, PCL) of the knee. You also have muscle tendons running directly down the back of the knee, as well as ones that run across the front of the knee enabling motion, and along both sides of the knee.

These injuries will usually not simply have pain at the joint but a little bit above or below, or even extending a good distance up the leg, where ligament and cartilage/meniscus injuries are usually defined by a more localized point of pain at the knee joint itself. From this information we can determine the style of taping necessary to help protect the knee and hopefully help reduce the chances of further injury, although there is never any guarantee that tape alone can do that. So, let's start with the ligament injuries of the knee.

Step 1

Start position for all ligament support tape jobs begins by placing a roll of tape (or other suitable object) under the heel of the leg to be taped. Ask the athlete to lean their weight (if possible) into the knee to be taped keeping the knee bent, to expand the muscles & reduce the chance of getting the tape too tight.

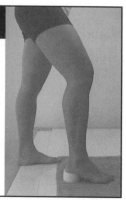

Step 2

Apply adherent spray & pre-wrap to entire area, including area above and below the knee.

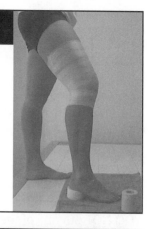

Step 3

Apply 2 "base strips" (to support the tape job), around the thigh about ½ way up the leg, pulling with steady tension but not too tight so as not to restrict motion. If this strip is too loose, the entire tape job will slide down the leg like a sock. Apply 1 strip around the lower leg between the knee and the bulk of the calf muscle. This strip is very easy to get too tight, so do it lightly.

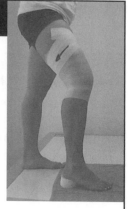

Step 4

Apply strips of tape creating an "X" directly over the point of pain at the joint line. Repeat with a second "X" moving the strips slightly closer to the patella (kneecap). If the injury is on the opposite side of the knee indicating a probable MCL injury, the same technique is performed on the opposite side.

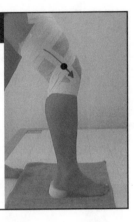

Step 5

If the athlete feels pain when they put their foot down to stop the motion and the thigh keeps sliding forward, it is highly probable that they have an ACL injury. For an ACL type injury you repeat the "X" on both the outer & inner sides of the knee, forming a diamond around the patella (kneecap). DO NOT put any of the tape strips directly over the patella (kneecap).

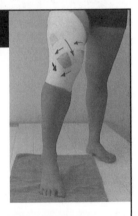

Step 6

Lastly, apply closing strips of tape, one rotation around the leg at a time. Tear tape and repeat until the entire area above the knee and just below the knee is covered and secured, as pictured.

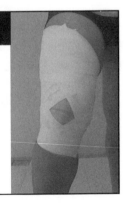

Taping for a hyperextended knee (which normally involves injured muscle tendons) is the same as taping for the Posterior Cruciate Ligament or PCL (which keeps the lower leg from sliding backwards at the knee when pressure is applied), or pain localized behind the knee, with the focus being on the back of the knee. First position the athlete as you did previously, with the heel on a roll of tape, knee bent, body weight in the involved knee. Then spray adherent spray over the entire area to be taped, both above and below the knee, front and back of the leg, trying to avoid spraying directly behind the knee. Apply the pre-wrap and base strips as previously described. Now, take your position to the rear of the athlete to complete the next few steps.

Step 1

Start your tape from the base strip high on the thigh, from either the front or side of the leg, taking the tape diagonally down and across the back of the leg and knee.

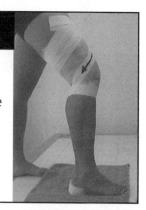

Step 2

Attach the other end to the base strip around the lower leg on the inner side of the leg. This strip is simply placed on the leg without any pulling or tightening. Make sure the end of the tape attaches to the base strip below the knee, not at the knee joint itself, as pictured.

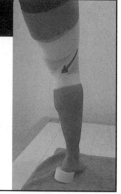

Step 3

Repeat from the opposite side. You can repeat Steps 1-2 to create a 2nd X for more stability if necessary. Return to the front of the leg & apply closing strips as with other knee tape jobs, being cautious not to pull tape tight around the lower leg.

Quite often I find another Certified Athletic Trainer who has developed a unique taping style that I end up incorporating into the many techniques that I use for various sports, but rarely do I learn of a new style from an athlete who I have been taping for years. But it does happen, and the next technique is a modification developed by one of my USA National Taekwondo Team members, Josh Coleman. Now, I have been taping various body parts of Josh since he was very young, as a Junior Team member and finally as a Senior National Team member. Josh injured his knee a few years ago, and we have been trying to put him back together for competition ever since. He finally had the knee surgically repaired, but when we started taping him for support while he was recovering he did not like the way the tape was restricting his movement, and yet he knew he still needed added support until it had completely recovered. The following technique is what he discovered and shared with me. By the way, Josh tapes himself quite often, as either he does not have the time to get taped or he does not have access to a Certified Athletic Trainer to do it for him, and does quite a good job (although I can't tell him that then he might never need me!).

Instead of criss-crossing the strips of tape over the point of pain at the knee joint, turn (causing a slight fold) the tape at the knee joint going back to the front of the leg when starting on the front, and towards the back when starting from the back, for the first layer. Josh likes to use a stronger form of tape Elastikon® by Johnson & Johnson. It is stronger than regular white athletic tape, and is allowed for use on the knee region by most martial art competitions. A second layer of white tape is applied over the Elastikon® in an X as previously described for added support.

Using Josh's technique versus the X style prevents the tape from going behind the knee and preventing full extension of the knee. It is a reduction in support, but gives enough support to reduce the chances of bending the leg out or inward. This is a very good taping technique when you need just a little bit of support, but still need to fully extend the knee, such as during poomse.

Result:

   vs.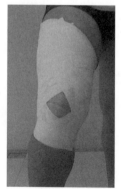

NOTE: not recommended for new injuries, high levels of weakness of the knee or for those preparing for surgery due to torn ligaments.

Knee: Patellar Tendonitis (Jumper's Knee) & Osgood Schlatter's Disease

Many jumping sports get a condition known as patellar tendonitis, or jumper's knee, from repetively jumping on a hard surface, putting stress and strain on the patellar tendon which attaches the four large quadriceps muscles (on front of the thigh) to a small bump (tibial tuberosity) just below the patella (kneecap). Pain is normally localized around this bump and the space between the patella and the bump just below the patella. Others get a similar pain because the bones of their legs are growing faster than the muscles can accommodate for, causing pain in the knee and just below in the area of the bump that the patellar tendon attaches to. This condition is most often seen in males, ages 10-15 years of age who have had a dramatic growth spurt in a short period of time. Martial artists are prone to both, even though it is not a jumping sport per se. A lot of the agility drills as well as jumping rope, can have the same effect, especially if they also run on a hard surface, such as concrete or asphalt. Now generally the best thing to do is to rest and ice these injuries, but sometimes practice and competition schedules are not that accommodating, and a pacifier for the injury is needed. You can purchase commercially produced CHO-PAT® straps, those brown straps that you often see basketball players wearing around the leg just under the knee, to help reduce the pain. You can also use pre-wrap, applied before any type of workout using the following technique.

Step 1

Using pre-wrap, circle the leg 10 times just below the patella (kneecap), being careful not to pull tight.

Step 2

Then take your hands and "roll" the pre-wrap down from the top and up from the bottom until you have a "strap".

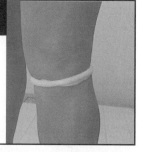

Step 3

To loosen, place your fingers between leg and strap and pull, stretching it to your own comfort. Simply tear to remove.

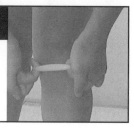

Hyperextended Elbow

In throwing sports, it is common to get your arm caught or "pinned" by your opponent's body forcing the elbow to bend beyond the comfortable extended (straight) position, damaging muscle tendons and ligaments. Hyperextension injuries can also occur from falling on an outstretched arm, or being struck in the outstretched arm when not prepared. This injury can be very painful, and take weeks, even months to heal. Taping is often a method of not only reducing the swelling and giving added support, but also reduces pain by not allowing the elbow to go beyond its normal range of motion. Even after the pain has subsided the elbow is still recovering and weak compared to what the athlete normally expects. When you have suffered a hyperextended elbow you need to see a medical professional such as your physician, physical therapist or certified athletic trainer to ensure that the joint itself has not been damaged (such as fracture), or the associated blood vessels or nerves. Such injuries if left untreated can lead to permanent damage and disability, so seek medical attention ASAP following a hyperextension injury of the elbow. You may be placed in a sling for comfort.

Step 1

First, position the elbow with a slight bend.

Step 2

Cover from mid-forearm to mid-upper arm with pre-wrap. Secure with 2 base strips above and below the elbow. Sometimes to better maintain the bend in the elbow, I position the athlete's hand under my arm and hold against my body.

Step 3

Take a strip of tape about the length from your shoulder to fingertips and twist, making it like a rope, leaving only the very ends not twisted.

Step 4

Attach one end of the tape to the base strip above the elbow on the back side of the arm, extending the "rope" diagonally down and across elbow.

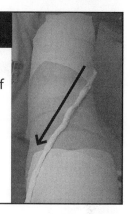

Step 5

Continue the rope around the forearm, then going diagonally up & across the elbow, attaching the end to the base strip of the upper arm.

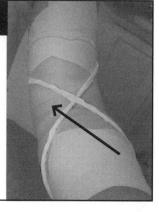

Step 6

Cover the rope with 2 single strips of tape creating an "X".

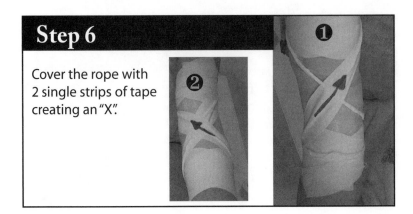

Step 7

Use closing strips on upper & lower arm to secure the "X" strips. Athlete should not be able to fully extend the elbow.

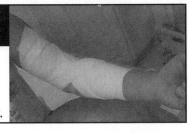

Tennis Elbow

Tennis elbow does not only occur in tennis players; that is simply where the first description of this injury came from. Tennis elbow, lateral epicondylitis, is pain on the outside of the arm just below or just above the elbow, and comes from repetitive activity which forces the arm to go out, such as reaching with a racquet for a tennis ball or holding a martial arts paddle while other athletes kick and punch it. In either case, it is usually an injury that takes a while to create as well as to heal. The taping techniques used for this type of injury mimic those used for patellar tendonitis of the knee, creating a CHO-PAT® style strap out of pre-wrap.

Even if the pain is below the elbow, create a "strap" just above the elbow, almost touching it.

Step 1

Using pre-wrap, circle the upper arm just above the elbow 10 times. Do not to pull tight, as this causes pain & tingling in the fingers.

Step 2

Next, roll the pre-wrap into a tube-like strap. To loosen, put your fingers between the strap and your arm and pull until comfortable. Tear off to remove.

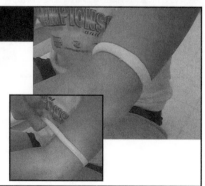

Wrist & Hand

The wrist takes a lot of abuse from punching and gripping in martial arts which is not actually what it was designed to do. A good weight training and strengthening program, as previously discussed, is the best prevention to injury in this region. Females, and low weight-class males, are often more susceptible to injuries in this area due to lack of large muscle content. Strengthening of these muscles does not mean bulking of muscles, but simply increasing the power of the muscles in the region, greatly reducing the chance of injury.

If an injury does occur, though, the following taping techniques can aid the athlete during the recovery period. In the sport of taekwondo the hands are not to be taped as for boxing, as this would give an unfair advantage, although other forms of martial arts require the hands to be taped. The taping technique below allows for taping of the wrist or wrist and hand without taping the knuckles of the hand and therefore avoiding a boxer's tape job as required by USA Taekwondo competition guidelines.

Step 1

Position hand with a straight wrist and fingers spread before applying pre-wrap.

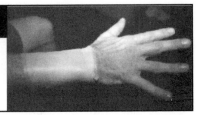

INCORRECT POSITIONS FOR WRIST & HAND FOR TAPING:

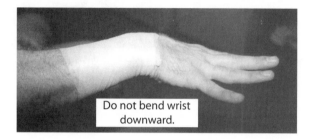

Do not bend wrist downward.

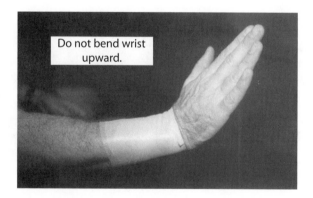

Do not bend wrist upward.

Step 2

Apply single strips of tape to the wrist.* Repeat layering 2-3 times.

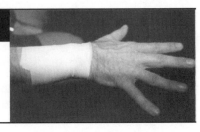

* DO NOT continuously wrap tape around the wrist or it will be too tight!

If you need a stronger tape job add in the hand by using single strips from the wrist across the palm of the hand running towards the thumb as in step 3 below.

Step 3

Place your thumb in the palm of the hand as you tape it in order to help prevent the tape from getting too tight, and causing the hand to curl.

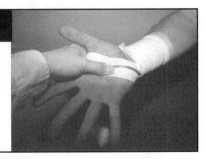

Step 4

Continue through the web of the hand next to the thumb & back to the wrist.* Repeat 2-3 times.

*You may want to fold the tape as it passes through the webbing to prevent blisters.

Step 5

You then add another layer of tape to wrist to close the tape job.*

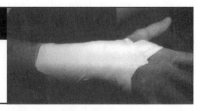

*Ensure tape does not pass over the knuckles as it is prohibited in some forms of martial arts competitions.

Fingers & Thumbs

Many martial arts athletes get fingers jammed or pulled in the wrong direction during competition or weapon use, or simply bend them the "wrong" way by getting them caught in their uniform. As Murphy's Law would have it, these are the exact same places which then get jammed time and time again, never truly healing. Jammed fingers can become very swollen and remain painful for long periods of time, some for as long as six months. Taping can help protect the injury, but needs to be supplemented with proper injury therapy and strengthening in order to be able to return to its original condition.

The following are several different techniques, which can also be used in conjunction with wrist and hand taping techniques for even further support of the muscles of the thumb and fingers. If a finger or thumb does become jammed **NEVER** pull it back out. This opens the joint causing a greater flow of blood to the area, leading to massive swelling, giving the feeling of a heartbeat in the joint. Simply Buddy Tape the finger to an adjacent finger. If a finger is dislocated you will need to have someone trained in reducing dislocations put your finger back into place. **DO NOT** attempt to reduce a finger yourself as you may catch a blood vessel or nerve in the process. **NEVER** reduce a dislocated thumb as a fracture is normally associated with a dislocated thumb. If your thumb does become dislocated, immediately seek the attention of a sports medicine orthopedist or go to a hospital for the joint to be properly cared for.

Buddy Taping of Fingers

Step 1

Have athlete hold injured finger near adjacent finger to be buddy taped with.

Step 2

Using 1" tape, wrap tape around finger between the last 2 joints of the injured finger,   NEVER TAPE OVER JOINTS.

Step 3

Continue with tape wrapping injured finger to adjacent finger between last 2 joints of the finger.

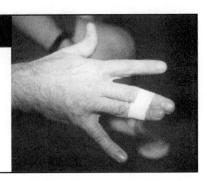

Step 4

Apply a 2nd strip of tape between finger and hand to better protect the finger from further injury.

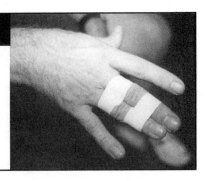

CAUTION: Never buddy tape all 4 fingers together, only 2 at a time.

Thumb Taping

Step 1

Begin by properly positioning thumb by asking athlete to grip your hand.

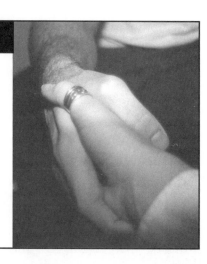

Step 2

Ask athlete to "uncurl" fingers from your hand but not the thumb, holding it in position as you remove your hand.

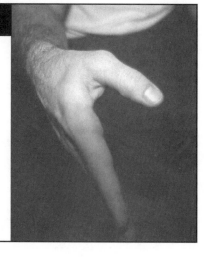

Step 3

With thumb in place apply 2 base strips to the wrist to anchor tape for thumb taping.

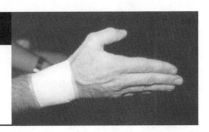

Step 4

Apply 1" or split 1 ½" tape by beginning on the wrist.

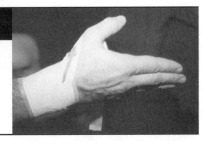

Step 5

Continue a single strip around thumb, pulling thumb towards palm without pulling tape tight.

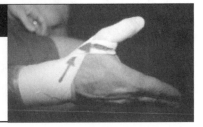

Step 6

Repeat steps 4 and 5 three to five times, tearing after each strip. Never pull tight.

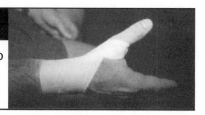

Step 7

Close by applying 1 ½" tape from thumb down and around the wrist to secure tape 2-3 times.

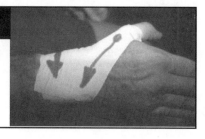

Donut & Horseshoe Pads

Certified Athletic Trainers (ATC's) have long since mastered the art of using padding to not only protect from further injury, but also to encourage containment of swelling, helping to reduce secondary injuries to surrounding tissue (such as reducing the swelling in the foot and toes following an ankle injury). Two of the tried-and-true methods of pressure padding are called donut pads and horseshoe pads. The donut is a round piece of foam padding with the center cut out, just like a donut. The horseshoe pad is a "U" shaped piece of foam similar to a horseshoe. Both can be purchased commercially from any sports medicine supply company or can be individually produced using various types of foam or felt padding cut to fit the athlete's needs. Below, these pads are cut from an Army bed roll purchased from an Army-Navy Surplus Store. It is very dense foam, so it holds its shape quite well. It is the same padding that we use to produce protective instep pads, as it does not absorb sound and may actually intensify the sound of a hit. One thing to warn the athlete about, though, is using pressure pads usually brings out the discolorization of a bruise much quicker. You might notice that the area around and under the horseshoe pad becomes extremely discolored, in many shades of blue, purple and yellow. This is normal and expected as the pad initiates the compression of the injured area. This "color" actually lets you know the area is going through the proper healing process while reducing the amount of swelling in the area. This is what is supposed to happen, so do not worry about it, and yes, they usually are ugly in appearance.

Donut Pad

Horseshoe Pad

The donut pad is used around an injury, such as a bad bruise or hematoma, with the opening of the donut being placed directly over the injury. The donut pad disperses the energy from a hit out and around the injury, allowing the injury not to sustain further insult or damage. The shin is a very common area that the donut is utilized. There tends to be a lot of bruising from "clashes" and very little muscle protection for the nerves in the area, so it is very painful when receiving multiple hits to the same point. Below is the use of a donut pad for a shin contusion or bruise. You can use either single strips of regular white athletic tape, or if the muscles are quite bulky, you can apply the pad using elastic tape (being sure not to pull too tight when wrapping) then cover with white athletic tape, as seen below.

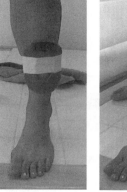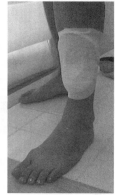

The horseshoe pad is used in conjunction with swollen joints or areas of the body to reduce swelling from proceeding into other local areas. The ankle is one of the most common areas ATC's like to use horseshoe pads, probably because we deal with so many ankle sprains that become very swollen if left untreated. In addition to the ice therapy and elevation (discussed later), the horseshoe pad can help reduce further swelling in the area or associated areas, reducing the chances of secondary injury occurring from the swelling. The following shows a horseshoe pad being used on an ankle in conjunction with an ace wrap, instead of tape. Remember to always remind athletes NOT TO SLEEP with the pad and ace wrap left on, as it may reduce circulation too much, and lead to further damage or permanent disability.

Step 1

Place the horseshoe pad around the ankle so the open end faces up the leg towards the heart (always face open end towards heart if possible).

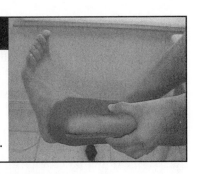

Step 2

Secure with a couple of strips of tape directly to the skin.

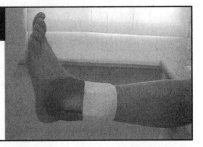

Step 3

Using the same basic technique as described for the figure-8 and heel lock for ankle taping, only this picture begins the wrap from the foot instead of from the ankle. Either method is correct as long as you are locking the heel from both sides.

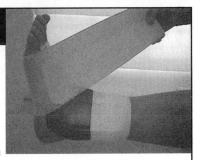

Step 4

Leave the toes exposed as any sign of the wrap being too tight (for example purple coloring) will be exhibited in the toes or toenails.

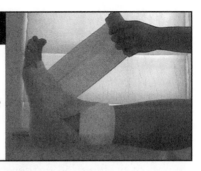

Step 5

You can cover the heel with the wrap (if using a 6-inch wrap this is going to happen), since this technique IS NOT for practice or competition, but for the initial stages of injury care immediately following the injury.

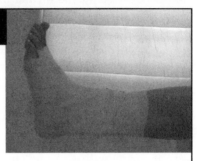

Padding an injured area to help reduce swelling

As with all new injuries, once the possibility of a fracture or dislocation has been ruled out ice treatments need to begin. The area needs to be kept wrapped or taped to apply compression and the limb needs to remain elevated as much as possible to reduce the chances of swelling and further damage to the tissue. Reduce the amount of time spent weight-bearing on the injured limb during the first three to five days to give the limb a chance to initiate the proper healing process. Taping and padding techniques, which are discussed in this chapter for various parts of the body, can aid in the treatment and support of an injured limb.

The pad lends support to the area making you feel better protected and supported. A horseshoe pad can be utilized basically for any area of the body that can be taped, wrapped or splinted. **Do not wear pad, tape or wrap** on an injured area to sleep in as it may slow the normal blood flow too much and cause pooling of blood and fluids in the injured area, the exact opposite of what you want to happen.

The above mentioned padding can be obtained from several sources, depending on the amount of money available to spend on such products. There are commercially produced pads in almost any shape (including horseshoe and donut pads) sold by sports medicine supply companies and athletic supply stores which can become rather pricey. When I do not have the funds to purchase such products I often contact local high school and college football programs and ask them to donate some old football pads that can be cut and used. One caution, when using football pads, make sure that you remove the hard plastic piece found inside of many football pads. A second place to obtain pads is from an Army/Navy/Military Surplus store by purchasing the foam bed-rolls used by our military personnel. These pads cut quite nicely, and can even make great instep pads. As a last resort you can always use cotton taped into a temporary pad. Use your imagination and you can probably find other sources of free padding.

Heel Pad & Taping

There are only a few instances which would allow for tape to be applied to the bottom of the heel of a martial art athlete, with the most prominent reasons being a bone bruise, bone spur or blister/cut of the bottom of the heel of the foot. With all of these the following technique should be used, but the athlete needs to be forewarned that as the tape collects dust and dirt it will become slippery, plus they will lose their "feel for the floor" from their heel.

Step 1

From a piece of dense foam cut a circle with a hole in it (donut pad). Place the opening of the donut pad so that the area of pain and/or injury is in the center, with the foam itself encircling but not touching the painful area. Use a piece of tape to hold in place.

Step 2

Using single strips of tape, first going around the foot.

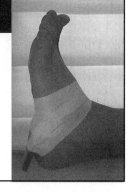

Step 3

Then make "horseshoe" strips (strips which look like a horseshoe, in which the ends do not touch) only going from one ankle under the foot to the other ankle, over the heel and back of pad.

Step 4

Follow up with 2 horseshoe strips running from the tape already on the foot behind the heel and back to the other side of the foot attaching to the instep tape.

Step 5

Close and secure the tape job with 2 more strips of tape around the ankle/leg, making sure that you are not overlapping layers of tape.

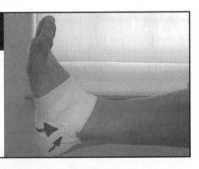

Step 6

Completed heel pad taping.

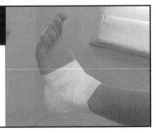

Elastic Bandage Wrapping

Elastic bandages are often used to wrap a brand new injury (within the first 72 hours) not only for support, but also for compression to help control some of the swelling that naturally occurs with an injury. Elastic wraps are also used to apply pressure pads, such as the donut and horseshoe pads just discussed, as well as splinting materials to help immobilize the injury until you can seek medical attention. You can use the elastic wrap to immobilize sprains, strains, dislocations, subluxations, separations and fractures. You can also use an elastic bandage to dress an open wound, helping to hold sterile gauze in place.

It is not recommended that you sleep with an elastic bandage on, unless told to do so by a medical professional, as swelling tends to increase during the night. The wrap can then cut off circulation to body parts beyond where the elastic bandage is being used, causing further injury, and on rare occasions permanent disability.

Sometimes you will see an elastic wrap used in practice or competition on the wrist, knee, ankle or hip/thigh/groin. For the wrist, knee and ankle it is preferred that you use a neoprene sleeve or tape, as the elastic bandage tends to slide down your arm or leg rendering it useless, and it is often very bulky. It is common, though, to use an elastic bandage to wrap the hip/thigh/groin region for practice and competition, although I still prefer an athlete to use a neoprene sleeve or tape as the strength lasts much longer. You can use an elastic bandage to wrap pretty much any injury or body part, but what I am going to show are the three areas you are most likely to wrap: ankle (usually a sprain), hip/thigh/groin (usually a strained muscle or tendon), and shoulder (usually a dislocation or separation, or muscle strain).

Elastic Bandage Wrapping: Ankle

You will apply the elastic wrap to an ankle in much the same fashion as the figure-8 and lock combo used when taping the ankle. The biggest difference is that you start the wrap on the foot rather than on the ankle, but if you do start it on the ankle instead of the foot it is okay. You can add a pressure pad in the shape of a horseshoe, just make sure that the open end of the horseshoe is pointing up the leg and not towards the toes, as then you only push swelling towards the toes. The preferable size of elastic bandage to use for an ankle is a 3" or 4" wrap, but a 6" is usually all that is available, so we will demonstrate the technique using a 6" wrap. If dealing with a very small foot, a 2-inch wrap may be optimal, or even a 3", if either one is available. If you have small children I highly recommend keeping a few smaller wraps in your first aid kit.

Step 1

Apply pad, if desired, securing with a single strip of tape to hold it in place. Begin the elastic bandage on the instep then circle down underneath the foot and come up on the outside of the foot. Take the wrap diagonally across the front of the ankle joint and then directly over the inner ankle. From here go behind the leg coming out as a heel lock just beneath the outside ankle.

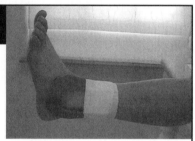

Step 2

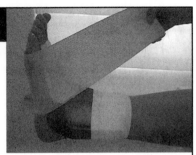

Continuing from the outside heel lock go under the foot bringing the wrap back out and up on the inside of the foot, taking it diagonally across the front of the ankle joint, going directly over the outside ankle, before taking the wrap behind the leg and emerging under the inner ankle as a heel lock. Repeat as many times as needed to use up the entire elastic wrap.

Step 3

Close with tape, or metal bandage clips. Notice you CAN cover both the ball of the foot and heel as this is not for competition.

Elastic Bandage Wrapping: Hip, Thigh, & Groin

The hip, thigh and groin region are very often injured in martial arts participation. The thigh muscles can be strained from the front (quadriceps muscle), the rear (hamstrings muscles), the outer edge (IT Band) or the inner thigh (groin muscles). The thigh can also suffer severe bruising, especially to the quadriceps muscle and the IT Band, particularly if you use your leg to block like one of USA Taekwondo's famous Olympians.

The ligaments of the hip can also be sprained, especially in the throwing forms of martial art, where legs and bodies tend to get all tied up together, often taking much longer to heal than muscle strains. Strained muscles also occur in the posterior hip or buttocks region, making it very painful not only to kick, but simply to move or turn the leg outwards. The hip can involve a strain of the hip flexor muscles which run up the front of the hip joint, or a bad bruise on the outside edge, better known as a hip pointer.

American football players wear pads in their pants to reduce the number of injuries from hits to the hip, but the martial artist wears no such protection. The hip joint, what is known as the ball and socket joint, can sustain repeated impacts to the bone leading to stress fractures in the area, or compression of the protective cartilage in between the bones. I presently have one case where the physician believes these repeated hits to the hip joint may have lead to the development of hip dysplasia, a condition of the hip in which the ball actually begins to break down and hip replacement surgery is often the end result. But I also had an athlete put into taekwondo upon being diagnosed with hip dysplasia at a very young age, to increase her mobility and flexibility to reduce her pain, and she eventually became a National Team member. She did later have hip replacement surgery once she retired and now runs her own martial arts program. In extremely rare cases the hip can be subluxed or dislocated, at which point a ride in an ambulance is necessary to have a physician reduce the dislocation, putting the leg back into the hip joint where it belongs. Unfortunately, the hip joint has very poor blood supply, and therefore often takes a long time to actually heal, in some rare cases never fully healing, case in point Bo Jackson. He took numerous hits to his hip from playing American football, suffering a serious hip pointer towards the end of the season. The hip pointer never truly healed as the bone became necrotic (bone death) and he eventually had to have hip replacement surgery ending both his professional football and baseball careers.

The difference between using an elastic bandage wrap for the various leg injuries which can and do occur in martial arts is the positioning of the wrap and the direction which you take the wrap on the leg. You always want to have the wrap pulling the muscle back into its normal position, not away from, so consider this when trying to determine which angle of pull you will need. For hamstring injuries and quadriceps injuries on the outer edge of the leg, IT band, hip flexor, and buttocks region, you will take the wrap from the front of the leg, through the space between the legs to the posterior and then up and around from the outside of the leg. For the groin, hamstring and quadriceps injuries on the inner portion of the leg you will begin the wrap from the posterior, pulling the wrap through the space between the legs, up and around the leg. The wrap can be used only on the thigh, or can also go up and around the waist to help keep the wrap from sliding down the leg, or for cases of high hip flexor pain. NOTE: applying the wrap above the hip joint, up and around the waist, will cause the hip to not fully extend, and may be annoying to some athletes while very helpful to others.

Begin as you do to tape a knee by having the athlete place their heel on a roll of tape, bending the involved knee and leaning slightly into the injured leg (if possible) to expand the muscles and reduce the chance of getting the wrap too tight.

Step 1

Use adherent spray over the entire area to be wrapped, to help the wrap stay in place better. Determine the position of the wrap and direction of pull.

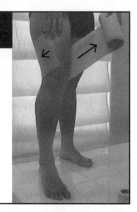

Step 2

Always begin below the point of injury or pain and work up to above the point of pain. Here is an example of a quadriceps wrap, where the injury/pain is towards the inner thigh region, so the wrap pulls it up and across, coming from the posterior through the legs, up and over the thigh.

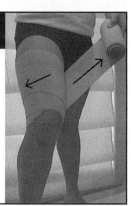

Step 3

Secure the end of the wrap with tape, applying the tape in the same direction you were wrapping, covering completely, working from knee up to the hip.

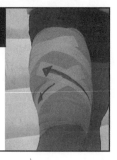

For the thigh alone, without wrapping up around the hip joint and waist, a standard 6-inch elastic wrap is sufficient. When wrapping up around the waist, a 6-inch double-length wrap will be required. For a groin injury, or other injuries high on the thigh/hip region, a 6-inch double-length wrap needs to be utilized as shown below.

Step 1

Wrapping is the same as previously described, only you will go around the hip & waist 1-3 times (to athlete's comfort).

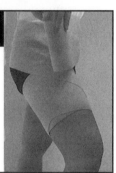

Step 2

For the groin come up between the legs from the posterior, wrapping diagonally up across the hip joint, behind the back then around onto the stomach, diagonally crossing the hip and circling the thigh.

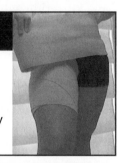

Step 3

Once again, secure with athletic tape, going in the same direction of the wrap, completely covering the thigh using single strips of tape, starting from knee and working upwards. Usually only one layer of tape is needed, but you can apply a second loosely at the bottom, middle and top.

It is always good to ask the athlete if they need to use the bathroom prior to wrapping them, as this becomes a difficult feat once wrapped, especially for females. Wrapping should be done over the athlete's underwear, and in some cases athletes will also wear tights, sliders, bike shorts or other tight fitting undergarments. It is not recommended you attempt to wrap over boxer shorts or other loose fitting garments as it will not be as effective or comfortable. The wrap should simply be laid upon the body part, as any tension, particularly in the first layers will become restrictive, causing pain, loss of mobility and eventual loss of proper blood flow. Be cautious, tighter is definitely not better here. Also, caution the athlete that when they first step down on the wrapped leg it is going to feel "weird" and maybe even a little tight and restrictive, but to try working out with it for a little while, long enough to sweat, as it often loosens with sweating anyway. The athlete should not feel any pinching or sharp pains, if so the wrap needs to be immediately removed. Although, sometimes if it is a hairy-legged individual there may be a little pulling from the adherent spray on the hairs as the wrap first begins to adjust. If it is painful it should be removed and re-wrapped.

Elastic Bandage Wrapping: Shoulder

The shoulder, much like the hip, is a very complicated joint which actually involves more than one joint, therefore complicating matters more. The shoulder is less likely to be injured in kicking and punching forms of martial arts than it is in throwing forms. Typically in kicking/punching forms of martial arts the shoulder is injured from being kicked or punched directly into the shoulder, kicked or punched from behind the shoulder, the arm is kicked hard putting pressure on the shoulder joints, or the athlete falls on an outstretched arm. The most common injuries from these mechanisms are a dislocated or subluxed shoulder, separated shoulder at the AC joint, rotator cuff strain, cartilage sprain or tear, or fractures of the humerus (bone of the upper arm), acromian or the clavicle (collarbone). In throwing forms of martial arts, the athlete often lands on top or back of the shoulder or has the arm forcibly forced beyond normal limits behind their back. They can also fall on an outstretched arm, dislocating the shoulder, as well as fracturing the forearm, and/or dislocating the elbow, often with their opponent falling on top of them complicating the injury even more.

Shoulder injuries are a "nagging" type of injury because we use our arms not only for martial arts participation, but for daily hygiene routines, such as brushing/combing the hair and teeth, eating/ drinking, washing our hair, etc., so if the joint is painful to move we then need assistance for these daily routines. The other problem is that we often, once injured, simply want to rest the joint, not using it at all, but this can lead to a more serious condition known as frozen shoulder, from the hardening of scar tissue in the joint.

So, flexibility work as soon as your medical professional will allow is paramount. Even after you begin stretching and strengthening the shoulder, you will probably still have some pain and fatigue, so wrapping it for support can be beneficial. The shoulder can also be taped, but it is a very difficult technique which some don't even benefit from, so it is not too often used. Instead of using an elastic bandage wrap, you can also purchase a commercially produced shoulder "harness", which restricts the movement of the shoulder to varying ranges. But if you do not have the money to spend on such an apparatus, wrapping can be the next best thing, especially to immobilize until you reach your physician, physical therapist or certified athletic trainer for further evaluation.

Step 1

First, position the arm in a comfortable position where you can move the wrap around the joint without it being too difficult. Usually having the shoulder and elbow bent at 30° is a good working position. As with the elbow, you may need to hold the arm in position.

Step 2

Begin wrap on upper arm near armpit, going around the arm twice, coming from under the arm and continuing up over the arm.

Step 3

On the third time coming from underneath the arm go diagonally across the top of the shoulder and contine diagonally across the back and under the opposite arm/armpit. Bring the wrap across the chest, (trying not to pull too tight over the breasts of females). Continue up towards the shoulder, crossing the shoulder and going down and around the upper arm. Repeat 2-3 times until the 6" double-length wrap is used up. Secure with tape or metal clamps.

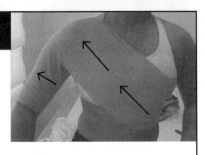

Step 4

If you need to completely immobilize the shoulder and/or elbow for transport to the hospital or physician's office you can add another wrap like a sling. Begin by positioning the arm in a comfortable position close to the body.

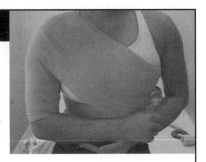

Step 5

With a new elastic bandage, wrap around the forearm twice. On the third rotation around the forearm, take the wrap up and over the opposite shoulder you just wrapped, taking it diagonally across the back to the already wrapped upper arm.

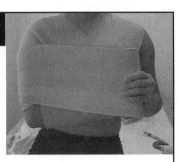

Step 6

Continue the wrap across the chest, passing the wrap across the forearm, leaving the fingers exposed. Take the wrap once more around the back, coming back to the front again, tying off the wrap at the forearm as pictured.

Chapter Four Key Points

✦ Taping cannot prevent injuries nor does it weaken joints.

✦ Taping should not be used in place of a conditioning and strengthening program to heal a weak or injured joint, but rather as part of a complete program.

✦ Tape loses approximately fifty percent of its supportive strength after only thirty minutes of sweating.

✦ Tape can provide compression of swelling after an injury and support weak muscles, tendons and ligaments during rehabilitation.

✦ Correct taping does not impede kicking performance, or movement of any joint.

✦ If you plan to tape a joint for competition, practice with the joint taped prior to the event to adjust to the feeling of the tape.

✦ Know the rules regarding the amount and type of taping permitted for your competition.

✦ Tape or spray adherent can cause skin irritation if you have an allergic reaction to latex, rubber or adhesive.

✦ A proper tape job is firm but not overly tight. Taping too tightly can cause many problems or even further injury.

Care of Injuries

5

care of common martial arts injuries

Injuries are an inevitable part of any athletic program if an athlete remains in the sport for any length of time. As already noted the best care of an injury is to prevent it from ever occurring, but in the event that injury does occur, the injury should be properly evaluated and treated as soon as possible. If the injury is more than a simple "minor" injury the athlete should always be seen by a certified and licensed sports medicine professional such as a certified athletic trainer (ATC), physical therapist (PT), or physician as soon as possible.

Like any other sport, there are several common injuries associated with participation in martial arts. These injuries will be discussed in the following pages. The most common injuries that occur in martial arts include, but are not limited to: ankle sprains, wrist strains/sprains, patellar tendonitis, turf toe, hamstring/quad strains, shin splints, hyperextended elbows, groin strains, low back strains & sprains, knee sprains, rotator cuff strains, AC separations, forearm/hand fractures, neck/spine injury, concussions/jaw injury, facial lacerations, shoulder dislocations, foot/toe fractures, dehydration, and board/weapon injuries. All injuries should be properly evaluated and treated as soon as possible.

For Coaches and Instructors

Response to injury or possible injury

There may be times when an athlete under your instruction is injured and a qualified medical specialist is not available to evaluate the injury. How do you as a non-medical person evaluate an injury situation without really knowing much about the human body? First, all instructors and coaches should be required to have First Aid (preferably Sports Medicine First Aid) & CPR Certification, and maintain this certification on an annual basis. Certification can be obtained through such organizations specializing in these certifications, including but not limited to the American Red Cross, American Lung Association, and the National Safety Council. All injuries should be approached in the same manner, by first analyzing the situation. Is this a possible life-threatening injury? Is the person conscious and breathing? If the person is not breathing or has no pulse you must immediately begin basic life support by using rescue breathing or CPR as needed while you send someone else to call 911.

If the person is breathing and is conscious then you begin by following some basic guidelines known as **HOPS**. HOPS simply stands for History, Observation, Palpation, and Special tests. Obviously if the injury is only a bump or a small scrape going through HOPS is not necessary. Clean the wound properly after determining it is only a simple scrape, and cover before allowing athlete to return to activity. Any bleeding wound must be covered for both the safety of the individual and those working out with the athlete. But for any other situation the following are the guidelines set forth by HOPS:

HISTORY — After calming the athlete, which with some may take a few moments, you need to ask some basic questions pertaining to the injury before ever touching or moving the athlete:

For Coaches and Instructors

1. What is the athlete's name? (especially if athlete was hit in the head)

2. What happened and how did it happen? Which way did it turn, etc. Get the details as the athlete remembers what happens. Remember though, the athlete may have no idea what happened or how it happened even if he or she did not lose consciousness.

3. Where does it hurt? Is this the only place? Is the pain sharp (stabbing) or dull (aching) or something in between? Get details

4. Have you ever hurt this before? When? Have you had surgery and/or rehab?

5. Did you hear a pop or snap, did it "give out" or "lock up" or did you feel something grab? Get details on everything the person heard or felt.

Try to get as much information about the situation as possible. If anyone else saw what happened then have that person describe to you in detail exactly what he or she saw.

OBSERVATION — At this point you are still **not** moving or touching the injury or the athlete, but simply observing the situation. You may also still be constantly reassuring and calming the injured person. You need to ask yourself the following questions as you observe the situation and injury:

1. What is the level of consciousness/mental state of the athlete? Does he/she appear to be off somewhere else or is completely able to answer all of your questions appropriately?

For Coaches and Instructors

2. Is there a noticeable deformity of the bone or muscle? Is the limb in a strange position? Does it look as though a joint is dislocated or out of joint? Is any of the skin torn, scraped or pierced?

3. Is there external bleeding or yellow body fluid coming from the injury or anywhere else? Where is it coming from? Is it oozing or squirting? If there is bleeding occurring the bleeding must be brought under control before any other testing is completed. At this point you need to use some gauze or other clean material to apply pressure to the area while elevating the limb above the level of the heart, if possible, and if no fracture is suspected until the bleeding has ceased, **unless a head, neck or spine injury has not been ruled out.**

NEVER MOVE AN ATHLETE FROM THE POSITION IN WHICH THEY FELL IN THESE SITUATIONS UNTIL IT HAS BEEN DETERMINED THAT THERE IS NO HEAD, NECK OR SPINE INJURY INVOLVED.

Simply try to apply gauze to control the bleeding while invoking your Emergency Medical Plan (discussed in Chapter 7). **IF A YELLOW FLUID IS SEEN, THIS IS POSSIBLY FLUID FROM THE BRAIN AND/OR SPINAL CORD AND YOU MUST CALL 911 IMMEDIATELY.** Do not move or allow athlete to move until the paramedics arrive. If a head, neck or spine injury is suspected, do not allow the athlete to eat or drink anything as they may need to have diagnostic tests or surgery and cannot within 6 hours of eating or drinking without the possibility of complications. NEVER REMOVE HEADGEAR (INCLUDING CHIN STRAP) OR CHEST PROTECTOR UNTIL HEAD, NECK & SPINE INJURY HAS BEEN RULED OUT.

PALPATION — Now you are going to begin palpation (gently touching) of the injured area, moving from a distal position (the farthest point on a bone from the point of injury) to the point

For Coaches and Instructors

of injury from both the superior (above the injury) and inferior (below the injury) regions. Ask the athlete what he/she is feeling as you palpate, with the athlete grading the amount of pain from one (least — barely any pain) to ten (most—being stabbed with a knife). Note any deformities (such as lumps, holes, jagged edges, etc) felt during palpation, as well as the level of pain upon palpation. Also note if you see any movement or change in the area of the injury as you are palpating, or if palpation in one area causes pain to shoot into another area. Be careful when doing palpations not to press too hard, in case there is a fracture you would not want to make it move.

If you see any movement or you cause increased pain there is good reason to suspect a possible fracture or dislocation even if you do not see a gross deformity. If a fracture or dislocation is suspected there is no need to continue evaluating, and instead the limb should be immobilized to reduce any movement while the athlete is being transported to a physician's office or hospital. Immobilization can be completed by using any sturdy substance such as a splint, board, rolled up magazine, etc tied to both sides of the injured limb and both joints above and below the site of injury, ensuring that the joints above and below the point of injury cannot move. This helps to prevent further damage from the movement of the fractured bone(s). The athlete should be seen by a physician, preferably a sports medicine orthopedist as soon as possible, either in the physician's office or the nearest hospital.

SPECIAL TESTS — These tests are performed to determine what has actually been injured and to what extent. **If a fracture or dislocation** is suspected these tests **should not be attempted.** These tests are simply used to see if the athlete will be able to complete the activity or competition, or whether treatment is necessary for the injury at that moment. These tests include several practical tests you can perform without having a medical background:

For Coaches and Instructors

1. Compression and percussion tests to determine if a fracture is present. When you tap on the bone at the point furthest from the injury does it cause increased or unbearable pain in the injury area? If you squeeze the bone gently at the opposite end away from the injury does it cause increased pain at the injury site? If either of these are a yes, suspect a fracture, immobilize the bone from the joints above and below the area of the injury and transport for further medical evaluation by a physician or in a hospital.

2. Active ROM (range of motion) tests to determine the amount of movement present. Ask the athlete to move the joint, but only if no fracture or dislocation is suspected. For example, for a possible sprained ankle ask the athlete to pull his or her toes and foot up and then point them down, followed by asking the athlete to turn the foot both in and out. Is there any great amount of pain on a scale from one to ten? Does the athlete appear to be able to move the joint without too much difficulty or not at all? Or does the athlete hesitate to move in a particular direction?

3. Passive ROM (range of motion) tests are where you take the body part through the same motions as you just asked the athlete to move a joint with your own hands, noting amount of and resistance to movement, and whether or not there is any increase in pain upon moving the joint.

4. Weightbearing ability and balance. If you do not suspect a fracture or dislocation, and if there is no great increase in pain when testing the range of motion, you need to determine whether or not an athlete can successfully stand and balance on the injured limb. This is particularly important during a competition when a decision must be made to continue or stop. If a person cannot bear weight on a limb or has poor balance the activity is ended at that point and injury treatment should be initiated immediately. Remind the athlete if he or she cannot move quickly and properly on a limb they cannot be expected to fight properly and therefore

For Coaches and Instructors

will lose the match and probably sustain further injury.

5. Functional tests which are specific to the needs of the activity. If the athlete is to continue the activity he or she must be able to demonstrate an ability to complete the necessary tasks of the activity, such as bouncing, spinning, kicking, punching, twisting, grabbing, etc. If the athlete cannot complete movements in a normal fashion the activity should be ended and injury treatment begun immediately.

Once treated, the injury, no matter how minor, needs to be recorded on an injury log sheet or on individual injury report form by the instructor present at the time of injury. This includes everything from a bandage to an ice bag to taping or wrapping, or requiring an athlete to be seen by a sports medicine professional.

For instructors and administrators, it is always wise to keep written records of all injuries occurring to athletes, and others, including the type of injury, what happened and what care (if any) was administered. This way if a person should say that they were not properly taken care of you have written proof of what happened and what was done for the individual. All such records should be maintained in a locking file cabinet in the office of the martial arts school, limiting access to the records to a few select responsible individuals.

Always follow up with the athlete at the next session to ensure proper treatment of the injury has been completed on a regular schedule. If the athlete has not followed proper injury care and management it is only going to prolong the amount of time before the athlete can return to normal activity. If ever in doubt as to the severity or extent of an injury, the athlete should be required to be seen by a sports medicine professional, preferably a certified athletic trainer and/or sports medicine orthopedist, before the athlete is allowed to return to normal practice and workout routines.

How do you determine the seriousness of an injury?

One of the things that is hard to determine when you are not a medical professional (such as a physician, ATC or PT) is how to judge the seriousness of an injury, and when to seek further medical attention for an injury. Sometimes what appears to be nothing to the untrained is an extremely serious injury, while others look very serious and are minor in nature. Often cuts to the face or head bleed dramatically and look horribly serious, but once the blood is cleaned up and controlled it is realized that it is only a cut, often less than an inch or so long. Some other injuries once the initial pain of the injury occurs, show no sign of pain and the athlete then believes it was nothing. Such is the case with many ligament ruptures of the knee, because the associated nerve is also damaged and can no longer send messages of pain to the brain. But the knee itself is unstable when trying to perform particular motions, such as spinning. So, here are some basic guidelines to get you started:

• If you have bleeding from anywhere on the body, including the nose, that cannot be stopped by applying pressure and ice within 20 minutes the athlete needs to be taken to a medical facility.

• If bleeding is occurring from a laceration (cut) greater than ½ inch wide or ¼ inch deep, it should be sutured (stitches). If the laceration is on the face, anywhere, but especially around the eye or chin, you should request that either a plastic surgeon or an oral-maxillofacial physician do the suturing to reduce the chances of leaving an ugly scar. If you can go directly to their office you will probably have the nicest looking stitches. Often times in an emergency room they have so many patients to attend to that they are going to close the wound up in the quickest, easiest fashion, which may mean fewer and larger stitches, staples or glue. The glue can work quite well, but with small children they tend to pick at the glue scab and end up with an ugly scar.

• If an athlete is known to have a "bleeding" disorder such as hemophilia, any time there is an injury, especially if bleeding is involved, they need to see their physician to reduce the chances of complications.

• Anytime you see a deformity, assume there is a fracture or dislocation, immobilize the joint and send them to get an x-ray immediately. Do not attempt "to put it back into place" or pull it out.

• Anytime the athlete feels a numb or tingling sensation following an injury to any part of the body they should be seen by a physician, ATC or PT as soon as possible. If this sensation is associated with a head, neck or spine injury DO NOT MOVE THE ATHLETE. Call for an ambulance. NEVER remove the headgear or chest protector as they may actually be immobilizing the injury, which you could make dramatically worse by moving the athlete or the equipment.

• Any time an injury has occurred to the mouth causing a tooth or teeth to loosen, be pushed up into the gums, or break, they need to be seen by a surgical dentist or an oral-maxillofacial physician within 6 hours if they hope to save the tooth/teeth.

• If a lot of swelling occurs in a joint within the first 10-20 minutes, the athlete needs to be seen by a sports medicine orthopedic specialist as there may be a fracture or torn ligament/muscle involved.

• If swelling has not begun to slow down or go down in 3-5 days the athlete needs to be seen by a sports medicine orthopedic specialist.

• If at any time a bruise begins to get a hard lump, especially if it causes pain when moving, the athlete needs to be seen by a sports medicine orthopedic specialist.

• If athlete shows any signs of a moderate to serious head injury (discussed later in this chapter) the athlete needs to be seen by a medical professional.

• Any joint that appears unstable, such as a knee that does not "hold you up" or gives out; or a shoulder that an athlete can purposely "pop out of joint" even when no pain is associated with it.

• If athlete begins vomiting within a few minutes to a few hours of an injury, they need to be seen at a medical facility immediately.

• Any time moderate to sharp pain is felt anywhere, the athlete needs to be seen by a medical professional

• Any suspected 2° or 3° sprain or strain (discussed next), should be seen by a sports medicine orthopedist. If the injury is to the foot or ankle, it is recommended that the athlete be seen by a sports medicine podiatrist (foot and ankle doctor) as this is all they do.

There are many other situations which should cause concern for further medical treatment, but this at least gives you a start.

What is the difference between an acute and a chronic injury?

We will often hear medical personnel asking whether an injury is acute or chronic when trying to evaluate the big picture of an injury, but what do these terms mean anyway? Well, an acute injury is a new injury, one which has recently happened, involves active swelling, and is a one-time occurrence, such as an ankle sprain. A chronic injury, on the other hand, is one which you have had for awhile, or one that keeps occurring without ever really healing, such as notoriously tight hamstrings or hamstring strains/pulls. A chronic injury can show a pattern of using poor mechanics or improper technique, or simply not taking ample time to warm up prior to participation in a workout or training session. It is wise when dealing with an injury that keeps occurring to look at your entire program, from the type of strength and conditioning program you do, to your flexibility program, to your style of kicking/punching/throwing for proper use of technique and mechanics. It may simply be that you need to change your stance to correct the problem. You can either videotape yourself, or have your coach or ATC watch your performance to analyze it for proper technique.

What is the difference between a sprain, a strain and a rupture?

There are three terms commonly used by medical professionals when discussing tissue damage to the muscle, muscle tendons, ligaments or cartilage. These terms are sprains, strains and ruptures. **Sprains** include all tissue damage to **ligaments and cartilage** including stretching, microfiber tears, partial tears or complete ruptures of ligament or cartilage. **Strains** are simply used to describe tissue damage to **muscle and/or muscle tendons** including stretching, microfiber tears, partial tears and complete ruptures. A complete **rupture** is what it sounds like, a complete tearing of a ligament, cartilage, muscle or muscle tendon.

Both strains and sprains are measured in degrees of damage with a 1° (minor) amounting to stretching with possibly some microfiber tears (small little tears of the tissue), and 2° (moderate) having partial tearing of the tissue, whereas a 3° (major) is almost a complete to a complete rupture of the tissue. Some medical professionals will also use a +/- system in addition to grading an injury by degrees. For example, a person could have a 1°+ sprain, indicating the tissue is stretched to its limit and may have some beginning tearing of the tissue, but one that is still considered minor in nature. Only a MRI (Magnetic Resonance Imaging) can definitively determine if any such tearing of the tissue has occurred. Often a physician will request a MRI to determine the extent of tissue damage before deciding if surgery will be necessary to properly care for an injury.

If you have never had an MRI or seen the machine, it can be one of two types: 1) is a cylindrical tube that is completely enclosed except for the open ends, which you "ride" into on a moving platform; or 2) a cylindrical tube in which the top has been cut out, referred to as an Open MRI. It is recommended that young children and those with a known phobia (fear) of small enclosed places request to use an Open MRI. Also, if you have very wide shoulders, ask if the MRI will accommodate a larger body structure, as some of the older MRI's are quite narrow. During the test you will have some bright lights and a lot of noisy "pinging" sounds, and you must remain absolutely still until the conclusion of the test (30 minutes to an hour). MRI's are like x-rays for soft tissue, as muscle and ligaments do not show up well enough on x-rays to determine absolute damage. The images taken will progressively take images of your body in cross-sections, as if you were cut in pieces going from your right side to the left, or from front to back, or from head to toe. This way damage within a joint can often be identified, but the only conclusive way to determine damage is to surgically open the joint. The MRI gives the physician an idea whether or not they need to "explore" the damage via cutting the area open.

What is the difference between types of fractures?

A **fracture** is a generic term for any injury causing discontinuity of the bone, which can involve displacement of portions of the bone, and disruption of the skin. Many people often associate a fracture with a bone completely broken into two or more pieces and displaced from its normal position, but a fracture can also simply involve a "crack" within the bone without displacement.

A **hairline fracture** or "crack" is a break in the bone that generally does not move from its normal position, or moves only slightly out of position, and is barely visible on an x-ray.

An **avulsion fracture** on the other hand is when a portion of bone is chipped or broken away from a bone, often from the tissue that is attached to it. Avulsion fractures commonly occur in the ankle or the thumb when the ligament rather than stretching "pulls" a piece of bone away.

A **stress fracture** is a fracture that lies within the bone without displacement, often lying within the interior portion of the bone. A stress fracture is often not seen on an x-ray until it has already begun to heal, laying down calcium deposits in the area of damage. A stress fracture, though, if not treated properly can fracture completely through a bone, causing a complete break and displacement of the bone to occur.

Fractures can also be classified as either **open or closed-wound fractures**. This simply describes whether or not the bone broke through the skin. If the bone breaks through the skin many other complications, including infection, play a role in the treatment protocol of the injured individual.

Treatment of fractures can be handled in different manners by a sports medicine orthopedist or other physician. The limb can be put into a cast immobilizing both the joint above and below the point of a fracture after reducing the displaced bone piece into its original position. The limb can be placed in a soft cast, walking cast or hard splint, which can be removed to shower and for rehab activities. The limb may also have to undergo surgery in which hardware such as pins, screws, rods or plates are used to hold the bone in its normal position while it is healing. Such hardware can be left in the body permanently or removed after the period of bone healing has been completed, usually after one year. The decision of what materials or procedures to use, and whether or not to leave hardware in temporarily or permanently, depends on the physician's preference and the extent of the injury. With any of these methods the physician will want the fractured pieces put in a position where they approximate (touch) each other in order to encourage bone growth and healing.

The most important thing to remember is that once a limb has been fractured an athlete needs to follow treatment of the fracture with rehabilitative and strengthening exercises prior to a full return to martial arts. If the joint has been immobilized for any length of time the muscles become weak from disuse and therefore make the athlete more vulnerable to re-injury, particularly in the martial arts, which often involves excessively strong blows to the limbs.

Secondly, even if a cast is only worn for three to four weeks, it may actually take up to six months or even a year for the bone to completely heal, leaving it susceptible to re-fracturing during this period of time. The athlete needs to be monitored for any signs of re-injury or weakness. A good strength program will help to reduce the risk of re-injury to the bone or associated muscles, tendons, ligaments and cartilage. For these reasons, a prescription for rehab with either a physical therapist or certified athletic trainer should be requested and completed before full return to athletic participation occurs.

For Coaches and Instructors

How to care for basic injuries

Once you have determined to some reasonable degree the extent of the injury, and whether or not the athlete needs further evaluation by a physician or at a hospital, then you can determine the treatment. If the injury needs to be transported by ambulance, follow your emergency medical plan protocol (refer to Chapter 7), making certain that you telephone the parents of the athlete to inform them of the situation. You should require that the athlete return to you a form releasing them to return to activity signed by a physician before allowing the athlete to participate in any activity. **The athlete who is sent for further evaluation should not be allowed to participate in activities without a written release from the attending physician.** If the injury is minor (1°) to moderate (2°) in nature, then treat the injury accordingly with guidelines known as ICERS:

1. Apply Ice directly to the injury for fifteen to twenty minutes, but never more than 30 minutes at a time

2. Apply Compression through use of plastic wrap or ace wrap while icing

3. Elevate the injury above the level of the heart, or as high as is reasonably comfortable for the athlete

4. Allow the athlete to Rest the injured area following ice treatment, using crutches, sling or other assistive equipment, if necessary

5. Apply Supportive taping, ace bandage or splint following ice treatment

For Coaches and Instructors

If blood is involved, be sure to take the necessary precautions while cleaning the wound (such as wearing latex gloves and using sterile gauze), bandage appropriately, and dispose of blood-tainted products in a biohazard waste receptacle (red plastic bag or red plastic box manufactured to store blood stained articles). Ensure that the bandage will stay in place by using tape adherent spray and/or tape around the wound area, but not in the wound itself, as adherent spray has large amounts of alcohol and will burn.

It is not only important to use these precautions for the athlete's safety (reducing the chances of contamination that could lead to infection) but also for you. Did you know that if an athlete left blood on you or a surface you come in contact with, that HIV is the least of your worries, unless you have direct contact to the athlete's blood coming from their body into either an open wound or mucus membrane (such as your eyes, nose and genitals) on your own body? Hepatitis is much more of a concern. Contracting it can lead to death if not properly recognized and treated early. Blood spilled onto a counter top, even after it dries, is capable of transmitting the Hepatitis infection to another person for up to 7-10 days! The HIV virus, on the other hand, is dead within moments of coming in contact with the air! So, it is extremely important for you to cleanse your hands before and after wearing latex gloves, cleanse and bandage the wound of the athlete, and then clean the entire area where the bleeding occurred with a substance such as a 10% bleach solution or other commercially produced products for blood clean-up. This includes the athlete's uniform. During most athletic competitions, all play is stopped once blood is seen, to have it cleaned up from all playing surfaces, players and their uniforms.

If the laceration (cut) is more than a ¼" deep or a ½" long, refer the athlete to the nearest walk-in clinic or physician's office for sutures (stitches). If suturing is going to be necessary, it must be done within 6 hours of the initial injury to be the most successful. A laceration less than this can be successfully closed using steri-strips

For Coaches and Instructors

(or butterfly bandages) and tape adherent spray. Be careful when using tape adherent spray not to spray it into the wound itself as it contains alcohol and will burn. Instead, spray some tape adherent onto a swab and then use the swab to apply the tape adherent around the outer surface of the injury before applying a bandage or tape. Remove the athlete from participation, including weight lifting and running exercises, until you are assured no further bleeding is going to occur. Anytime a person increases their heart rate through exercise the rate of blood flow also increases, so therefore exercise of any type is going to increase bleeding from a wound.

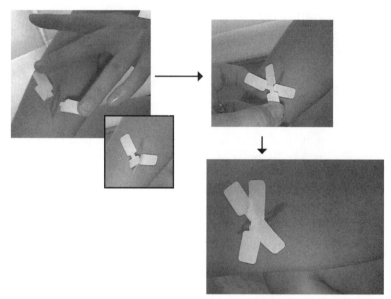

After thoroughly cleansing the wound, apply butterfly bandages by placing one on each side of the wound, angling in towards the cut, but do not adhere both ends of the butterfly yet. Now, take the two strips, gently pulling them into towards each other until the edges of the wound are touching each other, but not doubled over or wrinkling. Adhere the ends of the butterfly bandage, in an X formation once edges of skin approximate (touch). Repeat as necessary with 2 or more criss-crossing butterfly strips.

For Coaches and Instructors

If the laceration is to the head, evaluate for a concussion as well, and remove the athlete from participation until the next session (refer to head injuries later in this chapter). Inform the athlete that he/she needs to report to you prior the beginning of the next session. If there are **any** lingering signs of a concussion, do not allow the athlete to return to participation. If a fracture is suspected, immobilize the joint, and have the athlete transported to the hospital or physician's office by either the athlete's parents or call for an ambulance by invoking your emergency medical plan (refer to emergency medical plan in Chapter 7).

You should instruct any athlete about treatment for his/her injury, including the frequency and duration of follow-up treatments the athlete should follow for the next few days. This should include:

1. For any and all swelling and/or discolorization (bruising), ice needs to be directly applied to the area (except for children under the age of 8, elder participants with possible circulation problems, or at the elbow, instead put a wet barrier such as a wet paper towel or wet pillowcase between the skin and the ice) for fifteen to twenty minutes at least three to four times each day for the next three to five days or until the swelling has gone down. Make sure the athlete understands, though, not to leave the ice on any longer than fifteen to twenty minutes at a time or more damage can occur to the area. The athlete also needs to allow the area ample time for the tissue to return to a normal temperature (generally one hour).

2. Suggest that if the athlete has taken anti-inflammatory medications in the past, and **is not allergic to any form of ibuprofen, aspirin, etc.,** to begin taking anti-inflammatory medications of their choice as directed on the bottle with meals to help reduce pain and swelling. Inform the athlete, though, that you cannot supply any medication to them (if this is your policy), and if the athlete is a minor, parental approval is also required (if you are going to provide over-the-counter medications such as ibuprofen). You can

For Coaches and Instructors

opt to give out medications if you have signed consent forms on file from the athletes acknowledging they have no known allergies to such medications and they are allowing you to provide such over-the-counter medication. This should include obtaining a parent's signature for minors.

3. Inform athletes not to use any analgesic rub (pain-relieving), including Icy Hot®, Tiger Balm®, Ben-Gay®, Flex-All®, etc. as these products may increase the blood flow to the area (due to ingredients such as menthol) and therefore increase the swelling.

4. If the injury feels progressively worse the athlete needs to seek further medical attention from their physician or in a hospital as soon as possible.

5. If the joint is weak, then the athlete will need to tape the injured joint for a minimum of three to six weeks while the injury is healing. Strengthening exercises will also need to be used prior to a full return to complete activity.

6. **Have athlete restate your instructions to ensure that they heard and understood you,** or have the athlete sign a form that states what you have told him or her to do for treatment of an injury.

Following any injury, no matter how minor, enter the athlete's information onto an injury log sheet. If the injury is moderate to major in nature, involves the head/neck/spine, or is taken for further evaluation, be sure to complete the injury report form. **If you are ever in any doubt of the state of any injury, request that the athlete receive further medical evaluation by a physician before allowing a return to activity.** It is better to be safe than have regrets about not having the athlete see a physician and the injury becomes worse.

Using ice versus heat for injuries

The age-old question is how do you know when to use ice or heat? This one is easy to answer. If an injury is **less than 7 days old or is still actively swelling, new** in other words, **the only thing you want to use is ice no matter what part of the body is injured.** If an injury still has quite a bit of **swelling and/or pain,** even if more than 7 days old, you want to **use ice** following any workout, even if you are going to workout or fight later on in the day. If the injury is no longer swollen and simply sore or stiff after 7 days you can either use a moist heat pack (NOT DRY HEAT PACK) or analgesic rub prior to a workout to help increase the blood flow to the area. You should always use ice at the conclusion of the workout, usually for at least two to three weeks (or as long as it is painful or swollen) while the tissue is healing.

If **NO INJURY** has occurred and you are simply tight or sore from a previous workout **a moist heat pack or analgesic rub** can soothe aching muscles and help to loosen them prior to working out, and ice following the workout if you are still sore and aching, or have any pain. Whether using ice or heat prior to a workout ensure ample extra time to warm up and stretch prior to any workout or competition. Analgesic ointments which come in a roll-on form are often the easiest to apply to a muscle or joint. My favorite is made by Biofreeze®.

It is not wrong to use ice on an injury prior to entering the ring to fight or in the ring between rounds. In fact it is probably one of the best things you can do at that point as it will help slow the swelling process which will restrict your movement. The ice treatment should then be immediately followed by taping or wrapping of the area to maintain compression and further slow the swelling process. Remember, when an area of the body is injured it may take ten to fifteen minutes before you actually see any swelling or it may be immediate. The wisest thing to do when you "twist" or "pull" a muscle or injure a joint is to ice it immediately, and then get it wrapped or taped up. "Walking it off" can lead to greater pain and swelling in a matter of only ten to fifteen minutes, creating a more severe injury by continuing to put demands on it. So be intelligent and grab the bag of ice as soon as an injury occurs.

Ice can also be used when an injury causes external bleeding to slow the rate of blood loss. Apply sterile gauze, if available, to the open wound to help absorb the blood and then apply the ice over the gauze bandage. If you are going for further medical evaluation, secure the ice bag to the injured area with an ace wrap or plastic wrap. Try to use crushed ice or "half-moon-shaped" ice, if possible, as ice cubes generally have sharp corners that may further irritate or cause pain to the injury site.

When an injury occurs to the inside of the mouth, such as a "fat lip" or biting the tongue, sucking on an ice cube can also do wonders as opposed to putting a big bag of ice on half of your face. Try not to apply ice directly to the forehead when injured as this will become painful and give a feeling of "brain freeze", leading to a very painful headache. Instead wrap the ice bag in a wet paper towel or wet pillowcase. The same is true for the elbow, do not apply ice directly to the area without using a wet paper towel as a barrier. The reason being that the ulnar nerve (the one you hit when hitting your "funny bone") lies directly under the skin and can become damaged if allowed to get too cold. The reason you wet the barrier is to encourage the cold to transfer to the injured area, but at a slower rate than directly applied to the skin.

With pre-adolescent children (under the age of eight) do not apply ice directly to the skin without using a wet paper towel barrier as their skin may be too delicate to handle the cold. As for adolescents and adults, except for the forehead and elbow regions, ice can be applied directly to the skin unless there are known allergies or skin conditions (such as previous frostbite or Raynaud's Syndrome) that will not allow you to do so. The elder athlete (age 60 and up) may have begun to have some breakdown in their skin and skin circulation systems, so it is NOT advised to put the ice directly on their skin, if there is a known problem (such as circulation problems, diabetes, etc.), or if they are over the age of 70. Simply use a wet paper towel or wet pillowcase as a thin barrier.

Ice can be applied by using several methods other than an ice bag such as ice baths, ice whirlpools and ice massages. An ice bath is simply a cup, bucket or tub filled with ice and water in which to submerge the injured area. Ice baths in a cup are great for injured fingers and thumbs as the cold water better conforms around the injured area than a bag of ice and requires less time for treatment, generally only ten to fifteen minutes.

An ice bucket, on the other hand, is generally used for the ankle, calf, hand or elbow, as these are difficult areas to get an ice bag to properly conform to readily. If an ice bath is used, small digits such as fingers and toes, should be wrapped with an ace bandage or pre-wrap to help reduce the pain of them "freezing" before other areas during the cold treatment. Submersion of an ankle in an ice bucket also allows an athlete to complete range of motion exercises during the cold treatment. The athlete can complete circles (both clockwise and counterclockwise), or spelling the alphabet with his or her toes while the foot and ankle are submerged in the ice and water. This will help to increase the lost range of motion of the injured joint while reducing the chances of contributing to the swelling. Treatment time is generally fifteen to twenty minutes.

Ice tubs are used for larger body parts such as the hamstrings or quads that need cold treatment. Ice tubs should be maintained around 55°F (12°C) temperature with ice and water filling the tub to a level above the injured area. Athletes being treated using an ice tub need to be monitored at all times to ensure the safety of the individual, and that the individual only stays in the tub for twelve to fifteen minutes. Ice tub treatments are also great for re-vitalizing "dead legs" which have been beaten up during competition but which are not necessarily injured beyond the standard bruising or soreness from kicking all day. One word of advice, do not drink a warm or hot drink, such as coffee, while submerged as this generally causes the stomach to cramp.

Ice whirlpools are another version of a submersion ice bath with a twist. Inside a galvanized steel tub of ice and water is a motorized element that keeps the water in constant motion (same element as used in a standard hot tub). Therapeutic exercises can be completed while the injured area is submerged in the ice and water. Many athletes prefer the ice whirlpool to the simple ice bath as it gives them a "revitalized" feeling. This is especially true for sore and aching muscles of the leg, or strained hamstrings, quads and groin muscles. **CAUTION: Never turn the motor on for the whirlpool once you are submerged in the water.** A short could occur and you could be electrocuted. The wisest and safest plan is to turn the whirlpool motor on prior to entering the water, and then turning it off after the athlete exits the water. The water for a cold whirlpool should be the same temperature as an ice bath, around 55° F (12°C).

Ice massage is one other method of cold treatment that can be applied either by yourself or another individual assisting you. First, you will need to fill a small paper cup about half to two-thirds full with water and put it in a freezer. Once the cup of water is frozen it is ready for any injury. Simply take the cup and peel down the top until the ice is exposed. The cup acts as a handle or grip for the ice so you do not have direct contact with the ice. Using small circular motions, apply the ice to the injured area for twelve to fifteen minutes or until all of the ice is melted. This allows the injury to get the cold treatment needed for the early healing process while massaging and breaking up scar tissue which may be building up from the injury. Ice massages are especially beneficial for shin splints, knee injuries and other bony areas that become injured or sore.

Ice massage cups are also great to have on hand for insect stings and bites, as it will quickly cool the affected area, slowing the histamine response of the body, and reducing the pain and/or allergic reaction to the insect attack. Ice massage can be used in conjunction with an anti-histamine cream or medication (such as Benadryl®), if the athlete does not have any known allergies to the medication. This can be especially useful for athletes who have a low-grade allergy (minor swelling and itching) to such insect bites or stings. If an athlete has a known allergy to insect bites or stings, they should be carrying a prescription injection, known as an Epi-pen, that will need to be administered as quickly as possible. Ensure that you and other instructors know how to properly use the Epi-pen, by asking the athlete or parent to explain and demonstrate use, in case of such an episode. You should either have an Epi-pen given to you by the athlete to keep in your medical kit, or know where the athlete stores their own at all times. It could mean the difference between the athlete living or dying. Ensure, also, that you periodically check the expiration date, as all medications have a limited life span for use before disposal is required.

You can also create an ice massage by freezing water in a plastic soda or water bottle. This form of ice treatment is especially useful for arch injuries and plantar fasciitis (a condition of the tissues of the foot). Once the bottled water is frozen, lay it on the floor and roll your foot over the bottle, creating not only a cold treatment, but also a massage and a stretch of the muscles of the arch and foot.

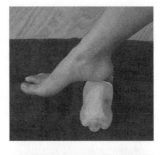

Any ice treatment is going to go through several basic phases: (1) The first two to three minutes will be an intense burning coldness that some describe as "pins and needles" followed by (2) an aching feeling with a dulling of sensation and

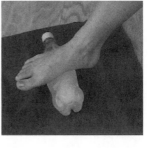

finally (3) reaching a point of cold numbness. These phases can start from phase one again if, once "numb", the athlete moves the limb or the water in which the limb has been soaking is disturbed.

Many of you have seen and or used the commercially produced instant ice packs and cold sprays available on the market today. Several warnings about these products before using them:

• Instant ice packs are designed **for ONE USE ONLY. Never** reuse or re-freeze an instant ice pack as they are developed from chemicals that can cause severe skin irritation and burns.

• Instant ice packs are only designed to assist for a short period of time, with the cold effect only lasting eight to ten minutes. If you are forced to use an instant ice pack because no ice is readily available you will need to use a second one after about eight to ten minutes to complete the standard cold treatment for an injury.

• Instant cold packs are great to have on hand if you do not know the availability of ice either in a dojang or at a competition site. Just remember to keep several on hand at a time as you will use at least two for every injury, and more if the injury area is larger than the cold pack.

Cold sprays are another form of cold treatment, but one that only lasts for a few moments. Cold sprays are only intended to last up to thirty to forty-five seconds, long enough to take the "sting" out of a bruise but not meant to replace the necessary cold treatment that ice provides. Several precautions about using cold sprays should be noted prior to use. Since cold sprays are either made from butane, ethyl chloride or fluromethane, all of which are explosive chemicals, use them with caution. These are compressed gases that can explode if handled improperly, overheated (such as leaving a can in the hot car) or dropped repeatedly. These cold sprays can also cause terrible skin irritation and burns if used improperly. Make sure you read all of the instructions before use and never use in place of traditional ice treatments for an injury. Note: Some forms of cold spray (such as fluromethane) have been linked with cancer-causing carcinogens.

Cold sprays should only be used during a competition fight to help a fighter "get through" the pain of a bruise or minor muscle/ligament injury pain. Be sure to hold the can or bottle at least six to twelve inches from the skin, never spray near the eyes, mouth, open wound or other mucous membrane (such as the nose or genitals). Do not use a continuous spray for more than five to ten seconds at a time in any one area to reduce the chances of skin damage. Also, never mix an analgesic rub and a cold spray, as this will inflict much unnecessary pain. If the cold spray does not take enough of the pain away to continue fighting, the injury is obviously more severe than initially believed, and the fight should be stopped. Always use good judgement when using cold sprays on an athlete, even if it means the athlete has to forfeit a fight. Always read the instructions written on the label carefully to ensure proper use.

Comparison of Ice Treatments

Ice is generally used prior to or following a workout

Treatment	Duration	When Used	Precautions
Ice Bags	15-20 min.	New injuries, swelling for 1st 7 days, continue as needed for pain & swelling management	Allergies/ Sensitivity
Ice Cubes	until melted	Inside mouth for swelling, cuts or abrasions	Allergies/ Sensitivity
Ice Baths/ Tubs	15 minutes	Large joint areas difficult to ice with a bag; can be done in conjunction with exercises	Allergies/ Sensitivity
Ice Whirlpools	12-15 min.	Large joint areas difficult to ice with a bag with desire to have water movement	Monitor at all times
Ice Massages	15 minutes	For large muscular areas needing combined cold treatment and massage; or for difficult to ice, bony areas	Allergies/ Sensitivity
Instant Ice Packs	8-10 min. (twice)	When ice is not available; must use one followed by another to get full cold effect	One use only

Cold Sprays	5-10 sec.	To take "sting" out of a bruise or minor injury	Chemical burns
Betadine® Soaks	10-15 min.	For blisters or open wounds needing cold treatment and "toughening" of the skin area	Allergies/ Sensitivity
Frozen Soda Bottle	15 minutes	Arch of foot; used for ice massage	Allergies/ Sensitivity

Comparison of Heat Treatments

Heat is used only prior to a workout, not following

Treatment	Duration	When Used	Precautions
Moist Heat Packs	10 minutes	Chronic "Old" injuries which cause stiffness or reduced flexibility	Allergies/ Sensitivity
Analgesic Rubs	Rub on	Chronic "Old" injuries which cause stiffness or reduced flexibility	Allergies/ Sensitivity
Warm Whirlpools	10-15 min.	Sore or stiff muscles	Monitor at all times

What is the difference between over-the-counter pain relief medications?

You go to the drug store to get something for the pain of your new injury, but how do you decide what is the right medication to take? Well, there are several "classes" of medications that are often used by athletes for injury relief. The two classes most commonly used are the NSAID's, non-steroidal anti-inflammatory medications, which includes Advil®, Motrin®, Aleve®, Orudus KT®, Ibuprofen, Excedrin® and Aspirin; and the antipyretics, like Tylenol® and Acetaminophen. NSAID's are best used for new injuries that involve pain and swelling, while the antipyrectics are used for fever reduction and pain relief. Tylenol® or Acetaminophen are what should be used when an athlete has a fever, has a headache from either dehydration or being hit in the head, or for people who have sensitive stomachs (and don't tolerate NSAID's without stomach upset and/or bleeding). Tylenol® or Acetaminophen, unlike NSAID's, do not "thin the blood", so therefore do not usually contribute to pooling of blood, as can happen in the brain following a hit to the head, or bruising. Both have side effects from long-term use, with effects seen in the kidneys and bladder of those using or abusing NSAID's, and the liver can see effects from long-term use of Tylenol® and Acetaminophen. Use as directed on the bottle for appropriate doses, being careful to use age-appropriate medications for children. All of the drugs in these 2 classes are legal to use and are not considered banned substances by USADA (US Anti-Doping Agency) or the NCAA, but neither should be used continuously for more than a few days unless otherwise directed by a physician.

Other classes of drugs that you may feel the need to use include anti-histamines, such as Benadryl®, stimulants, such as Pseudophed and Ephedra, and depressants, such as found in many cold medications, such as Robutussin-D® cough suppressant. Anti-histamines are used for allergic reactions to many things, from food allergies, to hay fever to sniffling/sneezing associated with an allergy to animals. Anti-histamines are available over-the-counter in creams, sprays and tablet/capsule forms, none of which are considered banned substances by either USADA or the NCAA. Stimulants, on the other hand, are found in many varying medications from non-drowsy cold medication formulas to diet pills to "all natural" energy supplements. These drugs need to be used with caution as acceleration of your heart rate is a component of the drug, with one of these substances, ephedra having been removed from the US market due to serious side effects of the heart. The NCAA does not ban these substances as of present, but USADA does have some restrictions of use by athletes, so check the USADA banned substance list before ingesting.

Depressants, on the other hand, slow the heart rate down, and often make you sleepy, and are found in many cold medications, particularly those that have a –D in the name. Depressants are not a banned substance by the NCAA or USADA for most sports, although certain sports, such as shooting in which the athletes would gain an advantage by slowing the heart rate, it is considered a banned substance. For a more complete list of the exact drugs banned, visit www.usantidoping.org, and www.ncaa.org respectively.

Many schools and programs do not allow the distribution of medications, even over-the-counter medications, within their facility. If you do decide to have pain-relieving medication available it is highly recommended that you have a signed release form from the athlete (which includes a parent signature for those under the age of 18) stating they have no known allergy or reaction from the use of such medications. Have the athlete list the allowable types of medications, and dosages you are allowed to distribute. Some ATC's and coaches will distribute over-the-counter medications to their own athletes while others will not. Chiropractors (DC), by the limits of their medical license, do not usually distribute medications not even over-the-counter medications, while MD's can recommend over-the-counter medications as well as prescribed medications for restricted use. NEVER share your prescription medications with anyone. Besides the fact it is illegal to do, you do not know their allergies or medical history, and the medication may not be appropriate for their needs.

Use of braces, splints, sleeves and Aircasts®

Many different versions of supportive equipment have been designed in recent years to assist an injured athlete during the healing process. Each brace or splint is designed to help support the injured area through use of sturdy materials such as metal, plastic, and other highly supportive material, in conjunction with flexible material such as neoprene. Every person has their own opinion as to the likes and dislikes of these products, and essentially it is up to the injured athlete and his or her medical professional to make the ultimate decision.

A brace or a soft splint is designed to hold its strength even when an athlete is sweating, whereas tape loses up to fifty percent of its strength within thirty minutes of sweating. Some athletes like the feel of tape better as they feel it is tighter, while others prefer the convenience of the brace or splint which is simply pulled on and either tied or velcroed into place. One thing to remember though is that no brace or splint that contains any hard substance, including shoestrings, hooks, plastic, metal, hinges, etc, is allowed in any martial arts competition for the safety of opponents. Neoprene-like materials, without any hard substances, are the only alternative to taping for competitions, and some competitions do not allow any form of protective or supportive bracing and/or taping. Braces and splints give additional support when doing daily life routines as well as training in the initial stages of returning from an injury, and therefore have a place in martial arts. Make certain that you are properly instructed on how to use the brace and are appropriately fitted for the brace by size and shape by a sports medicine professional.

Aircasts® are a specialized form of braces which contain an air bladder inside of a hard plastic supportive brace (either with or without hinges). The air bladder is intended for added compression, much like adding the horseshoe pad under tape or wrap, while the outer cover lends rigid support. This type of brace is often prescribed by physicians, physical therapists or certified athletic trainers for the initial stages of healing of a 2-3° sprain or strain. This brace is soon removed once strength and range of motion have been regained during rehabilitation, and should not be used during martial arts sparring as it could quite easily injure an opponent.

Neoprene sleeves have also become quite popular among athletes because of the ease of application to an injured or sore area of the body. Neoprene sleeves are now made to fit the ankle, calf, knee, thigh, buttocks/thigh/groin, low back, shoulder, elbow, wrist or thumb. These sleeves are simply made of compressive yet flexible neoprene-like material, or they can have flexible metal or plastic inserts that give added support. Please note though, if a brace has these substances inserted within the material it must be removed for competition as it is considered a hard substance and therefore illegal for use during competition.

Neoprene sleeves have a great compressive quality that aids in keeping the muscles warm. Neoprene sleeves are normally used in the last stages of healing or for areas that are chronically injured. Neoprene sleeves are also used for overuse injuries such as tendonitis and shin splints. **Never sleep** in a neoprene sleeve or brace as it may excessively restrict normal blood flow.

Blisters

For blisters of the foot and hand you can aid in the healing process and help toughen your feet and hands up by one of two methods. The first is to use an ice bath (ice and water in a bucket) and add a substance known as povidine or Betadine®. This is done by adding one part povidine solution to ten parts water creating a ten percent solution. Soak your entire foot or hand in this ice bath and solution for ten to twelve minutes, one to two times per day until the blisters heal and begin to toughen.

A second method is to simply replace the povidine solution with household bleach, in the same one to ten ratio, creating a ten percent bleach solution and soaking in the ice bath with bleach solution for ten to twelve minutes, one to two times per day. Both solutions will temporarily change the color of your skin, with the povidine giving a slight orange tint, whereas the bleach may lighten the skin a little. Once again, be cautious with children under the age 8, and those athletes with known skin allergies or sensitivity as they may have a reaction to these solutions.

A third method is use diaper rash cream in and around a blister. Just like with a baby's diaper rash, the cream helps to dry the blister without over drying or cracking of the skin. I prefer a product called Butt Paste.

There are several good preventatives for blisters that all athletes should consider. One, calluses that build up on the feet and hands, particularly the ball of the feet and palm of the hand, should be regularly shaved or filed down to keep blisters from forming between the tissue and the callus. You should not completely remove calluses but reduce them to a thin protective layer. Calluses can be shaved using a commercially produced callus shaver, callus file, or by using a pummus stone to file down the callus. Second, a cracked heel and skin lotion should be used on the area after reducing the callus to soften the skin to reduce the chances of cracking. Third, when switching from training on a mat or wood surface to a carpet (such as found in the warm-up areas of most competition sites), wear martial arts shoes for at least part of the time on the carpet (to reduce the chance of producing blisters or tearing of skin not accustomed to such an abrasive surface). If you are getting calluses on your hands from lifting weights or working with weapons, you need to consider wearing weightlifting gloves (leather gloves which the fingers are cut off, and may have some mesh components to keep hands cool).

Lastly, if your feet do not callus and tend to develop blisters easily there is a substance called New Skin® which is a liquid to be applied to the area before a blister occurs to create a second layer of skin much like a callus. Caution: Do not overuse or over-layer this product as it too can then cause a blister to form between the tissue of your foot and this product, just as a thick callus will do.

If a blister does occur on your foot, it is best to make use of a donut pad or heel pad (if involves the heel), to help protect the blister and underlying tissue until it heals (refer to Chapter 4). If the blister is on the hand, Second Skin® or Compeed® (gel pads of various substances) can be used to pad the area for participation in workouts and competitions, which also aids in healing. To help rebuild the tissue of the skin of the hand, you can use New Skin® a liquid skin-mimicing substance, but beware it will burn if the blister has been torn as it contains high levels of alcohol.

Fungal Skin Infections

Fungal skin infections (which often begin with the word "tinea") invade various parts of the body from the feet (tinea pedis or athlete's foot), groin (tinea cruris or jock itch), under the toenails (onychomycosis) or anywhere on the body from the face to the feet (tinea corporis or ringworm). Growth of these fungi occurs when the area is hot, moist, and lacks light to dry the body area. Fungal infections are highly contagious. You simply need to make direct contact with the infected skin (of say your opponent or training partner) or a contaminated surface (such as a mat or shared protective equipment).

Signs and symptoms of athlete's foot and jock itch include: scaly or blistered skin, swelling, itching, burning, and in some cases fluid draining from the sores. Ringworm appears as well-defined red rings on the surface of the skin with a clear center. Onychomycosis often discolors the toenail, along with causing deformity, thickening and detachment of the toenail. All can be treated with topical and/or oral medications, but prevention is better. Ensure that shoes and workout clothes have adequate time to dry out, wear clean cotton clothing (including under garments), use powders to absorb moisture (either commercially produced anti-fungals or baby powder with corn starch), shower frequently followed by a thorough drying with a clean, dry towel (including between the toes and the bottoms of the feet), and avoid direct contact with possibly contaminated surfaces by using shower shoes.

It is also important that when you are sharing protective gear, like headgear, that your thoroughly wipe out the headgear and then thoroughly dry it before using it. I keep baby wipes and tissues handy just for this reason, because you can contract ringworm on your face, back, arms, or anywhere on your body. Many tournaments require you to wear the provided gear. It is extremely important that this gear be cleaned prior to any use, every time, as it is often still wet with sweat from the previous user. Mats must also be cleaned with a solution which will kill bacteria, viruses and fungi after every training session or competition, to reduce the chances of spreading such fungi.

Arch injuries

Injuries of the arch can occur from various problems, ranging from flat feet, to a fallen arch, to plantar fasciitis. All are treated in basically the same manner with an icing regimen, strengthening program and taping. A modification of the normal ice treatment for arch injury and pain is to use a twenty ounce (half liter) plastic soda bottle filled with water and frozen (as previously described). Once frozen, the bottle can be placed on the floor to complete an ice massage by rolling the bottom of the foot back and forth over the bottle for ten to fifteen minutes. This modification not only ices but also massages the painful region and helps to gently stretch the tendons and fascia of the foot, aiding in the healing process.

In addition to the strength program and arch taping previously described, it is also highly recommended that you visit a sports medicine podiatrist (foot and ankle doctor) to be considered for orthotics. Orthotics are shoe inserts designed to adhere to your foot and your foot alone. They are often made from a mold created from the imprints of your feet in a molding foam. Orthotics are often costly, but are also often covered by your regular insurance coverage. When going to have the orthotics made, take various shoe types from running shoes, martial arts shoes, to any other type of shoe you wear on a regular basis to ensure the orthotics are going to fit properly into the various shoe types.

Stress fractures can and do occur in the foot, especially in the metatarsal bones (bones of the instep and arch). If you have pain that gets progressively worse, starting only when participating in activity to eventually being all of the time, whether or not you are on your feet, then a stress fracture may be the problem, and you need to see your physician, with a visit to your podiatrist highly recommended.

Bruising also occurs quite often in martial arts, especially to the arches and insteps, as they often take numerous hits, or are stepped on by an opponent. Sometimes, these bruises, especially when a new one occurs on top of an old one which has not completely healed, can lead to hardening of the tissue (scarring) which becomes highly sensitive any time pressure is applied to it. To help reduce the chances of bruises becoming a chronic problem, begin using friction massage to help break up the developing excessive scar tissue after the first 72 hours following the injury. To accomplish this, take either your thumb or a finger, and produce a circular motion in the center of the bruise or anywhere you feel a lump developing. This is easiest to do in a warm water shower or bath, but can be done at any time, as long as it is then followed by an ice treatment to reduce the chances of further swelling in the region. Breaking this excessive scar tissue down allows the body to rid itself of it, while encouraging the blood to bring in oxygen and nutrients for the healing process.

Foot and Toe Injuries

For fractures of the foot or toes which are not put into a cast or splint, the best way to reduce pain when you have to walk is to wear hard-soled shoes with a wide toe, such as leather casual or dress shoes. This gives much needed support to the fractured bone and provides relief. DO NOT WEAR sandals, flops, martial arts shoes or loosely fitted shoes. Even tennis shoes and running shoes do not always give rigid enough support to the injury to allow for relief.

As always, stay off of the injured foot and keep it elevated as much as possible. A fractured toe can take from ten days to three weeks to heal and gain pain relief. A fractured foot generally takes longer, particularly if the athlete continues to walk on the injured foot. Generally, fractures of the foot are placed into a walking cast for protection while healing, but also because the walking cast can be removed to shower and sleep.

Another common injury of the toes in martial arts is what is known as "turf toe", so named from an injury common among American football players from turf fields. Basically it is a "jamming" of the big toe or forceful separation of the big toe from the other toes, causing considerable pain and swelling of the joint at the base of the toe (MTP joint). Because the ability to balance our entire body is based at this joint, injury to this area leads to a great amount of pain, as most athletes will not get off of the foot long enough for the toe to heal. If allowed to become a chronic injury, surgical repair may be imminent. Ice massage therapy using the frozen plastic bottle, as well as taping techniques described in Chapter 4, and use of NSAID's in coordination with either using crutches or staying off of the foot all together will help this injury to more readily heal. When weight-bearing, you should wear a hard-soled, broad toe shoe to give the best support (as mentioned above). If the injury lingers for more than 2-3 weeks with little to no change, you need to seek the opinion of a sports medicine podiatrist.

Ankle injuries

The ankle has a mechanism of three ligaments that protect it on the lateral (outside) aspect of the lower leg, and one large triangular ligament on the medial (inside) aspect of the lower leg. In addition, there is also an expansive muscle and muscle tendon mechanism devised not only to move the ankle and foot, but to also protect it. The ligaments on the lateral aspect of the ankle are the ones generally injured in an ankle sprain, which include the anterior talofibular, calcaneofibular, and posterior talofibular. These ligaments often stretch, but do not usually completely tear in common martial arts injuries, as the ligaments and tendons are generally already stretched from use by the sport. An extra effort needs to be put forth to strengthen the muscles and muscle tendons of the lower leg to help reduce the chances of injury, such as the tubing exercises described in Chapter 2.

Surgery is very rarely needed to repair an injured ankle unless an athlete repeatedly injures the ligaments and bone. Then surgery is required to repair the area, remove lose bodies floating within the joint, and possibly tighten the overstretched ligaments. Surgery may also be necessary if an avulsion fracture occurs, with a ligament pulling a piece of the bone away from the ankle. Surgery to repair avulsion fractures normally includes placement of a pin or plate in the ankle joint to secure the bone fragment and associated ligament. Immediate injury care would include ICERS, crutches and NSAID's, and a visit to your medical professional for further evaluation and care.

Knee injuries

Knee injuries are what a lot of athletes fear, particularly in the martial arts, because they can lose a lot of time away from practice and competition due to injury. But what really happens when an athlete injures his/her knee? Well, it depends on what structure of the knee is injured, and how badly it is damaged. Injuries can range from a simple bruise and swelling of the muscle tissue, taking five to ten days to heal, to a complete rupture of a muscle tendon or ligament which can take six to twelve months to completely heal. So, let's talk about these injuries.

Like any joint in your body, your knee is made up of muscles, ligaments, cartilage (known as meniscus) and bone. Let's start with the bones. The long bone of the thigh is the femur. It is the most difficult bone in the body to completely fracture, but this does not mean it won't happen, or that it can't be chipped or cracked. There is also the patella, better known as the "kneecap" which floats over the knee joint. This is the bone that often becomes chipped or cracked when taking a direct blow to the knee. Lastly, there are two bones of the lower leg, the tibia and fibula.

The biggest problem with bones in martial arts, as with other sports, is that many athletes are still growing and therefore have growth plates in their bones located near every joint in the body. If growth plates are damaged it can lead to problems in bone growth, even causing these growth plates to close prematurely, stunting natural growth of that bone. Growth plates in females generally close between the ages of fourteen to seventeen, whereas growth plates in males tend to remain active up until age twenty to twenty-two.

The knee has several large muscle groups that cross over the joint, allowing movement of the joint. The main muscles of the knee include the quadriceps (muscles of the front of the thigh), the hamstrings (muscles of the back of the thigh), the popliteus (muscle which "unlocks" the back of the knee when bending), the gastrocnemius (better known as the calf muscle), the IT Band (which runs down the outside of the thigh to the knee), and the adductor muscles (which run from the groin down the inside of the thigh to the inside aspect of the knee). All of these muscles cross over the knee joint and thereby allow the knee to move.

Generally, the muscles that are injured the most often in martial arts are the muscles of the back of the leg, the hamstrings and popliteus. The popliteus muscle is a very small muscle found very deep in the back of the knee. This muscle is generally injured when the athlete has not properly warmed up and stretched before kicking full speed or against an object, or through hyperextension of the knee.

The hamstring is almost always injured from not properly warming up and stretching prior to kicking. Since this is a very large muscle group it tends to take longer to heal, particularly if an athlete continues to "push through the pain". Hamstring injuries can take as much as six months to a year to properly heal. When a hamstring ruptures (snaps or tears) it sounds like a gun being shot, very loud and extremely painful. Athletes who sustain injuries of this nature require several months of physical therapy in order to regain their original strength and flexibility, which sometimes includes surgery to reattach the damaged tendon.

The quadriceps muscle (front of the thigh), on the other hand, tends to suffer more from contusions (bruises) and conditions resulting from contusions rather than muscle strains, although muscle strains do also occur. Contusions often occur from being kicked in the quads, or from taking a knee, elbow or a shoulder to the quads. Athletes need to be especially conscious about bruising in this area, as the formation of a large hematoma (pooling of blood) can lead in some rare cases to a condition known as myositis ossificans. This condition involves small pieces of bone formation growing within the muscles, often associated with a large hematoma in the quadriceps muscle, which repeatedly is hit while trying to heal. This condition can become extremely painful, and limiting, if not treated properly and early. If you suspect such an injury you need to see a sports medicine orthopedist as soon as possible.

Muscle injuries to the front of the knee and leg often involve the patellar tendon, a small tendon connecting the four quadriceps muscles over the patella (kneecap) just below the patella. If you feel just below your kneecap on your lower leg you will feel a small bump (known as tibial tuberosity). This is where the patellar tendon attaches, and where the tendon tends to pull away from when injured. Injuries to this tendon occur from not properly warming up and stretching, running or jumping on a hard surface (such as concrete), a direct kick to the area, or in some cases from the bones growing faster than the muscle and tendons (Osgood Schlater's Disease). Injuries to muscle can take anywhere from three weeks to six months, even a year to heal, dependent on the extent of the injury and whether or not the athlete takes proper care of the injury, or is still growing which contributes to the problem.

The cartilage of the knee is known as the meniscus. The meniscus is a shock-absorbing cushion between the bones in the knee joint which prevents the bones from rubbing together. The meniscus is often torn when the leg is turning and strikes a hard object, such as in a spinning back kick. Meniscus damage can also occur when the leg is planted firmly and gets struck from an angle. When the meniscus is damaged, the athlete can often hear or feel a painful click or pop inside the knee. Pain tends to increase when walking down stairs, with the knee sometimes "locking up" or "giving way".

When the meniscus is torn an orthopedic surgeon will often remove it. If the tear is extensive the surgeon may opt to staple or suture (stitch) the meniscus back together. This is actually a very simple operation, with the athlete returning to participation within two to five weeks. The meniscus cannot heal itself once it is torn because it has a very poor blood supply and does not generally regenerate once damaged. If the damage is painful then the best solution is usually to have it removed. Just remember that now your knee will have less cushion between the bones, which can later lead to arthritis as the bones begin to rub together.

There is also cartilage located on the underneath aspect of the patella (kneecap) which can be crushed or torn from a direct blow or a twisting mechanism of the knee. This type of injury is often treated by surgery to scrape the damaged portion of the cartilage from the back of the patella. As with any surgery that removes cartilage from a joint this can predispose the athlete to possible arthritis development later in life due to the bones rubbing against each other without any protective "padding".

The cartilage underneath the patella can also be damaged from a condition known as chondromalacia, which technically is a softening of the cartilage due to excessive pressure or repetitive microtrauma occurring over many years. For this reason, many competitions that involve dance moves such as knee drops, must first hit their shin on the floor surface before the knee, with no direct drops to the knees being allowed. In martial arts, this type of damage can occur from repeated "clashing" of the knees, being kicked in the knees or falling onto a hard surface directly to the knees.

Lastly, there are four main ligaments of the knee: anterior cruciate ligament (ACL), posterior cruciate ligament (PCL), medial collateral ligament (MCL), and the lateral collateral ligament (LCL). The collateral ligaments are on the inner side and the outer side of the knee, protecting your knee from bending sideways. The cruciate ligaments are found inside of the knee, running from front to back and back to front preventing the thigh from sliding forward or backward on the lower leg.

Surprisingly, the ACL is sprained more often by female martial artists than males, as is the case in many other sports such as soccer and basketball. It is believed that this happens in part due to lack of strengthening of the hamstring muscles, compared to the quadriceps muscles, making the knee rely primarily on the ligaments for support rather than muscle. If the muscles of the knee are not strong enough, or the ligament is already overstretched (hyperflexible) when the athlete is struck by a kick the ACL tears because it is unable to hold the joint together. This often happens when an athlete is kicked from behind while her foot is planted, taken down while the foot is turned and planted, or when the foot is planted while the body is spinning, making contact with opponent.

When the ACL is completely torn it must be surgically reconstructed, taking from five months up to a year to recover (average six to eight months), depending on the protocol used by the physical therapist, certified athletic trainer and orthopedic surgeon. The protocol which has often been used by highly motivated athletes is known as the "Rapid Rehab Program" which is described by Dale F. Blair, MS, ATC, CSCS and Robert P. Wills, MD in *Athletic Training, The Journal for the National Athletic Trainers' Association* (1991, Volume 26, Number 1, Spring, pp 32-43), among many other great progressive programs. Care must be taken not to push too hard and too fast for the first 3-4 months, as you can ultimately stretch out the graph, rendering the surgery useless. Certified athletic trainers (ATC's) and physical therapists (PT's) will individualize a rehab program for each athlete, as each athlete has different needs for return to participation, not only for their capabilities, but also due to the demands of the sport. I always recommend that athletes provide a video tape of themselves, either during competition or practice, to both the physician and the person in charge of the rehab program, whether it be a PT and/or an ATC, so that they may gain a better understanding of what the sport entails and what your needs are. Many medical professionals simply are not aware of the demands of the various sports, whether it is aikido, judo, karate, taekwondo, or any other martial art.

The PCL can also be damaged, and tends to be damaged more in males than females, although females are beginning to have occurrence of PCL injuries as well. In the general public the PCL is rarely reconstructed, but for martial arts athletes this ligament must be repaired to continue participation in the sport. This is due to the fact that moving backward while spinning requires the protection of the PCL. The PCL generally takes the same amount of time to heal as an ACL, five to twelve months (average six to eight months), although many rehab programs have never worked with athletes returning from such surgical repair. Most protocols simply involve strengthening the muscles surrounding the knee for protection rather than surgical repair to stabilize the knee, which unfortunately is not enough in most cases for martial artists. If you damage your PCL, seek an orthopedic surgeon who repairs

PCLs on a regular basis, as many surgeons have not performed PCL reconstruction.

Damage to the MCL and LCL generally occurs when an athlete is struck from either the outside of the knee (damaging MCL) or from the inside of the knee (damaging the LCL), causing the knee to bend sideways. This injury can occur from being kicked while in a normal stance, getting the leg tangled up with an opponent during a throw to the mat, or when the supporting leg is kicked out from under an athlete who is either spinning or side kicking. These ligaments tend to stretch considerably ($1°$-$2°$) before actually rupturing. Unfortunately once a ligament is stretched it does not shrink to its original length like a rubberband would, but remains at least partially stretched permanently, making the knee joint loose. If the ligament is completely torn, reconstructive surgery is then the only alternative, although once again this injury is not often surgically repaired in the general population unless the ACL is also ruptured. In addition, the athlete will need to begin a strength program to strengthen the muscles of the area to better protect the ligaments from future injury.

Injuries of the knee and leg, like anywhere in the body, need to be treated immediately and handled with good sense. If you feel a sharp pain, or hear any snapping or clicking, your body is trying to tell you damage has occurred, and swelling is either occurring or soon will occur. Proper treatment should begin immediately with ice and be followed up by a visit to your sports medicine physician, physical therapist or certified athletic trainer to prevent further damage from occurring to the area, resulting in loss of time from practice and competition.

Hip and Groin Injury

The hip is what is considered a ball-and-socket joint, like the shoulder. Because this is the most complex type of joint found in the human body, injuries are never simple or small when the hip is involved. The hip allows motion in all directions, unlike most of the body. It is able to flex and extend, hyperextend, abduct and adduct, internal and external rotation, and circumduction (continuous motion through all possible movements). There are many large muscles which cross over the hip, having an effect on movement, all of which can become damaged from athletic participation. These include the external rotators, gluteals, hip flexors, IT band, quads, hamstrings, sartorius and muscles of the groin. The bones include the largest bone in the body, the femur, along with the bones of the pelvis which create the "socket" into which the "ball" of the femur rests. There are several major nerves that run through the area, with the most notorious being the sciatic nerve, running through the pelvis and down the back of the leg. And, of course, there are many ligaments and cartilage that can be injured as well.

Let's start with the muscles, with the quads and hamstrings, as well as the IT Band crossing both the hip and the knee, which we have already discussed. The IT Band, when it becomes injured, either from a direct hit or from overuse at the hip, begins to "pull" at the knee leading to knee pain. Those athletes who like to block kicks or advancements of their opponents by raising their leg are very prone to tight and bruised IT Bands. The IT Band can get so tight that it looks like a guitar string where it attaches just below the knee. The IT Band, though it is classified as a muscle, is basically a muscle tendon without any major muscle belly, and therefore may be more difficult to stretch, predisposing it to injury. The use of ice whirlpools or cold soaking baths is often recommended for treatment of this problem. Deep friction or sports massage is also recommended to help loosen the tendon and move out scar tissue and waste products. Many athletes today, get a weekly or bi-weekly sports massage of their legs, with concentration on the IT Band and hamstrings. Check out your local licensed massage therapists, who may have there own business, or operate through a physical therapy clinic or chiropractic office, or even your local health club.

The hip flexor muscle runs up the front of the hip joint and often is injured from hyperextension of the hip during a fall, causing the muscle to strain. It rarely ruptures, but frequently develops $1°$ and $2°$ injuries. As always, ICERS will aid in the healing of this injury, as well as a good strengthening and flexibility program. The sartorius muscle, on the other hand, also crosses both the hip and knee, but it is mainly responsible for allowing us to cross our legs by externally rotating and flexing the hip and flexing the knee at the same time, often referred to as the tailor's muscle. Wrestlers are more prone to injuries to the sartorius than most martial artists, as they begin many maneuvers on their hands and knees, wrapping their legs around the legs of an opponent. As with the IT Band, the sartorius can put pressure on the knee, creating pain, even when the injury actually occurs at the hip.

Groin muscles are injured quite often in martial arts for various reasons, including not properly stretching before kicking or doing straddle moves, being kicked in the groin while muscles are fully contracted (such as during a spinning back kick), or simply because the groin muscles are often some of the weakest muscles on the athlete's body. Because these muscles are often weak to begin with they can take longer to heal than other muscles. Using the wrapping technique previously described or a neoprene sleeve will help reduce the pain and swelling of the area in conjunction with ice, ice whirlpools or ice baths. It is very important to include strengthening exercises for the groin in your strength and conditioning program to reduce the chances of or return from such an injury.

The external rotators and gluteals are the main muscles of the buttocks and outer edge of the hip, creating a lot of power and movement necessary for kicks, as well as being able to stand your ground against an opponent who is trying to throw you from your feet. Often, though, martial artists strengthen their external rotators and gluteal muscles, and forget they must maintain an equal muscle balance of opposing muscles, the internal rotators and groin muscles. Remember you MUST ALWAYS strengthen opposing muscles (muscles with opposite actions, often on opposite sides of the body) in order to have balanced strength and reduce the chances of injury.

As for the bones, it is very difficult to fracture either the femur or the pelvic bones (with some exceptions in the pubic bone region), with bruising more common, and dislocations or subluxations rare (but not impossible). One of the common injuries is better known as a hip pointer, which is essentially a bone bruise, coming from a direct hit to the hip joint or a fall directly onto the hip joint. The problem in this area, unlike most areas of the body, is the bone has very poor blood supply, and therefore heals very slowly, and often very poorly. Repeated hits to the same area of the bone, especially before they have completely healed, can lead to necrosis, or cell death, of the bone. If this happens, hip replacement surgery is not far away.

Another degenerative condition which can occur in the hip is known as hip dysplasia, where the head of the femur actually begins to break down, creating a lot of pain and instability. It is possible that over time, numerous repetitive hits to the hip region could lead to either bone necrosis or hip dysplasia, both ultimately ending in hip replacement surgery. If you have hip pain not associated with flexibility issues alone and have received some good hits to the hip region, it would be wise to visit a sports medicine orthopedist who specializes in hips to rule out these conditions.

Unlike the knee, the cartilage of the hip does not tend to become injured quite as easily from athletic participation. It takes a forceful hit driving the femur up into the socket, especially if it is then forcefully rotated, to seriously damage the cartilage. There are though, many ligaments in the area that can be damaged, but which are far less likely to become damaged than the ligaments in the knee. But, if the hip joint simply does not feel "right", is painful, or restricted in movement, it is time to visit your sports medicine orthopedist who specializes in hips.

Many people have heard the term "sciatica" or sciatic pain syndrome, stemming from pressure or damage to the largest nerve in the body, which runs down the back of the thigh, originating at the spine in the lower lumbar region. Sciatic pain syndrome or sciatica are generic terms for a condition which causes sharp pain and sometimes numbness, running down the back of the leg, often felt as high as the low back to behind the knee. What happens is that the nerve runs through the pelvis which often does not have adequate room for the nerve, so it becomes compressed, "squished". This can follow a low back injury, an injury stemming from increasing your muscle mass without maintaining your flexibility, and pregnancy, among many other things. Often the best way to relieve the pain is to lay on your stomach with a pillow under your hips, and an ice pack applied directly to the area for 20 minutes, in addition to the use of NSAID's.

It is also important to have your kicking styles and/or stances evaluated, as it may be a matter of improper technique. Instead of kicking the leg up towards the chest you may be bending the torso towards the legs to aid in your kicking, putting pressure on the low back and pelvic region. It is extremely important to ensure that you have both back strengthening and abdominal strengthening as part of your strength and conditioning program, but also maintain and increase your flexibility. Yes, females are much more flexible in this region than males in many cases, because female bodies are created for giving birth to babies, therefore everything needs to be flexible in this area, but this does not mean males cannot gain great levels of flexibility in the hip region.

Sciatic nerve pain that occurs during pregnancy usually occurs from a combination of pressure from the baby, weight gain and the fact that all of your joints are "loosening" from the release of a hormone called relaxin. This is why pregnant women "waddle", although most will never admit they do! Pregnant athletes should be especially aware of this condition, spending a lot of time not only stretching, but strengthening the abdominals and back to help better support the developing fetus so it does not apply as much pressure to the area until time for delivery. If you have a tight low back or tight hamstrings, I highly recommend both pregnant and non-pregnant athletes to receive a sports massage to help increase blood flow to the area to loosen things up, while breaking up scar tissue created from multiple microtraumas to the area. I also recommend ice treatments daily, especially after any type of workout, or when any pain is felt in the area.

Low back pain and injury

The low back is one of the worst places to have an injury. A low back injury affects your entire body since it is the center of the majority of the weight of your body. You can either strain the muscles of the lower back (which run from the base of the skull to your buttocks) or sprain the small ligaments in between each of the vertebrae of your spine. You can also damage the specialized cartilage, the discs, which lie in between each vertebra. Damage to any of these structures, though, is completely debilitating and requires your immediate attention to reduce the chances of further injury.

There may be several reasons for your low back pain other than injury from a hit or move during practice or competition. One reason may simply be that your hamstrings are too tight. The hamstring muscles attach in your lower back/buttocks region and can pull on your lower back if not stretched out properly before kicking, leading to pain in the lower back. You also may not be kicking or throwing properly, putting undue stress and strain on the muscles of your lower back to help you to accomplish a kick or throw. Just as you are taught about lifting heavy objects, your stronger leg muscles, not your low back muscles, should be the main muscles used for kicking. You may also be doing an abnormal amount of spinning or rotation when kicking, or overarching your back when trying to throw your opponent, putting too much pressure on your lower back from poor mechanics.

Have your instructor watch your kicking and/or throwing mechanics to ensure you are using proper technique and not putting added pressure on your back. Try to even out the number of spinning kicks you complete as opposed to other kicks such as side kicks and axe kicks or try to throw equally from each side of the body to reduce the chances of injury. Your abdominal muscles may also be too weak making the low back muscles the main support structures of your upper body when kicking or throwing, causing you to compensate by overarching the back and therefore your pelvis to tilt forward.

Or you may be overarching your back because your abdominal and upper body strength are not to the level needed to properly overtake and throw your opponent. The abdominal muscles should be just as strong if not stronger than the lower back muscles in order to help support your upper body, as well as to help maintain proper posture enabling you to best use proper mechanics for kicking and throwing opponents. You may be "overstretching" your low back, or improperly stretching your low back and/or hamstrings. Have your instructor watch as you stretch out or have a certified athletic trainer or physical therapist instruct you on proper stretching techniques. If you are "too flexible" it is time to add some back strengthening exercises, as well as abdominal exercises, to your daily routine, especially some of the core strengthening exercises previously discussed.

If you have truly injured your low back a visit to your physician, physical therapist or certified athletic trainer is required in order to get you back on track. You will also need to begin an ice treatment routine, as well as a strengthening and stretching program before returning to a full workout. When you do return to a full workout you will have to begin at half speed, with kicking hard into the air being added last. It is better to first work on kicking paddles, bag or opponent as opposed to simply kicking air. The back has to work much harder to slow the leg down when kicking into the air.

Another option for working out and kicking while your back is healing is to complete the kicking portion of a practice in waist-deep water, such as in the shallow end of a swimming pool. The force of gravity on your joints and muscles is greatly reduced and often allows movement with little to no pain. In addition, the drag effect of the water gives you a great workout, even if your lower back is not injured. Aquatic therapy can be used with many injuries during the later healing stages of muscular or ligamentous injuries. Aquatic therapy can be utilized even if you cannot swim, as no swimming has to be included in the workout and you only need to be in waist-high water, usually about three feet deep for adult athletes.

NOTE: Don't be in a hurry to have surgery on your back unless you have lost all sensation in your leg or foot, or develop a condition known as "drop foot" in which you cannot flex your foot upwards. In many cases, with proper rest and then strengthening the body will absorb the damaged disc. Be certain to seek the care of a neurosurgeon for any back injury.

Shoulder Injuries

The shoulder, known as the glenohumeral joint, is a complex ball-and-socket joint, enabling athletes to move their shoulder in any direction, from flexion to extension, hyperextension, horizontal flexion and extension, abduction, adduction, internal and external rotation and circumduction. In addition to the glenohumeral joint is the shoulder girdle. The shoulder girdle allows the shoulder to be elevated (shrugged) and depressed (dropped shoulders), protracted (pushed forward) and retracted (pull shoulders back). So, you can see there are many different directions from which the shoulder can be injured. Now, in kicking forms of martial arts the shoulder is not a common injury, normally being injured from a kick or punch to the shoulder (and clavicle/collarbone), or from falling on an outstretched arm. Throwing forms of martial arts are more likely to lead to injury of the shoulder and shoulder girdle from being thrown directly onto the shoulder, getting the arm pinned or caught in an abnormal position, being hit from behind forcing shoulder abnormally forward, another athlete landing on the shoulder as they fall during a throw, or from falling on an outstretched arm. So, let's talk about what kind of injuries can occur.

The muscles, there are plenty of them, not only have an effect on the shoulder, but the arm, neck, chest and upper back. These include the muscles of the rotator cuff, the deltoids, the traps, the biceps (long head), the pectoralis muscles, rhomboids and lats, to name a few of the major ones. Any of these muscles can be strained or ruptured from abnormal movement of the shoulder and shoulder girdle, especially if the movement is forceful. I once had an athlete rupture (snap) the large pectoralis major muscle of the chest simply because he did not think. He was returning from 6 weeks off from weightlifting due to vacation, and walked up to the bench press and decided to set the rack up for the weight he was lifting when he had left. At about the third troubled rep it sounded like he had been shot by a gun in his chest, as the pect snapped and quickly coiled up in a ball in the center of his chest, immediately turning the entire area black and blue. He lost the next 6 months from athletic participation unfortunately, as the muscle had to be re-attached surgically, and some serious rehab followed. So, see, it is not only your martial arts participation that can cause injury but also your other workouts, if you don't take proper precautions to reduce the chances of injury.

The bones in the area are also at risk of injury. Generally, the humerus, the long bone of the upper arm which articulates with the shoulder, rarely fractures and usually only fractures when the arm is in an abnormal position and blunt force is applied to the bone. The clavicle, better known as the collarbone, is highly susceptible to fracture, particularly from a direct punch or kick. The problem with this bone fracturing is that there is a large major artery just beneath it that can also be damaged if the bone is fractured and forced into it. If immediate care is not sought, the person can suffer from serious internal bleeding, which can become life-threatening. Often the fracture is evident just by looking at the athlete as there will be a large sunken hole and possibly black and blue discolorization. If the opposite end of the collarbone from the fracture site is pressed, the end of the collarbone which is fractured will raise just like a piano key, when it should have no motion. This injury generally takes about 6-8 weeks before you are allowed to return to regular kicking martial arts participation, and often longer for the throwing sports.

The bone the clavicle articulates with is the acromian, forming what is known as the AC joint. This bone can become fractured or chipped from a direct hit, but this is not common. More often it is the soft tissue holding the acromian to the clavicle that becomes injured in the notorious separated shoulder. A separated shoulder is a very painful injury in which you lose the ability to lift or move your arm without pain. You will need to first put the injured shoulder into an arm sling or wrap to protect the area and take the pressure off the joint from the weight of the arm before even applying ice. Later a shoulder harness may be used to support the shoulder and arm as it goes through the healing process. Any suspected separated shoulder needs to be seen by a sports medicine orthopedist specializing in shoulders as soon as possible.

The shoulder joint can also either sublux (partial dislocation that reduces itself back into the joint) or completely dislocate, as the head of the humerus does not sit in a deep socket like the femur does in the hip. The biggest problem with a subluxation or dislocation of the shoulder is that it then becomes much easier to repeat the injury, from weakening of the associated ligaments and cartilage, known as the labrum. And each time this happens it only further breaks down the joint until eventually a person will go to pick up a piece of paper and the shoulder will dislocate. Any athlete who purposely dislocates their shoulder for a laugh should be highly discouraged. This damages the joint, even if there is no pain. Eventually surgery is often necessary to repair the torn labrum (cartilage) and tighten up the ligaments that have been damaged allowing for the multiple dislocations.

If an athlete dislocates their shoulder you should NEVER attempt to reduce or put the shoulder back into place unless you have been properly trained to do so as you may impinge (catch) either the nerve plexus (group) or large arteries in the joint, leading to temporary and/or permanent disability. An athlete with a dislocated or subluxed shoulder should always seek proper medical attention to reduce the shoulder, as well as have other diagnostic tests run to ensure there are no problems with the nerves or arteries and veins surrounding the joint. Strengthening exercises, some of which were described previously in Chapter 2, should be performed to help reduce the chances of such an injury occurring or re-occurring. As always, when an injury does occur, utilize ICERS, and immobilize the arm in the most comfortable position to be transported for further medical attention. The most comfortable position may NOT be with the arm against the body. ALWAYS seek the medical advice of properly licensed medical professionals (such as physicians, PT's and

ATC's) when an injury to the shoulder does occur to ensure proper recovery and reduce the chances of the injury occurring again. You will also need to evaluate your mechanics and technique to ensure that improper technique or mechanics were not the reason for the injury, and therefore need to be adjusted to reduce the chances of such an injury occurring again.

One last injury to the shoulder I want to discuss is what is known as the "frozen shoulder". A frozen shoulder is one in which the person has reduced or limited range of motion and flexibility due to tightening and pain in the shoulder region, and may occur without any direct force applied to the area. A frozen shoulder can occur at any age, but is more common in those over the age of 40, or those who have developed arthritis and/or large amounts of scar tissue due to a previous injury. Essentially, the frozen shoulder does not allow a person to move the shoulder through its normal range of motion, and in the worse cases renders the person unable to perform daily hygiene skills, such combing or washing their hair, reaching back towards their buttocks, or raising their arms to put clothes on. In rare cases, surgery is required to remove some of the scar tissue build-up, but this injury is more commonly handled with patience and persistence.

A frozen shoulder is an injury in which moist heat is necessary, either in the form of moist heat packs (NEVER DRY HEAT PACKS), warm whirlpool or hot shower. Generally, the condition is worse in the morning upon rising, somewhat loosening as the day progresses. What I do with an athlete with a frozen shoulder is ask them to first thing in the morning take a hot shower, warm whirlpool bath or use a moist heat pack to bring a sweat to the area, raising the body temperature and heart rate, so as to better pump blood to the area. I will then ask them to do a series of shoulder stretches while still in the shower or whirlpool, including shoulder pendulums (previously described), and wall or chair-assisted shoulder stretches. In some cases, wall-assisted shoulder stretches are performed by asking the person to "walk" their fingers up the wall as far as they can go without "hunching" the shoulders to rise higher on the wall. Internal and external rotation stretches are best completed while lying on a bed or table with the affected shoulder hanging slightly over the edge. A partner can gently stretch the shoulder, or small weights (even unopened soup cans) in the hand. Stretches can also include towel-assisted exercises in which the opposite end of the towel is grabbed by the uninvolved arm to aid in pulling the arm behind the back from both high and low.

The important thing is never to give up or give in, as motion should be something you easily maintain until the day you leave this earth. Do not allow anyone to say that you need to expect it due to previous injury or your age, as that is simply not true in most cases. You may not regain your complete original flexibility but you should be able to come pretty close, at least to a point that is comfortable and enables you to perform whatever tasks you desire, including athletic participation. Precautions should be taken when using moist heat if you have any infection or cancerous cells, as heat can increase the spread of an infection or cancerous cell growth, or if you have a problem with over-heating or cannot judge temperature properly, as adverse events could occur rendering you unconscious or causing serious burns to the shin. Always speak with a medical professional if you are unsure of the possible effects of heat on your body.

Elbow Injuries

Elbow injuries in the martial arts are not all that common, but are not rare either. As with any other area of the body the elbow can suffer from overuse, leading to chronic pain around the joint area. Typically, when this pain occurs on the outer edge of the elbow and arm, it often is referred to as "tennis elbow" while pain on the inner edge is known as "little leaguerer's elbow" based upon the mechanics that lead to this overuse syndrome. Typically, mechanics which put pressure on the outer edge of the elbow leads to tennis elbow, are often seen in those athletes that hold paddles a lot. Little leaguerer's elbow comes from pressure applied to the inner edge of the elbow, such as motions in which you lead your arm with the inside of the elbow before snapping the arm. This condition needs to be treated with ICERS and often NSAID's, but you need to remember this is one area of the body that no one should apply ice directly due to the close proximity of the ulnar nerve just under the skin which could be damaged. The taping technique of creating a "strap" for this condition was previously discussed in Chapter 4.

The elbow can also be dislocated, usually from a fall on an outstretched arm, the same mechanism often found with dislocated shoulders. Falling on an outstretched arm can cause multiple injuries from a fractured hand, wrist, or lower arm to a dislocated elbow or shoulder, due to the transmission of energy up the arm from the force of the fall. NEVER attempt to reduce or put the elbow back into place, nor attempt to ask the athlete to move the arm. The elbow and arm needs to be immobilized in the position it is found in and the athlete made as comfortable as possible until medical attention can be obtained at the hospital or sports medicine orthopedic physician's office. Be careful not to create any more movement in the limb than possible as there is often an associated fracture of the olecranon (ball part of the back of the elbow) with elbow dislocations.

The elbow can also be hyperextended from either falling on an outstretched arm, or having the arm suddenly twisted or kicked backwards. This is another one of those painful injuries, due to the fact that the safe guards to preventing the abnormal motion (hyperextension) have been loosened, putting pressure on highly sensitive nerves in the elbow region. The use of ICERS and NSAID's as always is highly recommended with proper precautions, as well as taping the elbow for prevention of hyperextension (described in Chapter 4). Sometimes the arm is placed into a sling for the first few days to take the pressure and weight of the arm off of the elbow, giving it a chance to begin the healing process. Remember, though, actual healing takes at least 3-6 weeks, and longer if it is aggravated or re-injured or not properly rested.

Wrist, Hand, Finger & Thumb Injuries

The wrist is a common site for injuries from sprains and strains, to fractures, to chronic weakness and pain. Martial arts typically does not spend much time specifically trying to strengthen the muscles of the hand and forearm, although this strength is necessary to punch and to grip opponents. Many injuries come from simply not taking the time to strengthen this area of the body as described in Chapter 2, especially among younger and lighter weight athletes. Bones of the forearm, the ulna & radius, as well as the numerous carpal bones of the wrist, are susceptible to fracturing from punching, being kicked during a block or falling on an outstretched arm (do you get the idea you should never put your arm out to catch yourself when you are falling?).

If the ulna and radius are fractured, it often will appear that the wrist has moved further up the arm, bending at the point of fracture. This type of fracture is known as a Colles' Fracture when it occurs near the wrist, and a Nightstick fracture when it occurs further up towards the middle of the forearm. Both are extremely painful and debilitating, although we have had some of our older elite athletes attempt to compete with the arm only supported by padding wrapped entirely around the forearm. Obviously, this injury is going to need to be seen by a physician or at a hospital, where it can be set and cast, and in rare cases metal hardware surgically implanted to hold the bone in place while healing. Remember, when splinting this injury for immobilization of the fracture site, you must extend the splints so that neither the elbow nor the wrist move, as this might cause the fractured bones to move causing additional pain and further injury. I generally splint the arm with the elbow bent, with the splint extending to the fingers and the splinted arm placed in a sling to reduce the chances of movement.

The hand, fingers and thumb can also be fractured, with the most common fracture being the "boxer's fracture" to the 5th metacarpal, the bone of your hand between your "pinky" finger and your wrist. It is given its name because boxers often fracture this bone from punches such as the left hook that apply force from the side of the hand as well as the fist. Martial artists often sustain this injury when trying to block a kick and are struck on the side of their hand. The navicular bone, one of the carpal bones at the base of the thumb, is another common fracture occurring from punching opponents. In the cases of broken fingers, thumbs or bones of the hand, we will often tape a dense piece of foam to the palm side of the hand to support the fracture, taping it into place, and allowing the athlete to complete the competitions if they desire. Remember, though, NEVER tape the hand closed into a fist as this increases the risk of fracturing bones in the hand and fingers.

You can greatly reduce the risk of injuries to the wrist, hand and fingers/thumb by strengthening the muscles that support this area, including the muscles of the hand (squeezing exercises, including squeezing putty, tennis ball and grip strength apparatus), wrist and forearm (as previously described in Chapter 2). Always begin treatment of an injury with ICERS, and seek medical attention if you feel there is a possible fracture, or the injury simply does not appear to be getting better over time.

Torso Injuries

The torso encompasses many tissues that can be injured including many of our organs, along with bone, muscle and ligaments. Generally, bruising is the common injury to the torso, with an occasional fractured rib. Rarely is there a serious injury to the organs outside of bruising and inflammation. The bones of the torso include the ribs, the sternum (breastbone), and the spine (already discussed), all of which are susceptible to fracturing, and those fractures can become displaced. The ribs are the most commonly fractured bones in martial arts from kicks, punches, falls, and maneuvers which either squeeze or lift the ribcage. Fractures of the ribs, if not displaced, are not put in a cast or splint of any type (although some may be put in an elastic wrap known as a rib belt), but there are some precautions which must be followed. If you have a known or suspected rib fracture:

• Avoid lifting your arms or any objects in your arms above shoulder level as this will cause pain and can lead to displacement of the fractured ribs.

• Try to avoid laughing, coughing or sneezing as this also inflict pain.

• Avoid physical activity for at least the first 10 days following injury as it is possible to displace the fracture or damage other nearby tissues while the rib is trying to heal. This includes running, weightlifting, martial arts participation, other sports, etc.

• DO ice the area 3-4 times/day for 15-20 minutes directly on the skin, take NSAID's for pain and swelling if nothing contraindicates their use (no allergies or reasons for not taking).

• You can purchase a neoprene or elastic "rib belt" created for quarterbacks injured in American football that will apply compression, giving some relief.

• Watch for any bleeding in your stool or black bowel movements when you use the bathroom as this will signal possible internal bleeding.

Organs can also become injured from martial arts participation, particularly the kidneys (from punches and kicks) and the gall bladder (from improper weight loss), as well as the lungs, heart, appendix and pancreas. Any of these organs can be damaged from blunt impact to the area, such as from punches, kicks and elbows or can be damaged due to poor health habits, such as dropping weight improperly, use of alcohol, nicotine or other drugs. In ALL cases of possible organ damage or injury, you need to seek the medical attention of a physician who deals with the organs, starting with your family physician who can refer you to a specialist. You should seek immediate medical attention from a physician or at a hospital if at any time you have blood in your urine or stool, blood in vomit, severe abdominal cramping, if your stomach becomes rigid (hard) in any area, or you suffer from pain of unknown source. In some cases you have a limited amount of time (often less than 6 hours) to seek treatment before permanent and/or fatal damage occurs, so seek medical attention immediately! Luckily these types of emergencies are few and far between.

For Coaches and Instructors

Head Injuries

Since some martial arts allow hits to the head, including the face, as legal scoring areas, minor to traumatic injuries occur to the head and face from kicks or punches, as well as hitting the mat or floor. As an instructor or coach, there may be incidents when immediate medical care is not available for an athlete who has suffered a head injury. The following guidelines can help you, as a layperson, follow the proper procedures until the athlete can receive professional medical care.

All head injuries should be considered serious injuries until proven otherwise. If an athlete has suffered a suspected injury to the head/neck/spine region, **do not move the athlete until you or medical personnel have determined the extent of the injury**. If an athlete is knocked unconscious or has sustained a hit to the head, **NEVER REMOVE THE HOGU OR HEADGEAR**, only remove the mouthpiece to allow for easier breathing by the athlete without causing movement to the head or neck. The hogu and helmet help to keep the head in good alignment with the rest of the spine giving it support. If there is a fracture of the skull or spine removing the helmet or hogu will cause further damage to the athlete by allowing the head to drop lower than the spine, possibly causing permanent disability or even death. If the athlete is transported to the hospital for further evaluation, the athlete should be strapped to a spine

For Coaches and Instructors

board with the helmet and hogu still on and the cervical collar placed under the helmet and chin strap. **Do not even loosen the chin strap as this helps the helmet keep the head in line with the rest of the spine.** If there is a fracture, any movement of the head or spine could cause permanent damage or disability. When EMS arrives request the paramedics or EMT's not remove the helmet or chest protector, and to transport the athlete to the hospital in this manner. The physician at the hospital will make the determination as to when it is safe to remove the gear.

If any deformity, loss of sensation, or unusual sensation should be noted, or the athlete's pupils (dark center portion of the eye) are unequal (one larger than the other), unresponsive (do not move or do not change size in response to a light stimulus), or fixed (do not move in response to light or image stimulus), you should begin your emergency medical plan immediately (refer to emergency medical plan in Chapter 7). If none of these signs exist then, you will need to test for signs of concussion, and degree of such a concussion.

Concussion

A concussion is injury to the brain from a hit to the head, usually from the brain sliding across the skull and hitting the opposite side of the skull from which the original blow came. Swelling of the brain tissue and damage to the various blood vessels can soon follow, creating further injury to the brain tissue. Swelling can take up to 6-8 hours to cause noticeable damage when an athlete suddenly becomes unconscious. If an athlete has lost consciousness, or was semi-conscious at any point, the athlete has most likely suffered a concussion. If the athlete loses consciousness for more than thirty seconds, he/she needs to be transported to a hospital as soon as possible. Begin emergency medical plan (refer to Chapter 7) at this point. While another designated individual is contacting EMS you need to begin to not only evaluate the athlete but to also stabilize the

For Coaches and Instructors

athlete from moving. Have a designated person remove all coaches and spectators away from the athlete to give medical personnel room to work upon arrival.

Check for any bleeding or yellow fluid coming from any part of the head, ears, mouth or nose. If you find the source of bleeding try to control for excessive bleeding using sterile gauze pads. If a yellow fluid is seen though, **do not try to stop the flow.** This yellow fluid is what is called cerebral spinal fluid and it is coming either from the skull or spine region. Stopping the flow will only complicate the injury.

You and at least one other person need to stabilize the position of the athlete to prevent movement of the head, neck and spine. You, as the designated leader, need to position yourself at the head of the athlete. On your hands and knees, and without moving the head, slide your arms in beside the ear holes of the helmet, bracing your hands on the athlete's shoulders, with you fingers underneath and your thumbs clamping the shoulder from on top, gently squeezing the head and helmet with your elbows for stabilization. In this position you are locking the head and spine from movement if and when the athlete wakes up. Do not try to simply hold the head with your bare hands as an athlete can often move their head inside the helmet. If the head is turned in an awkward position, do not try to move it unless the athlete is not breathing. If the athlete is not breathing you will have to follow instructions for a log roll and rescue breathing taught in your CPR certification program.

As you stabilize the head have a second person (and a third if available) position themselves to hold the body and/or legs down in case the athlete regains consciousness and attempts to get up. If the athlete regains consciousness before paramedics arrive try to keep the athlete as calm and motionless as possible. The athlete is probably never going to remember getting hit, may not know where he/she is, and is very often scared and somewhat combative.

For Coaches and Instructors

It is your job to keep the athlete calm and not moving until the paramedics arrive and take over. Try to calculate the amount of time the athlete was unconscious and anything unusual that occurred while the athlete was unconscious to report to the paramedics. Also, have a coach or parent with all of the athlete's personal information close by to answer any other questions the paramedics may have. This may simply be information contained within the athlete's file for the dojang. Make sure that someone in your dojang also begins to complete an injury report form as you will want to have everything documented that happened and what you did for the athlete. Ask others to sign as witnesses on the form.

If the athlete does not lose consciousness, or loses consciousness for less than thirty seconds, further evaluation must be completed to determine the degree of damage that has occurred to the brain. A concussion can range in severity from "ringing their bell" (no loss of consciousness, 1°) to complete loss of consciousness (3°).

Treat all head injuries as the worst case scenario until you or medical personnel determine otherwise. If there is no neck or spine injury indicated from examination and testing including fractures or dislocations, you need to determine if a concussion is involved by asking a few simple questions before further evaluating or moving the individual:

1. What is your name? How old are you? Where are you from?

2. Do you know where you are? What day is it?

3. Can you tell me what happened? If the athlete does not know, reassure them that it is all right if they can't remember

4. Do you feel sick to your stomach or dizzy? Do you need to throw up?

For Coaches and Instructors

5. Do you hear any ringing in your ears? Or anything weird like buzzing?

6. Do you see anything unusual, like bright flashes of light or dark spots?

7. Can you feel your fingers and your toes? Can you wiggle them for me?

8. Do you have any pain anywhere, or feel funny in any way?

9. Do you have a headache? Where does the headache run?

If the athlete has any problem answering these questions or replies yes to any of the symptoms, chances are he/she has at least a 1° degree (minor) concussion. You should next test the athlete's eyes for reaction to light and ability to track an object using either a penlight or a very small key chain-size flashlight while the athlete is still lying on the ground.

1. Using a penlight, quickly flash the light from above the eye down across each eye, watching for restriction (shrinking) and dilation (enlarging) of the pupils — compare the right pupil with the reaction of the left pupil. They should both react & react equally in response and speed to the light source.

2. Have the athlete follow your finger with their eyes and without moving the head — watch the athlete's ability to follow your finger — do the pupils appear fixed and unable to follow your finger?

3. Hold several fingers up about 6-8" from the athlete's face and ask the athlete to tell you how many fingers there are. Do the same from several different vantage points to also check peripheral vision

For Coaches and Instructors

If the pupils are not equal in size (and are not normally two different sizes, which a few people exhibit naturally), do not react equally to light, cannot track your finger as you move it, or have problems with normal vision, the athlete should be taken to the hospital for further evaluation, due to possible injury to the brain, optic nerve or the eyes themselves. Do not move the athlete, while calling EMS to transport the athlete to the hospital.

If no neck or spine injury is suspected, nor a skull fracture, you can allow the athlete to get up.

Next you will need to check the athlete's balance. This can be done using typical roadside sobriety tests (be ready to catch a swaying athlete to prevent further injury to the athlete from falling during tests):

1. Rhomberg's Test — have athlete stand and put both feet together and then close their eyes, with arms at their side. Does the athlete sway? Can the athlete stretch arms out and then touch the end of their nose with the tip of their finger with the eyes still closed? Does the athlete still sway once he/she opens eyes?

2. Can the athlete walk heel-to-toe along a straight line without looking down and without losing balance?

3. Can the athlete subtract seven from one hundred, or count backwards from one hundred? (This is one of those age appropriate tests that may not be appropriate for younger athletes or those with a learning disability.) Or you can ask the athlete to name the president of the United States and other such cognitive questions that require the athlete to recall common information.

If the athlete appears to be having balance or cognitive problems, he/she probably is suffering from some degree of a concussion. If these problems are extensive or lingering beyond twenty minutes,

For Coaches and Instructors

the athlete needs to be further evaluated by a physician and is considered to have at least a 1° concussion, the mildest form.

If any degree of a concussion is determined, the athlete must be removed from all activity until **all signs** of a concussion have **disappeared**, usually a **minimum** of twenty-four hours.

The athlete should not be allowed to sleep for six to eight hours without being fully awakened every thirty minutes to an hour to ensure further swelling is not occurring to the brain. You should complete the long version of the injury report form, and then give the parent or athlete's roommate a copy of the head injuries guideline sheet (refer to forms in Chapter 7). Be sure to put where you can be contacted if they have any further questions or where the nearest hospital is located should they need to take the athlete for further evaluation.

If you question how extensive the injury is, don't hesitate, send the athlete for further medical evaluation. Once a martial arts athlete has sustained a concussion lasting more than twenty minutes or has suffered from a knockout, that athlete is not allowed to participate in any contact practice or competition for at least thirty days. It is recommended that all athletes sustaining a 2° concussion or greater, or who have been knocked out to be evaluated by a physician, not only at the time of sustaining the injury but also at the end of this thirty day period, prior to being allowed to return to participation in activity. It should be mandatory for an athlete to obtain a "return to play" release from the attending physician prior to allowing the athlete to return to practice or competition after this 30-day period has ended. **This thirty-day rule applies to head injuries occurring during any workout or competition.** It is for the safety and well-being of the athlete and should not be ignored.

You need to explain to both the athlete and the parent (if the athlete is a minor) or responsible adult the chances of second impact

For Coaches and Instructors

syndrome if the athlete returns to participation before all signs of the concussion have resolved. **Second impact syndrome** is a rare condition that can occur while an athlete still has lingering signs and symptoms of a concussion/head injury. If the athlete takes another hit to the head, or suffers from a second case of whiplash, the athlete can suffer from catastrophic events, including internal bleeding, respiratory arrest, unconsciousness and even death. Several recent deaths in various martial arts and boxing competitions have been thought to be attributed to or in conjunction with complications from second impact syndrome. **Please stress the extreme importance to not return to any form of athletic participation before all signs of a concussion have been resolved.** It may take minutes, hours, days even weeks before all symptoms have subsided. This is why USA Taekwondo and USA Boxing have a thirty-day out rule before returning to competition following a knock-out or substantial concussion.

Facial Injuries

Many injuries can occur to the face from blows sustained during practice or competition in the martial arts. Since the head does not have a lot of bulky muscles the blood vessels tend to be close to the surface of the skin, and therefore bleed readily and excessively. A very small cut of the face can look like something out of a Hollywood horror movie. Even though the wound may look ugly you have to try to remain calm while you assess and treat the injury. First try to determine where the bleeding is coming from: a cut of the mouth, the eyes, nose, ears, etc. Gently clean the bloody area with sterile gauze to determine the extent of the injury while trying to determine if there is a fracture associated with the bleeding. If no fracture is suspected then treat it as a normal injury as previously explained earlier in this chapter.

If the bleeding is coming from the nose and the nose shows no signs

For Coaches and Instructors

of deformity you can take some cotton rolls (like the cotton used by your dentist to put in your mouth, or use small tampons) and place them into the nostrils of the athlete. You can apply some petroleum jelly or skin lubricant to the end of a cotton roll to help it slide into the nostril easier. Also place another cotton roll just under the front lip, which is a pressure point for such bleeding. Have the athlete lean slightly forward, not backward, while pinching the bridge of the nose or applying ice, if it is available, to the nose. Leave the plugs in place for a good twenty minutes before removing to see if the bleeding has stopped. If the bleeding continues, re-plug and wait another fifteen to twenty minutes to re-evaluate. Monitor the athlete for signs of a concussion, because facial injuries are often associated with head injuries such as concussions.

If the nose is out of line or "crooked", do not attempt to "put it back into place" as you may damage other structures of the face by doing so. Simply pack the area in ice and seek the attention of a physician who specializes in the ear, nose and throat (ENT) as soon as possible. If the nose swells too much before reaching the physician they will not do anything for it until the swelling goes down in about three to five days. So, do not delay seeking medical attention. At that time, if the nose is still out of alignment from a fracture, the physician may choose to re-fracture the nose in order to properly align it, or the physician and athlete may choose to simply leave it as is, a battle wound from participation in martial arts. If the athlete feels blood or fluids running down the back of the throat, regardless if the nose looks deformed or out of place, the athlete should be seen by an ENT (an Ear, Nose, & Throat Specialist) or a maxillofacial specialist (both are specialized physicians for the face) to ensure that the nose has not been broken or the septum (cartilage dividing the nostrils of the nose) has not been deviated or damaged.

Injuries can also occur to the eyes and the bones supporting the eyes. Be extremely careful when palpating around the eye if a fracture

For Coaches and Instructors

is suspected as you may cause a fractured piece of bone to fall into the eye itself causing further damage. If no concussion is suspected but an athlete is having vision problems (lack of sight, spots, bright lights, etc) or a fracture is suspected, seek the attention of an ophthalmologist, maxillofacial specialist or the nearest hospital to reduce the chances of permanent damage to the eye. Apply an ice bag to the area and transport as soon as possible. Eye injuries are not as common in the martial arts as in other sports, but when they do occur they generally are more serious in nature, including fractures of the orbit (bones around the eye), torn retina, and corneal lacerations, often times from simply getting poked in the eye by an opponent's finger or thumb, or punch to the face.

Injuries to the jaw and zygomatic arch (cheekbone) are very common in the martial arts with the athlete often being kicked while the mouth is wide open and no protective mouthpiece is in place. The bones of the jaw and cheekbone can be bruised, dislocated or fractured, all of which can be very painful. If the zygomatic arch has been fractured it will often appear as a sunken pit in the center of the athlete's face. If the jaw has been fractured usually the athlete's teeth will not line up normally when you look directly into their mouth. When the jaw is dislocated the athlete may not be able to open or close their mouth, or it may appear to sit off to one side or the other. **DO NOT ATTEMPT TO REDUCE AND PUT BACK INTO PLACE A DISLOCATED JAW** as a fracture is often also associated with a dislocation and you can cause further injury.

If the mouth is bleeding, attempt to determine from where the bleeding is originating without excessively moving the mouth. Use a tea bag moistened by cold water to apply to the inside of a bleeding mouth to help slow the flow of blood (there is an acid in tea that when moistened with cold water encourages blood to coagulate or clot) and then pack with cotton rolls or sterile gauze. Apply an ice pack to the outside of the face and offer ice for the athlete to suck on while transporting for further medical evaluation. If the athlete can

For Coaches and Instructors

be seen by an oral surgeon it would be more beneficial than simply going to the emergency room of a hospital. An oral-maxillofacial surgeon can often perform the necessary surgery in their own office at the time of the evaluation, reducing the time the athlete is in pain. Always assume other head injuries, such as a concussion, has occurred and monitor athlete for signs and symptoms while preparing to transport for further medical attention.

When a facial injury involves the teeth there are some simple guidelines to keep in mind:

• If a tooth or part of a tooth is dislodged or broken, try to find it and store in either a tooth preservative kit, in milk, or the athlete's own saliva (spit) until you are able to reach a dentist for repair.

• Never store the tooth in tap water or saline solution as these may contaminate or dry out the tooth.

• If an entire tooth is dislodged never touch the root end of the tooth with your hands. Instead handle the tooth from the crown end (the part you normally can see above the gum-line). If possible, rinse with the athlete's own saliva and put the tooth back in the hole in the gum line.

• Seek the care of a dentist or dental surgeon as soon as possible in order to increase your chances of saving the tooth. Seeing a dentist within an hour of the injury is highly recommended. The chance of the tooth being saved decreases with the passage of time.

• If it is loss of a baby tooth, you may simply want to have the dentist check the area to assure that no other damage has occurred to the area.

• Place a cotton roll or sterile gauze in the bleeding hole and give the athlete some ice to suck on to try to slow the flow of blood.

Dehydration

Martial art athletes are often involved in more activity during competitions than they are normally accustomed to, often in the heat and humidity of small quarters designated for warm ups. These athletes usually do not drink adequate amounts of water throughout the competition day, are already dehydrated from making their weight class or choose to drink carbonated caffeine-loaded drinks instead of water. It is a good idea to bring at least one-gallon jug or three liter bottle of drinking water to be consumed throughout the competition day, beginning immediately after weigh-in.

If you become dehydrated, remove yourself from the activity area, into the hall, another room, or someplace cool and quiet. Sit down and immediately begin drinking lots of water and/or sports drink. You can also take a glucose tablet (diabetic sugar tablet) or electrolytes tablet (sugar and salts tablet) to help boost your blood sugar levels, but you must then drink at least a ½ liter of water or you will get a terrible cotton-mouth feeling. You also need to have someone get you a small bag of ice and apply it to the back of your neck. Ice bags can also be placed on the wrists, behind the knees, and on the lower abdomen if you are excessively overheated. You should also elevate the feet while lying on your back. If you cannot adequately become rehydrated you should remove yourself from participation for the remainder of the day.

After a bout of dehydration it is important to continue drinking water throughout the rest of the day as well as the next few days. You should drink enough water that your urine is clear in color. If you are not allergic, take a couple of Tylenol or acetaminophen (as directed on the label) for the headache that accompanies dehydration. If dehydration leads to light-headedness or fainting, a trip to the hospital is necessary to have an IV administered to replenish lost fluids and nutrients. If dehydration is excessive, then organ and tissue damage, some of which can be permanent, will occur, which can possibly lead to organ failure.

Also remember that dehydration can lead to injured muscles more readily than an adequately hydrated body. Think of it this way, your muscles are a lot like a sponge. When a sponge is moist and full of water you can bend and twist it in any direction at any rate of speed without having a great deal of tearing. Now take that same sponge when it has dried out and try to twist and bend it. The sponge now tears and cracks rather easily, just like your muscles do when you are dehydrated. Dehydration also reduces your ability to think and to react quickly, both of which are necessary in the competition ring. Always consume lots and lots of water. It can be one of the greatest preventatives to injuries in martial arts participation.

Some signs and symptoms of dehydration:

1. Thirst is not an indicator of dehydration, as you are well beyond the beginning signs of dehydration by the time your body tells you it is thirsty. It takes a minimum of twenty to thirty minutes for the message to get to your brain to signal that you should drink.

2. "Cotton-mouth" feeling of dryness in the mouth.

3. Tired or weak feeling, often simply want to lay down and sleep, or do not feel like you can continue participation.

4. Flushed face which becomes quite pale as dehydration becomes worse.

5. "Hot" sensation which later leads into a cold, clammy feeling as dehydration progresses from excessive sweating as the body attempts to cool the body.

6. Dizziness and nausea, sometimes vomiting.

7. Reactions and responses become slow, sluggish speech may occur.

8. Loss of appetite.

9. Become incoherent, can lead to semi-consciousness and even unconsciousness.

10. In worst case scenarios, cardiac arrest can and does occur along with kidney failure.

The key is to maintain hydration and prevent dehydration from ever occurring by consuming large amounts of water prior, during and following participation in competition. If dehydration begins to occur, immediately begin drinking large amounts of water, apply ice to key points, get to a cool area, lay down with feet up. If dehydration becomes worse, seek immediate medical attention.

Never go into a sauna or steam room by yourself to drop weight, particularly if you have been depriving your body of adequate water intake. Dehydration in a sauna progresses rapidly and you may become too weak to get out of the sauna, leading to greater danger.

Chapter Five Key Points

✦ For anything but minor injuries, seek professional medical advice and care.

✦ After a serious injury like a fracture, athletes must commit to a rehabilitation and strengthening program for a full recovery.

✦ Never move a fallen athlete until it has been determined that there is no head, neck or spine injury.

✦ For injuries less than seven days old, always use ice to treat pain and swelling.

✦ For general soreness and tightness, moist heat may be used before a workout. If the pain remains after a workout, use ice.

✦ Ice may be used for pain relief prior to a match or between rounds.

✦ Apply ice to new injuries as soon as possible. Do not wait for swelling or bruising to appear and do not try to "walk off" the injury.

✦ Cold sprays should be used only during a match, never in place of ice.

✦ Bring a one gallon jug or three liter bottle of water to competitions to prevent dehydration.

✦ Signs of dehydration include: dry mouth, weakness, flushed face, dizziness, nausea, excessive sweating, sluggish speech and disorientation.

Common Conditions

6

medical conditions that may affect athletes

As with the general population there are many disorders and ailments that athletes bring to sports participation of which instructors and coaches need to be aware. These disorders should not be considered a weakness of an athlete, but rather a characteristic of the athlete which must be dealt with and in some cases monitored. The scope of this book is not large enough to dedicate time and space to all ailments and disorders, but a few of the more prominent ones will be discussed.

As a coach, instructor or parent of an athlete with one of the following conditions, you should understand the effects the condition might have on that athlete and your role in helping the athlete manage his or her condition. While the wording of this chapter is geared toward instructors and coaches, athletes with any of the conditions discussed will also benefit from reading the appropriate section and discussing any concerns with his or her coach or instructor.

Asthma

Asthma is a condition prevalent among athletes in recent years (some estimates are as high as 5% of the total population). An athlete may be born with it, develop it in adulthood or develop it as the result of athletic participation (exercise-induced asthma). Some of these childhood asthma cases actually outgrow the problem by early adulthood while others are afflicted with the condition the rest of their life.

Asthma generally involves shortness of breath due to bronchioles that lie within the lungs being unable to gain adequate amounts of oxygen for normal breathing due to an obstruction or narrowing in the airway. Athletes may wheeze, choke, cough, have shortness of breath, hyperventilate, become increasingly panic-stricken, pass out or even die from an asthma attack. Asthma sometimes involves allergies associated with animal hair and dander, cold air or food, tobacco smoke, molds/pollens, medications or other environmental factors. It can also be induced from stress, respiratory infection, lack of proper sleep, improper nutrition or improper use of daily asthma medication and inhalers.

Asthma is a very serious condition that should not be ignored by the athlete, parent or instructor, but need not be emphasized to the point of making the athlete self-conscious about being "different". Many people with asthma will not use their inhalers (usually Albuterol based) in front of others, so do not restrict the athlete's right to take their inhaler to the restroom to use and do not "fuss" excessively over them. People with asthma normally control asthma attacks with daily medication as well as by use of rescue inhalers.

Never forbid or restrict an athlete the opportunity to use their inhaler when they feel it is necessary to use. In fact, it is a wise idea to have the athlete give you an extra inhaler to keep in your first aid kit that is kept in the dojang and travels with you to tournaments. In this manner you are assured that the proper medication is always readily available. The athlete should get two full "puffs" holding each one in their mouth for approximately thirty seconds. This inhaler should be held approximately six inches from the mouth, NOT IN THE MOUTH for best results. This way the medication can be properly inhaled. To prevent overdosing from panic an athlete should never have more than two full puffs every two hours unless otherwise directed by their physician. The effects of using an inhaler can last as long as four to six hours. Overdosing from an inhaler could lead to an overstimulation of the heart and contribute to a heart attack. On the other hand, an athlete or instructor should never ignore an asthma attack, using an inhaler to prevent a major attack from occurring.

If an athlete forgets to bring an inhaler and has an asthma attack, seat the athlete on the floor and allow them to rest back against you. Encourage the athlete to take deep breaths, bringing it all the way from their "belly button", dragging out each breath as much as possible. Breaths should come in through the nose and exhale out through the mouth. Try to calm the athlete while having everyone else continue with their activities away from the person having the asthma attack.

If the athlete begins to hyperventilate (short, quick breaths) have the person breath slowly and deeply into a brown paper sandwich bag by asking them to breathe in through their mouth and out through their nose. This allows the air to be warmed before entering the lungs, aiding in the control of the asthma attack since cold can trigger an attack in some individuals. Once an attack has subsided the athlete will probably be too tired to continue any activity. Encourage the athlete to rest and drink lots of water, and not to worry, that he or she can pick up the next time where they missed out on the present activity.

The important thing to remember is that asthma is a very serious condition, and an athlete should never be punished by removing their inhaler or preventing an athlete from using their inhaler, as this can endanger their life. Rather an athlete should be encouraged to use their inhaler whenever they deem necessary returning to activity as quickly as possible once they feel they can.

Even though an athlete may not have had any recent asthma attacks it does not mean that one will not occur, particularly in a competition setting where the chest may be repeatedly struck. Always ensure an athlete has an inhaler readily available if an attack should occur, if they have been diagnosed with asthma.

If the athlete is going to be participating in an Olympic sporting competition, or where drug testing may occur, have the athlete register with the anti-doping committee (in the United States it is the US Anti-Doping Agency) their legal use of the inhaler with forms (TUE - Therapeutic Use Exemption) their physician must complete and have put on file with the anti-doping committee. This may be in addition to other medications, such as steroids, used to help control the asthmatic attacks.

Diabetes

Diabetes mellitus is a disorder involving the metabolism of carbohydrates caused by a deficiency of insulin readily available in the body. Insulin is required to metabolize glucose, the basic component of sugar and carbohydrates found in many foods necessary for proper nutrition. Diabetes is normally controlled by proper diet, exercise, medication, and sometimes insulin injections. When diabetes is not properly controlled the person can go into diabetic shock. Diabetic shock takes many different forms in each individual but can include trembling, irritability, hunger, excessive sweating, confusion, convulsions and loss of consciousness.

Since diabetes is controlled by a balance of food intake vs. amount of exercise, any change in food intake or amount of exercise can affect a person with diabetes. Athletes with diabetes in the martial arts have to be particularly aware of this and monitor both their weight loss from change in eating habits prior to competition as well as the increase in activity that is part of the normal competition day. Athletes should have their physician regulate the amount of medication and insulin accordingly to avoid any chance of going into diabetic shock during competition or competition preparation. Often physicians will recommend administering insulin into the abdomen rather than the arms or legs during periods of increased activity and/or reduced food intake to reduce the chances of diabetic shock during these periods of time.

If an athlete begins to show signs of diabetic shock and has not yet lost consciousness you need to get them seated in a cool dry area, and give them either orange juice or another sugar loaded drink, glucose tablets, or candy to help bring their blood glucose levels back into line where they should be. Do not encourage the use of drinks with caffeine as this may further complicate the situation.

If an athlete progresses into convulsions **do not** try to restrain the person. Instead clear the area of any items that may cause injury to the athlete if struck during the convulsions. **NEVER PLACE ANYTHING INTO A CONVULSING PERSON'S MOUTH,** including sticks, fingers or anything else. The athlete may bite down so hard as to break it off and then choke on the item. Monitor the athlete for any breathing difficulty and invoke CPR if the individual stops breathing as instructed in your CPR certification course.

If the athlete remains unconscious or has difficulty breathing begin your emergency medical plan (refer to Chapter 7) immediately. If the athlete does not lose consciousness, he or she will probably be too tired to continue any activity at that time. Allow the athlete to rest in a cool area, checking on them periodically to ensure that they are not getting progressively worse. On the other hand, under normal day-to-day circumstances, never "baby" a person with diabetes as most do not want people to know they have diabetes. It is a personal matter to them, not to be shared with everyone in the school or on the team, so do not share this information with other students unless you have been granted permission by the athlete or the athlete's parent.

Epilepsy & Seizure Disorders

Epilepsy and seizure disorders are still very common disorders in our population today, but are better controlled than in previous decades, with many "outgrowing" the disorder and leading normal productive adult lives. A seizure or convulsion is a condition that occurs to a person affecting the majority of their brain for a limited amount of time. Since these disorders involve the brain instructors should obtain a recent physical exam and release for participation in martial arts before allowing the athlete to participate in competition. If the athlete chooses to only train and not compete, there is a much lower chance of having to worry about a seizure occurring due to a hit to the head as in competition. If the athlete has been released for all participation by their physician, no restrictions or concerns about this athlete are necessary.

Often a person with a seizure disorder will have a feeling of the ensuing convulsion moments before it begins in what is known as an "aura". An aura is a sensation of sound, smell, sight, taste or general feeling that is a warning to the person that a convulsion is about to occur. Generally this sensation only lasts seconds before the convulsion begins, sometimes just enough time for the person to sit onto the ground.

If an athlete does have a seizure you should never try to hold the person down. Instead, move any objects out of the way that may injure them if struck. **NEVER STICK ANY OBJECT INTO THE MOUTH OF A CONVULSING ATHLETE,** including sticks, fingers, etc. The athlete may bite down so hard as to break the object in half and choke on the object as it becomes lodged in their throat during the convulsion. Monitor the athlete to try to prevent further injury, and to ensure that the athlete does not stop breathing. If the athlete stops breathing and does not begin breathing upon the seizure stopping, you must begin rescue breathing as instructed in your CPR certification course upon conclusion of the seizure.

If the athlete does not have any problems breathing there is probably no reason to take them for further medical evaluation and the athlete needs to be reassured that you are not going to force them to go for further medical evaluation. Many people with epilepsy and seizure disorders want to be treated as normal as possible, and know when they have crossed their limits. If an athlete does stop breathing or remains unconscious for more than thirty seconds further medical evaluation is warranted.

Instructors must realize that athletes are at higher risk for seizures when put in situations of high stress or extended exercise, such as competition. Individuals should not be prohibited from participation in martial arts but should be monitored for any change or increase in the number of seizures occurring. An athlete must be completely honest with their physician to the amount of exercise the sport involves and how they feel during participation in order to properly regulate the medication that reduces the chance of having a seizure. Instructors must be informed of such a condition in order to be prepared for any seizures that may occur. Otherwise, treat these individuals as normal athletes, without restrictions upon written release for participation as part of an annual athletic participation physical exam conducted by their physician.

Migraine Headaches

Not much is known in the medical community about the source of migraine headaches, but it is known that many people suffer from migraines, especially females. Migraine headaches are very intense headaches that come on suddenly and feel like they not only take over your entire head, but your body and mind as well. People suffering from a migraine headache will not only be sensitive to loud noises, but also bright lights and motion. If the athlete takes a medication regularly for migraine headaches (whether over-the-counter or prescription form) know where it is (or have your own supply given to you by the athlete to keep in your medical kit) at all times, as the pain comes on suddenly and can completely incapacitate a person. If possible, put the person in a cool, dimly lit or dark room, that has little to no noise and allow them to rest undisturbed. The headache sometimes will pass rather quickly or can last hours, even days. Do not tell the athlete you believe they are faking, as the pain is for real, and you are more likely to increase the pain they are feeling.

In many cases, even if the headache is not associated with stress (as it is in many cases) the stress of knowing you can't continue the workout increases the pain and pressure. Try to calm and reassure the athlete that they can return to participation once the migraine episode has passed or in the next session. As always, if the athlete is taking any medication and competing in a nationally or internationally sanctioned event, they need to check with the anti-doping agency responsible for drug testing to see if their medication is on the banned substance list.

Chapter Six Key Points

✦ Athletes with special medical conditions should not be seen as having a weakness but as having a condition to be monitored and managed in training.

✦ Asthma should not be ignored. An athlete should have access to his or her inhaler whenever necessary during training.

✦ Athletes with diabetes need to monitor their eating and activity levels, especially on competition days.

✦ The stress of competition can raise the risk of an athlete with epilepsy/seizure disorder having a seizure. Athletes should discuss this risk with both their physician and their instructor or coach.

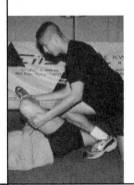

For
Instructors

Injury Care Programs

a program for your school or competition

Annual Medical Exams

One of the best ways to prevent injury is to know an athlete's health limitations or restrictions. This is most commonly done in all sports activities by requiring a physical exam by an MD every year for continued participation in a sports program. This not only helps the athlete to know the status of their health, along with any restrictions in activity, but also informs the instructors of any health problems the athlete may have that needs to be monitored. These physicals should be completed and signed by an MD every year, and kept on file in a locking cabinet of the office of each martial arts school. Keeping such records may also help to reduce liability insurance costs as the school owner has taken extra steps to secure the safety and well-being of all participating athletes. A sample physical exam form that may be used for athletes by a school is the following:

SAMPLE MEDICAL HISTORY QUESTIONNAIRE

NAME:_____   NICKNAME_____

DATE OF BIRTH_____   SOCIAL SECURITY NUMBER_____

ADDRESS_____

HOME PHONE:_____ E-MAIL ADDRESS_____

IN CASE OF EMERGENCY:

CONTACT:_____   PHONE #_____RELATIONSHIP_____

****

PLEASE RESPOND TO ALL OF THE FOLLOWING QUESTIONS, GIVING DETAILS AS NECESSARY
— ALL INFORMATION PROVIDED WILL REMAIN STRICTLY CONFIDENTIAL.

FAMILY HISTORY

	AGE(S)	HEALTH	OCCUPATION	HISTORY OF DISEASE
FATHER:				
MOTHER:				
BROTHER(S):				
SISTER(S):				
OTHER:				

PERSONAL HISTORY

PLEASE CHECK ALL CONDITIONS WHICH CURRENTLY HAVE OR HAVE HAD A PREVIOUS PROBLEM WITH:

		MEDICATIONS CURRENTLY TAKING
NERVOUS SYSTEM	_____	_____
HEART/BLOOD PRESSURE	_____	_____
BLOOD	_____	_____
ANEMIA	_____	_____
VISION	_____	GLASSES OR CONTACTS (circle)
THYROID/ENDOCRINE	_____	_____
GASTROINTESTINAL	_____	_____
DIABETES	_____	_____
SPEECH	_____	_____
MENTAL	_____	_____
RESPIRATORY	_____	_____

****ASTHMATICS MUST PROVIDE AN EXTRA INHALER

URINARY/KIDNEY	_____	_____
GENITAL/REPRODUCTIVE	_____	_____
HEARING	_____	_____
BALANCE	_____	_____
CANCER	_____	_____
EPILEPSY	_____	_____
SICKLE-CELL TRAIT	_____	_____
DENTAL	_____	_____

WEAR DENTAL APPLIANCE, CROWN, BRIDGE (CIRCLE)

FAINTING/DIZZINESS	_____	_____

HERNIA	_____	SURGICALLY REPAIRED	_____
BACK PROBLEMS	_____		_____
SKIN PROBLEMS	_____		_____
OTHER	_____		_____

HEAD INJURY INFORMATION:

Have you ever sustained a concussion without loss of consciousness?   YES   NO
DATE(S)_____

Have you ever been knocked-out, unconscious?   YES NO
DATE(S)_____

If yes, do you remember what grade concussion it was? 1st 2nd 3rd

Have you ever had a CT scan or MRI associated with a head injury?   YES   NO
DATE(S)_____

Have you ever been placed on a spine board & transported to the hospital to be evaluated for possible damage to the head, neck or spine?   YES   NO
DATE(S)_____

Explain any problems or complications associated with your head injury:

_____

_____

_____

ORTHOPEDIC HISTORY:

In the following section, list all injuries from the previous 5 years that resulted in treatment being necessary for continued participation in athletic competition, whether or not related to participation in taekwondo. For example, fractures, damage to muscle, tendon, ligament or cartilage, and/or surgical repair of any of these areas, or metal implants. *PLEASE INCLUDE ALL DATES of INJURY or SURGERY.*

HEAD/FACE/JAW _____

NECK/THROAT _____

BACK _____

CHEST _____

ABDOMEN _____

SHOULDER _____

UPPER ARM _____

ELBOW _____

FOREARM _____

WRIST/HAND _____

THUMB/FINGERS _____

HIP/IT BAND _____

THIGH (QUADS/HAMS)_____

KNEE _____

SHIN/CALF _____

ANKLE _____

FOOT/TOES _____

OTHER _____

Date of your last medical physical exam _____

Name of the attending physician _____

Date of your last tetanus shot _____

List/explain any conditions or medications not previously disclosed, including over-the-counter drugs and vitamins:

_____

_____

_____

_____

List/explain any allergies which you may have (for example, codeine, penicillin, food, insects, etc.)

_____

_____

_____

I hereby acknowledge that the above completed information is correct and complete to my best knowledge.

_____

      ATHLETE'S SIGNATURE   DATE

INSURANCE INFORMATION:

Primary Insurance Company_____

Insurance Address_____

Insurance Phone#_____

POLICY # _____   GROUP #_____

Claimant's Name (Print)_____

Policyholder's Name (if different)_____

****
****

I, _____, consent to medical treatment for athletic related
     (Print Name Clearly)
injuries/illnesses by _____ and/or Hospital Medical Staff. I
authorize treatment by such personnel in the event of injury or illness.

_____
ATHLETE'S SIGNATURE   DATE

As a parent or legal guardian of _____, who
is under the age of 18, I hereby authorize medical treatment in the event of an
injury or illness while participating in activities and competitions associated with
_____ by _____ and/or Hospital
Medical Staff.

_____
PARENT/GUARDIAN SIGNATURE   DATE

****

*Athlete must provide a copy of primary insurance company
card (front & back plus any secondary insurance company card
information)*

PHYSICAL EXAM
(to be completed by attending MD or DO)

GENERAL MEDICINE

CLEARED FOR ATHLETIC PARTICIPATION	*CLEARED WITH RESTRICTIONS*	*FURTHER EVALUATION IS NECESSARY BEFORE BEING CLEARED*

Height: Weight: Body Fat Content:

RHR: BP:

HEART: LUNGS:

GENITALS:

URINALYSIS: Carbohydrates:
                          Proteins:

Problems:

Doctor's Initials_____   DATE_____

Doctor's Name_____

Doctor's Address_____

Doctor's Phone Number_____

****

ORTHOPEDIC

CLEARED FOR ATHLETIC PARTICIPATION	*CLEARED WITH RESTRICTIONS*	*FURTHER EVALUATION IS NECESSARY BEFORE BEING CLEARED*

Problems:

Doctor's Initials_____   DATE_____

Doctor's Name_____

Doctor's Address_____

Doctor's Phone Number_____

Emergency Medical Plan

Every martial arts program and school should have already set up a plan of action in case a major injury occurs in the dojang. This is better known as an *Emergency Medical Plan*. To ensure the best care of athletes, the following guidelines should be used to organize and create an emergency medical plan.

The emergency medical plan should be predetermined prior to the beginning of a session for cases of traumatic injury, put into writing and placed in an area of easy access should a traumatic event or injury occur. Remember, whoever is the first person to begin care of a traumatic injury will be unable to leave the athlete, and must depend upon others to follow instructions, so it is best to have a carefully planned outline of action in case such an event should occur. Ensure that all instructors and senior students know where this plan is located and how to follow it. Doing a mock practice twice a year is a good idea.

First, at least one instructor who is present at all times in the dojang should be certified in CPR and First Aid care by either the American Red Cross, American Lung Association, National Safety Council or other certifying organizations. There needs to be at least one person certified in the dojang at all times. Often, if you have several instructors and students wanting to become certified such organizations will come to the school to do the training and certification. It is best to get the Community First Aid and CPR training or Sports First Aid and CPR training as these two courses cover the needs of pediatric, adolescent, and adult care. Having personnel certified in CPR and First Aid often also helps to reduce your cost of liability insurance as you are showing prudence in the safety and care of all individuals participating in the program.

Secondly, know where the nearest telephone is located in order to direct designated instructors or students to call 911 (in most areas of the United States) for the Emergency Medical Service (EMS). Every school should have written in the Emergency Medical Plan and discuss with instructors what information he/she will need to relay to the Emergency Medical Service operator. If 911 is not used in the area, find out what the emergency medical phone number is, and make sure it is located near the phone along with school address, phone number, and directions to school. A good plan would include a sheet with the following information for caller to provide for the 911 Operator:

• Address and phone number (as listed by the telephone)

• Directions to the site (as written, located by the telephone)

• Exact location where the injured person is located

• Details of the accident (including when and how happened), as well as any of the known injuries (cardiac arrest, head trauma, unconscious, etc.) and any care being administered to the person at that time

• Name of person placing the call

DO NOT HANG UP THE TELEPHONE BEFORE THE 911 OPERATOR HAS HUNG UP THEIR LINE.

In the event the 911 Operator needs more information he/she will be able to contact the staff member who originally placed the call.

Thirdly, find out if any of your staff has any athletic training or sports medicine background, as this knowledge can be very beneficial in caring for injuries and traumatic events. Plan who will be asked to help in case of any emergency. There is no need to actually discuss it with them, but have a plan, at least in your head. Obviously some staff members will be more helpful to the situation than others.

Fourth, find out if any gates or doors on the premises will need to be unlocked in the case paramedics or ambulance must be called.

Predetermine who must be contacted for this to be done. Have the name & phone number of who is to be contacted written down in your emergency medical plan and by the telephone. Have one person designated to meet the paramedics and/or ambulance outdoors, bringing them inside to the location of the injured person.

Lastly, have an instructor retrieve an injury report form and record your evaluation for you. You can sign it later, but it is important to get the information in writing before the athlete is transported. The person initiating the original treatment of the individual must remain with the athlete, stabilizing the injury, until the paramedics arrive and take over. **Under no circumstances do you release the injury until told to do so by Emergency Medical Service Personnel to anyone unless you are physically incapable of continuing life support treatment.**

After releasing the athlete to the care of Emergency Medical Services Personnel, get a copy of the directions to the hospital for the parent or family member if necessary. Ask the parent or family member to bring back a release form for participation and a report on the injury. This report and release is filed with the injury report form that you completed. Make sure all injury report forms are filed in a locking cabinet with limited access, as these are considered confidential files not to be shared with anyone without the athlete's (and parents') written consent.

Attached you will find copies of the injury log form, injury report form and head injury care form designed and used by the USA Taekwondo for all injuries. It is a wise idea to keep written record of any injuries or incidences occurring to athletes for liability reasons as well as to simply be able to keep track of athlete's health.

DAILY INJURY LOG FORM

Date	Name	Body Part Injured/ treated	Treatment

CONFIDENTIAL ATHLETIC INJURY/ILLNESS REPORT FORM

NAME_____ DOB_____ GENDER_____

ATHLETE___ COACH____ OFFICIAL___ PARENT___ OTHER_____

DATE & TIME OF INJURY_____ STATE/COUNTRY _____

NAME OF COMPETITION_____

INJURY NATURE: ACUTE___ CHRONIC __ RE-INJURY___ (date of 1ST INJURY_____)

OCCASION: WARM-UP____ COMPETITION_____ NON-SPORT_____

WEIGHT CLASS_____ WTF or OLYMPIC WGT___ BELT COLOR/DAN_____

CLASSIFICATION: PRE-ADOLESCENT___ JUNIOR___ JUNIOR ELITE__SENIOR____

SENIOR ELITE_____ GOLDEN SENIOR_____ NON-ATHLETE_____

===

VITALS: TEMP_____ BP_____ PULSE_____ RESP_____ PUPILS_____ LOC_____

ALLERGIES_____

DIAGNOSIS/EVALUATION_____

HISTORY & EVALUATION_____

_____

_____

_____

SENT TO HOSPITAL____ X-RAY___ FURTHER EVALUATION____FOLLOW-UP____

TREATMENT_____

CLEARED FOR PARTICIPATION___ 30-DAY OUT HEAD INJURY____ RETURN _____

SIGNATURE_____

TITLE_____

CIRCLE ONE FOR EACH:

Was the injury sustained from:
- ❑ blocking a kick
- ❑ blocking a punch
- ❑ attacking with a kick
- ❑ attacking with a punch
- ❑ charging opponent, no kick or punch
- ❑ unblocked kick or punch
- ❑ stepped into kick
- ❑ stepped into punch
- ❑ recovering from missed kick
- ❑ attacked with back turned
- ❑ kicked/punched while falling
- ❑ kicked after fall/on the ground
- ❑ hitting playing surface
- ❑ colliding/clashing with opponent
- ❑ warming up
- ❑ unknown origin
- ❑ non-sport related

Body Part:_____
    Right   Left   Both
             Posterior Anterior
Specific Structure:_____

Injury Nature:_____

If concussion, what grade:___

**wearing
mouthpiece?**   **YES**   **NO**

Was the injury sustained during:
- ❑ previous injury prior to event
- ❑ 1st round
- ❑ 2nd round
- ❑ 3rd round
- ❑ warm up/between fights
- ❑ non-sport related

Type of kick causing injury:
- ❑ spinning/swing
- ❑ thrust
- ❑ axe
- ❑ punch/no kick
- ❑ non-sport related
- ❑ fell onto, no kick involved

Was the injury sustained during:
- ❑ previous injury prior to event
- ❑ during fight number _____
- ❑ warm up/between fights
- ❑ practice
- ❑ non-sport related

Has athlete ever sustained a head injury before?   YES   NO
Date(s) of head injury_____   Type of head Injury_____
Evaluated at hospital   YES   NO   Stayed overnight at hospital YES NO
Complications_____

When released for return to participation/competition?_____
by whom? _____   In writing? yes no

HEAD INJURY GUIDELINES

This is a follow-up sheet for your health and safety. Quite often, signs of a head injury do not appear immediately after trauma, but hours after injury. The purpose of this fact sheet is to alert you to the symptoms of significant head injuries, symptoms that may occur several hours after sustaining a head injury.

It is common to have a headache following trauma to the head or face. If you feel the need to take a medication to relieve this discomfort, you may take **2 acetaminophen tablets (Tylenol®) every 4 hours for the pain and NOTHING ELSE!!!! DO NOT TAKE ASPIRIN OR IBUPROFEN (Advil ®, Motrin®, Aleve®, Nuprin®, etc.)** If in doubt, contact your physician before taking any medication.

If you experience one or more of the following symptoms following a head injury, contact your physician or go to the nearest hospital:

1. Difficulty remembering recent events or meaningful facts
2. Severe headache, particularly in a specific location
3. Stiffening of the neck, causing sharp pain
4. Bleeding or clear fluid dripping from the ears or nose
5. Mental confusion or strange feeling
6. Nausea or vomiting
7. Dizziness, poor balance, or unsteadiness
8. Weakness in either arms or legs
9. Abnormal drowsiness or sleepiness
10. Convulsions
11. Unequal pupil size
12. Loss of appetite
13. Persistent ringing of the ears
14. Slurring of speech
15. Lethargy, the "blahs"

The appearance of any of the above symptoms tells you that you have had a significant head injury that **requires medical attention**. If any of these symptoms appear, contact your physician, or report **IMMEDIATELY** to the hospital. Do not eat or drink anything at this point until evaluated by medical personnel.

_____   _____
          Evaluator   Phone/Pager Number

REPORT TO YOUR INSTRUCTOR THE FOLLOWING DAY BEFORE BEGINNING PARTICIPATION IN ANY ACTIVITY

IF YOU HAVE SUFFERED A CONCUSSION OR KNOCK-OUT YOU WILL NOT BE ALLOWED TO PARTICIPATE FOR 30 DAYS IN CONTACT ACTIVITY OR COMPETITION.

YOU MUST BRING A RELEASE FORM FROM YOUR PHYSICIAN TO BE ALLOWED TO RETURN AFTER THIS 30-DAY PERIOD HAS BEEN COMPLETED— NO EXCEPTIONS

What do you put in a first aid kit?

Everyone knows that they should have a first aid kit fully stocked in their school and for travel to tournaments, but very few actually know what should be in it. A first aid kit needs the essential items for caring for and/or preventing injuries, easily accessible for use by athletes and instructors. Only those items whose correct usage your are familiar with should be included in the kit. Although you can purchase expensive pre-packed first aid and trainer's kits it is generally better to create your own kit to include the following:

- ☐ 2-3 rolls of 1½" white athletic tape (more for competition)
- ☐ Roll of pre-wrap or underwrap
- ☐ Can of tape adherent spray
- ☐ 3"x 3" sterile gauze pads (can be used for bleeding or taping)
- ☐ Skin lube or petroleum jelly
- ☐ Several ace wraps — 3", 4" & 6"
- ☐ Bandages of various sizes and shapes
- ☐ Steri-strips® or Butterfly bandages®
- ☐ Swab sticks or Q-tips®
- ☐ Foam or felt padding
- ☐ Noseplugs (get cotton rolls used by your dentist)
- ☐ Small tube of antibiotic ointment
- ☐ Bottle of saline solution (for contacts and wound cleaning)
- ☐ Contact case & small mirror
- ☐ Small jar of diaper rash cream (to help dry up blisters)
- ☐ Small bottle eye drops/re-wetting drops (for irritated eyes or contacts)
- ☐ Small bottle of povidine or Betadine® solution (for disinfecting open wounds)
- ☐ Latex gloves (lots!)

❑ Bandage scissors (blunt-end)

❑ Tweezers

❑ Fingernail clippers

❑ Penlight (small flashlight used to examine the eyes)

❑ Plastic bags for ice & several instant ice packs (in case no ice is available)

❑ Brown paper sandwich bag (for hyperventilating athlete)

❑ Plastic wrap (may be too expensive but nice to have)

❑ Jar or tube of your favorite analgesic rub (roll-ons are best)

❑ Tongue blades or popsicle sticks (for fractured or dislocated fingers & toes)

❑ Tea bags (for a bleeding injury inside of the mouth; wet with cold water and place on wound to help stop the bleeding from acid in the tea)

❑ Bottle of glucose tablets (for diabetics, dehydrated athletes, loss of energy)

❑ Alcohol gel for hand cleansing

❑ Small bottle of acetaminophen (Tylenol®) if you choose to give medication

❑ Small bottle of anti-inflammatory medication (Advil®, Motrin®, Orudus®, etc) if you choose to give pain-relieving medication to athletes

❑ Spray bottle of ten percent bleach solution (for cleaning blood off of uniforms)

Many other items are nice to have, even beneficial, but these are the minimum necessary items, at the lowest cost to you. It is wise to make a letter for the parents of your athletes as well as for local medical offices and clinics asking for any of these items to be donated. You will be surprised how much you can get for free! Then, if you do not want to actually purchase an expensive trainer's kit, simply go to a home improvement store and purchase a small plastic tool box for anywhere from ten to twenty dollars to put all of your supplies in. This is much cheaper than buying the commercially produced kits and it will have everything you want in it. You can often get grocery stores to donate a roll of vegetable bags to use for your ice bags if they know it is for a good cause.

It is also a wise idea to keep a contact case, mirror and saline solution on hand so athletes do not waste time trying to find some place to store the contacts that become too irritated to continue to wear. Saline solution can also be used to flood an open wound or an irritated eye, as the spout allows you to directly target a small area with a sterilized solution. The saline takes the place of needing hydrogen peroxide in your kit. As for foam padding, ask your local high school football team for any used pads they are going to throw away that you can cut into smaller pieces to use for injuries or injury prevention. Be forewarned though, you may have to cut the pads open to remove the plastic insert found in most football pads.

How do I determine what type of medical attention is needed & where do I find it?

Okay, you say, now I have a better understanding of when to seek medical attention but how do I know who to go to and where to find them. Here are a few pointers:

1. Certified Athletic Trainers (ATC) – these individuals have a national certification from the National Athletic Trainers Association, and in most states a state license or registration from the Board of Allied Health Professions or related boards, to handle sports-related injuries for people of any age, any ability, any sport. The care ranges from preventative taping, strength & conditioning, immediate injury evaluation (usually on site), follow-up treatment and/or referral to a physician, and rehabilitation and strengthening for return to athletic competition. ATC's can be found in many high school athletic programs, college programs, all pro-sports programs, rehab clinics, wellness programs or in private practice. You can contact the National Athletic Trainers Association (NATA) to help you find an ATC in your area. ATC's cannot prescribe drugs or perform surgery but often work at a physician's side in the office, clinic and athletic competitions.

2. Physical Therapist (PT) – nationally board certified by the American Physical Therapy Association, and in most states registered or licensed by the state; try to choose a PT that works specifically with sports medicine and athletes as many work predominantly with those injured on the job, from auto accidents or the elderly, rather than athletes who generally work harder and faster to recover. They also cannot prescribe medications or perform surgery, and they work under the direction of a physician. In order to be seen by a PT you must have a prescription for therapy from a physician (MD, DO or DC).

3. Physicians – board certified first in general medicine and then in their specialty:

MD's:

a. Sports Medicine Orthopedists – physicians who specialize in bone and joint injuries occurring to those who participate in sports; often are surgeons as well, and can prescribe medications. Check out who your local university or pro team uses as their orthopedist, and see if they are allowed by your insurance. They are less conservative, meaning they are less likely to tell you to just stay off of it; rather they will send you for appropriate rehab therapy through either an ATC or PT. The orthopedist has further specialties pertaining to the part of the body they prefer to deal with, such as the shoulder, knee, back, etc. It is wise to choose a sports medicine orthopedist who specializes in the joint injury that you have sustained, so shop around before settling on a physician.

b. Sports Medicine Podiatrist – physicians who specialize only in problems of the foot and ankle, nothing else, with those specializing in sports medicine gearing their practice to athletes or those who are actively involved in sport activities. Once again, contact your local university or pro team to find out who they use, as they are often at the top of the list to choose from.

c. Sports Medicine Pediatrician or Pediatric Orthopedist – very hard to find as they are rare – physicians that deal with bone and joint injuries and disorders of child athletes, and the specialized problems that can arise from the young sport participant. If you can find one, and you have a child under the age of 14 they are the recommended choice.

d. Family Medicine or General Medicine – physicians who generally deal with a little bit of everything from illnesses to injuries, with few of them specializing in one area. Often your insurance company will require you to visit them first before getting referral to a specialist.

e. Oral-Maxillofacial Physician – physicians who specialize in working with injuries and disorders of the face, mouth and jaw, and the one you want to see if you have any serious injury to the area, especially if surgery is recommended or a fracture is involved.

f. Plastic Surgeons – physicians that specialize in reducing or changing the appearance of the skin, shape of the face and body. Often plastic surgeons are also maxillofacial physicians as a lot of plastic surgery involves changing or fixing facial, jaw and mouth features. The plastic surgeon or maxillofacial physician are the ones you want to see for sutures (stitches) on the face, especially around the eyes for females, and around the chin for males. They do beautiful work and leave little to no scarring.

g. ENT – physician specializing in the treatment of only the Ears, Nose & Throat. This is one of the physicians you should consider seeing when you have an injury to the nose, or have an illness of the nose and throat.

h. Dentist – physician that deals with problems of the teeth and gums. Dental surgeons are the ones that will perform corrective surgery for injuries to the teeth and gums, whereas the regular dentist is the one you go to for cavities, root canals, and general dental health.

i. Opthalmalogist – specialized physician that deals with the eyes from illnesses to injuries that may lead to surgery or other treatments. The optometrist is the physician you go to for eye examinations, eyeglasses, and general eye health.

j. OB/GYN – physician that specializes in female's health, with the GYN (gynecologist) caring for general female health and the OB (obstetrics) specializing in working with pregnant females and their health as well as the health of their developing baby.

Non-MD Physicians:

k. Doctor of Osteopathy (DO) – physician whose background combines the education of an MD and a DC (chiropractor) enabling them to perform surgery and write prescriptions as well as do adjustments of the joints. The DO is nationally board certified and state licensed like an MD or a DC.

l. Doctor of Chiropractic (DC) – physician whose background is related to what is considered non-invasive treatment (do not do surgical treatments), involving adjustments, massage and counseling among many others specialties. Like the DO & MD, they are nationally board certified and hold a state license. They cannot write a prescription for medications, but they can write prescriptions for diagnostic tests such as MRI's, or for rehab therapy. Some have further training in strength and conditioning or nutrition. They also have various specialties, including sports medicine. As an athlete I prefer to have you seen by a DC whose has the further education, experience and certification in chiropractic sports medicine, and one who is accustomed to working with athletes.

m. PhD – Doctor of Philosophy – not a medical degree but the highest degree that can be obtained from a university in sports medicine without going to medical school. These ARE NOT physicians, although you call them Dr. So-in-so, and their degree DOES NOT equate to a degree obtained from medical school although it does have its merits. Both ATC's & PT's can obtain a PhD, with PT's calling their PhD a DPT (Doctor of Physical Therapy). There knowledge base must be at a high level in order to be able to obtain the degree, with a greater understanding of the body and how it functions than those who have only a bachelor's or master's degree in the same field, as well as interest and ability to complete necessary research in the field.

So, that is just a few of the medical personnel you may seek for further evaluation. Their are also various assistants to the physician working in their offices, clinics, hospitals and in surgery with them that can also be a good source of information and/or direction to the best medical professional for the injury. These include:

• **Physician's Assistant (PA)**

• **Orthopedic Extender (OE)** – often they are ATC's

• **Nurse and Nurse Practitioners** – various levels of education with Nurse Practitioners and Nurse Midwives having the highest levels

• **Physical Therapy Assistant (PTA)** – work under the direction of PT

• **Occupational Therapist (OT)** – work with fine motor skills rehab

Chapter Seven Key Points

✦ Requiring an annual medical exam for athletes is an excellent way for athletes and instructors to prevent injuries by being aware of an athlete's physical condition.

✦ Requiring an annual medical exam for athletes may reduce liability insurance costs for school owners.

✦ Every school should have an emergency medical plan in place and all instructors should be aware of the plan.

✦ At all times when the school is in operation, there should always be at least one instructor or coach present who is certified in CPR and First Aid.

✦ Always complete and sign an injury report for all injuries that occur in the school.

✦ Only include items in your first aid which you fully understand how to use or apply.

✦ A low cost alternative to a pre-stocked first aid kit is to pack a plastic tool kit with donated and/or purchased supplies.

Sports Medicine Teams 8

organizing a team for your tournament

If you have ever been to a USA Taekwondo National Event you have probably seen the medical care provided in the Sports Medicine Area and on the competition floor by medical volunteers that I organize. Many competition organizers feel they could never have that same kind of coverage at local, state or regional events, but this is not true. Getting licensed/certified medical personnel to handle the medical care at your events is not so terribly difficult. The USA Taekwondo Sports Medicine Committee has set criteria on which coordination of medical personnel are based for national events which anyone can use as a guideline for organizing medical coverage of an event. Here are a few easy guidelines to follow:

1. Have **at least one MD** (orthopedist preferred), **DO** (doctor of osteopathy) and/or one **PA** (physician assistant) on the competition floor at all times; add a orthopedic pediatrician if you have a large number of pre-adolescent or adolescent competitors; a second MD/DO/PA should be in the Sports Medicine Triage Area if available.

2. Have at least **one ATC** (NATA Certified Athletic Trainer) **for every two to three mats** of sparring at all times plus at least one additional ATC for your medical treatment area. ATC's will also be responsible for all athletic taping of both pre-competition and injury care taping for all athletes. Generally all ATC's will be utilized in the Sports Medicine Area prior to the beginning of the event in order to expedite the taping of athletes prior to the event, before

taking up there duties of injury recognition on the floor.

3. Have at least **one DC** (Chiropractic Doctor) — Sports Chiropractic Certified preferred if available as they have further training for competition venues.

4. Add an RN (registered nurse) or Nurse Practitioner, PT (physical therapist), DDS (dentist) or other medical staff if available **if they have had sport competition experience.** If they have not worked in a competition atmosphere they may not be comfortable with the speed at which injuries are evaluated and treated, but can be beneficial to have in the medical triage area.

5. Include student athletic trainers, chiropractic students, and medical students to increase the number of volunteers **in addition to your licensed/certified medical volunteers.** The licensed medical professionals can sign off for these students as they need the hours of experience for their license and/or certification.

6. Add **Paramedics/EMTs** if possible. Request a volunteer standby unit or pay to have a squad on standby (as opposed to simply having an ambulance on site). The difference amounts to paramedics being trained to use advanced life support equipment, oxygen and life supporting drugs to sustain life until the patient has reached the hospital if a traumatic event should occur as opposed to basic first aid care while being transported. This is also beneficial if one of the spectators should suffer a heart attack or other medical emergency while at the competition. Often you can get a reduced price to have a unit stay on site if the company knows that there is a physician on site directing care of the injured athlete. Simply call the local fire department to make arrangements for a paramedics unit, asking for the department that handles coverage of sporting events. You may also get a reduction in your liability insurance rates by having a paramedics unit present.

Now I am sure you are wondering how to go about getting these people to volunteer their time. First you will need to send a letter asking for medical volunteers, include the dates, times, location, number of participants and how many volunteers are needed. Here are a few places to send your letter to request for medical volunteers:

1. Contact the Head Athletic Trainer (ATC) at your local university, college, junior college or high school athletic training room. This person can usually either help provide you with personnel from their own training room (including ATC's, MD's & DC's) or give you phone numbers of contacts that can help you. Don't hesitate to contact these ATC's as they are accustomed to volunteering their time or helping to coordinate volunteers for local events. The Head Athletic Trainer can also have some of their upper level student trainers volunteer for the event as part of their required hours of experience.

2. Contact the Sports Medicine Coordinator at a local physical therapy clinic such as HealthSouth, Rehability, PhysioTherapy Associates or any private practice rehab clinic. These clinics are also accustomed to assisting with coordinating medical volunteers for events.

3. Contact local orthopedic practices as many love to have the opportunity to work sporting events of this nature. Simply ask them to volunteer as many hours as possible if they cannot work the entire day.

4. Contact local chiropractors trained in sports chiropractic medicine (such as ProSport Chiropractic or members of the Sports Medicine Division of the ACA- American Chiropractic Association) via the internet. These organizations have member chiropractors all over the USA who are sports chiropractic certified and who routinely work sporting events in addition to rodeo events and race car events, and who have additional training for working sporting events, including emergency care basic need. Do not replace your MD or DO with a DC or vice versa, but rather have both to better benefit your athletes and staff.

5. Contact your local hospital director to post a notice requesting volunteers for your event. You can often get a variety of medical volunteers, including nurses, doctors, ATC's, etc. You can also request the hospital to become a sponsor and donate needed first aid supplies for your event

6. Contact your sport's national governing body as they often have a medical coordinator (like myself) for events that can give you added guidance and direction. I often coordinate the volunteer medical staff (for a small fee) for events even when I myself do not work the event, as I do "rent out for hire" jobs.

Many of these medical volunteers will also gladly donate some first aid and taping supplies in addition to or instead of volunteering for the event. Most medical volunteers simply wish to have their organization recognized as a sponsor of your event by allowing them to hang a company banner. It is also a nice gesture to give each medical volunteer a certificate of appreciation for volunteering, which can be hung on his or her office wall. If you can figure it into your budget, an even nicer gesture is a monetary per diem or honorarium to help cover there expenses.

It is important, though, that you ensure that your medical volunteers have the proper medical credentials and are licensed or certified by the proper governing medical board. For instance, in order to be considered as a USA Taekwondo Medical Volunteer for national events each person must submit a resume or curriculum vitae, in addition to a copy of their medical license/certification or medical liability insurance for review before being considered for any event. This ensures your athletes have the best possible medical care available to them. You can also determine whether or not that individual has worked athletic events in the past or not.

Generally you want to stick with those individuals with some type of sporting competition experience since these medical volunteers must be able to evaluate a competitor in under 60 seconds, not an easy thing to do. Those without competition experience often can be best utilized in the Sports Medicine Triage area, or they may simply need to pair up with one of your experienced volunteers for a while to "get their feet wet" before jumping into the actual on mat evaluations. Each medical volunteer needs to understand the rules pertaining to medical treatment of athletes, including medical time-outs, taping restrictions, and the limitations of what you are allowed to do for any athlete. Some competitions do not allow you to actually treat the athlete, but rather you must instruct the athlete how to care for the injury if they wish to continue. Other competitions do not allow an injury time out for the athlete's lack of conditioning, such as cramps occurring from dehydration, so make sure all of the medical staff are clear on the rules of the tournament as it pertains to them.

Finally, one convenient resource for medical care for your dojang is to make a "deal" with a certified athletic trainer or student athletic trainer from the local university to trade basic sports medicine care for your students in exchange for martial arts lessons. Simply contact your local university athletic training room about getting an upper level student (in the last four semesters of school) to help you out if no ATC is available. This student will often travel with you and your students to events, as well as help you coordinate medical volunteers for your events. This is just one of many ways to care for the medical care needs of your athletes.

Chapter Eight Key Points

✦ A sports medicine team for a tournament should consist of at least one MD, DO and/or one PA plus at least one ATC for every two to three rings of sparring. Additional staff can include DCs, RNs, PTs, medical students, and paramedics/EMTs.

✦ Volunteer staff can often be obtained through local colleges/ universities, physical therapy clinics, orthopedic practices, chiropractors, hospitals, or your sport's national governing body.

✦ The above organizations may also be willing to donate supplies in exchange for recognition at the event.

✦ Ensure that all medical volunteers have the proper medical credentials and are currently licensed or certified by the appropriate board or licensing agency.

✦ Inform the medical staff of the rules pertaining to medical timeouts, treatment of athletes and taping.

Pregnancy and the Martial Arts

9

precautions and modifications

Many people believe that martial arts participation should not be part of a pregnant woman's schedule, but I disagree. From my own experience as a mother-to-be along with numerous pregnant athletes I have worked with, I have found martial arts participation to be very beneficial for both the mother-to-be and the developing fetus. Yes, of course, some modifications and precautions need to be considered, but many women who are athletically involved prior to pregnancy can and do continue to be involved throughout their pregnancy. In fact, the more toned your muscles are, especially those of your abdomen and legs, the easier labor and delivery will be for you as you have more strength and endurance to aid in the delivery. Here are the main points you need to consider before continuing with or beginning training in martial arts as a mother-to-be:

• **You must first and always get approval from your physician** for participation prior to any form of athletic involvement to ensure the safety and well-being of both you and your baby. It may take some discussions with your physician before he/she is comfortable with the concept, but as long as you assure him/her that those things which might endanger the safety of either you or the baby will not be performed, you often can convince the physician it is in your best interest. There may be conditions of your body or that of the developing fetus such as diabetes, high blood pressure, history of miscarriage or difficult pregnancies, though, which would limit or preclude your participation because it may cause harm. So, listen and talk to your physician.

• Always ensure that you consume at least 1-liter of water prior to any type of work out: strength & conditioning, cardiovascular (such as running, swimming or biking), or martial arts practice

• Always ensure that you have adequate water to drink during your workout, drinking even when you do not feel thirsty. I know this means you make more visits to the bathroom, but better there than to the hospital for an IV to replace the fluids you were not drinking. Also, in the later stages of pregnancy, if you do not drink plenty of water and you become dehydrated (and you may not even realize you are dehydrated) you can go into premature labor or begin to have complications due to overheating. So, drink, drink drink!

• If you suffer from "morning sickness" or "all day sickness" in my case, take additional time when sitting up from a workout completed lying on the floor, bench or table, as the sudden movement will often trigger nausea, especially if you have been sweating. Once again, make sure you are getting plenty of fluids, even if it is in the form of ice cubes (of water, sports drink, juice, etc.).

• You should also be aware of the fact that your blood pressure (BP) often progressively decreases over the course of your pregnancy, so this means rising from a lying or seated position too quickly can trigger nausea, dizziness and even fainting episodes. Be very conscious of not moving too quickly for this reason.

• Some physicians prefer that you not exercise while lying on your back, especially after about the 5th month or towards the end of your second trimester. The size of your belly may also preclude much exercise from this position. As always, discuss this and your concerns with your attending physician.

• It is very important not to allow your body to overheat, as you do not want to "overcook what is in the oven" so to speak. You should **not allow your body to get too warm**, so keep activities that make you sweat to short time intervals. Your heart rate should not go much above 140 BPM (beats per minute), and should not be sustained for more than 15 minutes at a time before resting, as this could harm the developing fetus. Overheating and dehydration are the two biggest fears of physicians for pregnant women participating in physical activity.

• Remember that at around your 4th month of pregnancy the hormone relaxin begins to make all the joints in your body loose, and therefore there is a greater chance of you falling or injuring a joint, so you must be extra careful with your movements. And yes, this hormone is what is responsible for making pregnant women waddle, as it loosens the joints by softening the ligaments and connective tissue in order to make it easier for them to expand and stretch during childbirth. Unfortunately, this hormone does not only target the joints involved during childbirth but all joints of the female body!

• You may need to remove yourself from practices which involve sparring or throwing, opting for more traditional non-combative training or maybe in a new form of martial art that you have yet to experience, such as Tai Chi. Check out your options before removing yourself totally from martial arts training.

• In most cases, a physician is not going to want you to compete past your 1st trimester, and you may not be capable of it anyway, depending on your developing shape. You do not want to risk harming or losing the baby.

• Nutrition is extremely important, but **don't eat as if you are eating for two people because you are not.** You need an additional 300-400 kcal/day for the developing fetus, which is not much. So eat your normal portions of healthy food (not the entire pie!), and eat more times throughout the day. Try to avoid eating right before going to bed as you will end up with heartburn, another problem prevalent during pregnancy. It is important to eat plenty of fresh fruits and vegetables (avoid canned and boxed, too much salt!), low-fat dairy products and low-fat protein. Even if you are a vegetarian (or simply do not eat red meats) you need to supplement your diet with additional protein in the form of fish, poultry, beans, soy, etc. as the developing fetus needs protein to properly grow. Also, take your daily vitamin supplement, recommended by your physician, which often can simply be a children's chewable vitamins. Avoid products with caffeine, such as coffee, tea, chocolate, dark sodas, etc. as this may increase not only your heart rate but that of the baby, leading to complications. If you are having problems knowing what is best to eat, visit a nutritionist to help get you started. Continue to eat healthy after the baby is born as you will need your strength and energy gained from healthy foods.

Strength & Conditioning:

• No lifting of heavy weights. Instead reduce the amount of weight and either increase your reps or your sets. You may also need to consider doing the lifts from a seated position rather than a standing position due to balance issues, or problems with dizziness.

• The exercise ball may become difficult to do by the middle of the second trimester. Be careful, and use a partner if your are having balance problems.

• Yoga and pilates are highly recommended, as there are classes strictly devoted to pregnant women. They help to maintain your flexibility, strength and endurance, all of which you need during labor and delivery.

• Fast walking may need to replace jogging once you develop a tummy, but if you do continue to run make sure you purchase specially designed tummy supports for your pregnant belly. Even walking 30 minutes every day is beneficial in keeping your heart rate healthy.

• Swimming may become too difficult, although some women swim until their 8th month. Doing your strength and conditioning program in the water may be a good switch. Check with your local gym for aquatics programs designed for pregnant women.

• Core strengthening should be continued throughout pregnancy, but many physicians do not want you lying on your back to complete the exercises as it encourages your blood pressure to go down, and that increases your chances of dizziness, fainting and nausea, things you don't want or need. You may need to modify some of the exercises, particularly the abdominal work, and switch to an upright machine or apparatus, including using the Total Gym®. But, remember, the tighter you keep the core, the easier the labor and delivery, and the easier the return to normal after the baby is born. Some even believe the more fit you remain during the pregnancy the less postpartum effects there will be on you and your system.

The important things to remember are to stay physically active throughout your pregnancy without putting you or your baby's safety at risk. Good nutrition and hydration are also extremely important both before, during and after pregnancy. Physical activity, including dancing, tend to calm the developing fetus, as they get a chance to be active with you and then take a nap (as you may also choose to do!). Listen to your physician's advice, but don't be afraid to discuss your concerns or desires, as you may have thoughts he/she has not considered. Remember also, injury is more likely to occur from working out while pregnant than normal, as you lose your balance easily, and things just don't seem to move the same as before. Conditions such as sciatic nerve pain, diabetes, high blood pressure, asthma, as well as many other conditions may appear during pregnancy and limit what you can and are allowed to do. Athletic participation in activities that have a high risk of falling (such as rollerblading, roller skating, ice skating, balance beam work, etc.) should be avoided and traded for activities of lower risk that involve low impact aerobic exercises (such as yoga, pilates, etc.).

Good Luck for a healthy and happy pregnancy.

Conclusion

Well, you now have the basic knowledge to help prevent and care for basic injuries that occur to the martial arts athlete. This does not mean you are an expert by any means, but at least you have some of the fundamentals which every athlete, parent and instructor should know. There are many great publications out there which are directed towards sports medicine, athletic training, injury care and management, as well as strength and conditioning or nutrition which can also be beneficial for you to read if this book has not fully answered some of your questions. I hope you utilize this book as a beginning guidebook leading to the exploration of further knowledge to better yourself as a participant in the martial arts and person in general. Good luck and stay healthy!

Trish Bare Grounds, Ph.D., ATC/L

About the Author

Trish Bare Grounds is the USA Taekwondo (formerly the USTU) Medical Committee Chairman, Medical Coordinator & Head Athletic Trainer for the US National Taekwondo Team. She has worked in this capacity since 1994, soon after Coach Han Won Lee became the USOTC Head Taekwondo Coach. She has traveled with the Junior and Senior National Teams for international competitions, including World Cup Championships, Pan Am Championships, World Championships, and Olympic Qualifying Events, as well as various Open Tournaments in Europe. Trish has also coordinated all of the medical staff and supplies for all National Events since 1996, given the position just before working the Olympic Games in Atlanta. She spends the year convincing medical supply companies to donate the supplies and equipment used at National Events as there is no budget for such items. Trish also convinces various medical personnel from doctors to athletic trainers to paramedics, to volunteer their time for events without compensation, as well as donating her own time without compensation. Trish conducts Sports Medicine Seminars for athletes, parents, coaches and referees at various USA Taekwondo National Events, as well as at dojangs and conferences for medical personnel through her company Bare Essentials Sports Medicine. Contact her if you would like to have a seminar conducted at your school or event.

Trish works for the National Cheerleaders Association and National Dance Alliance through the National Spirit Group & Varsity Brands as the medical coordinator and athletic trainer for camps, special performances, and competitions. Since becoming employed by the NCA in 1997 she has been named Athletic Trainer of the year for eight consecutive years.

Trish also creates strength and conditioning programs, as well as nutritional eating programs for athletes of various sports, from pee-wees to elite Olympic & Paralympic athletes to the elderly population. Trish is also a doping control officer for the United States Anti-Doping Agency (USADA).

During the course of working on her doctoral degree, Trish has been an instructor at the University of Florida in the Sports Medicine/Athletic Training Program, as well as an instructor at the University of West Florida in the Athletic Training Program, and an instructor Pensacola Junior College in the Exercise Science Department, Education Department, and Psychology Department.

While at the University of Florida completing her studies, Trish was the Head Athletic Trainer for the UF Wheelchair Basketball Team, member of the GatorSports Committee, the Strength & Conditioning Advisor for the UF Living Well Program, and worked with It's G.R.E.A.T. Hippotherapy Program (using horses for rehab therapy). She came to the University of Florida following a Visiting Professorship and Assistant Athletic Trainer position at the University of Miami, and Head Athletic Trainer/Instructor position at Lynn University, initiating the first Sports Medicine Program there.

Trish is a Certified & Licensed Athletic Trainer (ATC/L) and Strength & Conditioning Program Designer. She holds a BA degree from DePauw University in Psychology & Pre-Med/Biology, along with an MS degree from the University of Miami in Sports Medicine. Along with these, she is finishing up an MS ED degree at the University of Florida in Secondary Science Education while concurrently completing a PhD in Sports Medicine/Athletic Training. Her doctoral research involves taekwondo athletes in a biomechanical study of forces applied to the head during kicks to the head, and the injuries sustained by these forces.

Trish is married to Mark A. Grounds who is in the U.S. Air Force. Trish and Mark welcomed their first daughter Olivia in April 2001, in addition to Mark's daughter Heather from an earlier marriage.

This reason I do this…..for all of "my kids", present & future stars!

Olivia at 20 months

Olivia at 3 ½ Years

Index

Also Available from Turtle Press:

Timing for Martial Arts
Strength and Power Training
Complete Kickboxing
Ultimate Flexibility
Boxing: A 12 Week Course
The Fighter's Body: An Owner's Manual
The Science of Takedowns, Throws and Grappling for Self-defense
Fighting Science
Martial Arts Instructor's Desk Reference
Solo Training
Solo Training 2
Fighter's Fact Book
Conceptual Self-defense
Martial Arts After 40
Warrior Speed
The Martial Arts Training Diary for Kids
TeachingMartial Arts
Combat Strategy
The Art of Harmony
Total MindBody Training
1,001 Ways to Motivate Yourself and Others
Ultimate Fitness through Martial Arts
Taekwondo Kyorugi: Olympic Style Sparring

For more information:
Turtle Press
PO Box 290206
Wethersfield CT 06129-206
1-800-77-TURTL
e-mail: sales@turtlepress.com

http://www.turtlepress.com